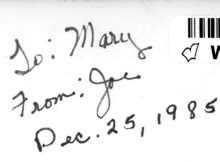

To: Mary
From: Joe
Dec. 25, 1985

Patricia Smith's

DOLL VALUES

Antique to Modern
Series III

COVER CAPTION: 20" American Character
"Alice in Wonderland". Marked: A.C., on
head. All hard plastic. Courtesy Elizabeth
Montesano.

COLLECTOR BOOKS
P.O. Box 3009
Paducah, KY 42001

The current values in this book should be used only as a guide. They are not intended to set prices, which vary from one section of the country to another. Auction prices as well as dealer prices vary greatly and are affected by condition as well as demand. Neither the Author nor the Publisher assumes responsibility for any losses that might be incurred as a result of consulting this guide.

Additional copies of this book may be ordered from:

COLLECTOR BOOKS
P.O. Box 3009
Paducah, Kentucky 42001

@$9.95 Add $1.00 for postage and handling.

Printed by IMAGE GRAPHICS, Paducah, Kentucky

CREDITS

The author wishes to thank the following for their help and information. Each collector took his own photographs unless noted after their name, in preference.

Hazel Adams, Jayn Allen, Joan Amundsen (Dwight Smith), Ruth Anderson (Carol Friend)(Dwight Smith), Jackie Barker, Anita Belew, Louise Benfatti, Sally Bethscheider, Irene Brown, Valna Brown, Kay Bransky, Sylvia Bryant, Elizabeth Burke (Gunner Burke), Mildred Busch, Magda Byfield, Millie Chappelle, "Tete" Cook (Dwight Smith), Linda Crowsey, Renie Culp, Beth Donor, Barbara Earnshaw, Marie Ernst, Edith Evans (Carole Friend), Eloise Godfrey (Robert Walker), Jo Fasnatch (Leon Folse), Joleen Flack, Carole Friend, Beverly Harrington (Dwight Smith), Bernice Heister, Mimi Hiscox, Pauline Hoch, Diane Hoffman (Steve Schweitzberger), Phyllis Houston, Verna Humphrey (Sally Freeman), Virginia Jones (Dwight Smith), Dorothy Judge, Elaine Kaminsky, Pat Lindis (Sally Freeman), Theo. Lindley, Beres Lindus, Nancy Lucas (Sally Freeman), Margaret Mandel, Zoura Martinez, Jeannie Mauldin, Billie McCabe, Mary McGinty, Marge Meisinger (Dwight Smith), Shirley Merrill (Brent Merrill, Woody Evans), Mrs. Frank Miller, Karen Miller, Wendi Miller, Lois Miluis, Arlene Mitgel, Dorothy Mulholland (Sally Freeman), Florence Black Musich, Cynthia Orgeron, Shirley Pascuzzi (Mike Stehlin), Penny Pendlebury, Piecewicz (Joseph J. Mishley), Anne Rankin, Jim & Fay Rodolfos, Evelyn Samec, Barbara Schilde, Robin Schmidt, Sheryl Schmidt, June Schultz, Lenora Schweitzberger (Steve), Betty Shelly, Trudy Shelly, Charmaine Shields, Jeannie Shipi, Martha Silva, Carroll & Bob Skell, Jessie Smith, Wanda Smith (Lisa Kindrick), Pat Spirek, Helena Street, Sally Swain, Martha Sweeney, Mary Sweeney, Phyllis Teague, Pat Timmons (Cecil Timmons), Virginia Travis, Treasure Trove (Dwight Smith), Pat Potts, Marjorie Uhl, Arlene Wacker, Jane Walker, Kathy Walters (Dwight Smith), Ann Wencel, Lorraine Hancock Weston (Lin Flowers Weston), Mary Wheatley, Mary Williams, Glorya Woods, Yesterday's Child.

CONTENTS

A WORD ABOUT PRICES

Unfortunately few read the forwards to the price guides, but we shall repeat a number of things that we have said over and over, in the hope that a few will stop to read it.

ALL price guides are based on "antique" dolls (bisque, etc.) being undamaged, clean, well groomed and dressed and ready to go into a collection. Composition doll prices are based on mint condition with no crazing, cracks, well dressed or original, wigs in very good shape and ready to place into a collection. Modern dolls are based on mint condition, unplayed with or nearly unplayed with, with original hairset and clothes.

PRICES MUST VARY DUE TO THE CONDITION OF THE DOLL. Bisque with hairline cracks, eye chips, broken bodies, dirty, in need of restringing, undressed, anything that detracts from the doll must be much lower in price than shown in any price guide. The same holds true for composition and modern dolls, or dolls made from any material.

A price guide is just that, a GUIDE, so the collector can see what area of value the doll is placed in. The collector may pay less and thereby be getting a bargain, or pay higher and still be getting a good deal, as the doll may be exceptional in some way. The final judgment of what to pay for a doll remains with the buyer, and the seller.

This book is divided between "ANTIQUE" and "MODERN" by sections, with the older dolls in the first section and the newer dolls in the second section. To be an antique, an item must be over 100 years old, but we have placed the breaking point of these two sections in the 1920's.

REVISED PRICES: VOLUME I

The following prices are updated, and reflect the current market values. The listing is by page, so it will be easy to go through Volume I and jot down the current prices.

COLOR SECTION

Page 8
1079, 20″	425.00
1909, 18″	485.00
Paris Bebe, 27″	4,000.00

Page 9
Dolly Dimple, 25½″ .	2,800.00
Open mouth China ..	700.00
Bru Jne, 17″	8,500.00

Page 10
Super Man	125.00
Little Girl, 29″	145.00

Page 11
Half Figure........	100.00
Parian, 6″	550.00

Page 12
Composition, 11″ ...	75.00
Walker, 13″	65.00

Page 13
Celluloid, 6″	22.00
Open mouth China, 15″	700.00

Page 14
P.S., 10″	225.00
351, 26″	800.00
Ball head, 20″	1,100.00

Page 15
Jumeau Fashion, 19″	3,000.00
Jumeau Fashion, 20″	3,100.00
Belton, 15″	1,200.00

Page 17
Gigi, 7½″	22.00
Majorette, 7½″	3.00
Heindel, 8″	3.00

Page 18
Donna Doll, 10½″ ..	22.00
Doll To Dress, 7½″	2.00

Page 19
Wanda Walker, 17½″	65.00

Page 20
Dionne Quints:
Current prices
in this Volume.

Page 21
(Composition)
Madalaine, 14″	285.00
Alice In Wonderland	
9″	200.00
14″	250.00
18″	300.00
Bride, 9″	165.00
15″	200.00
21″	275.00
Bridesmaid, 11″ ...	200.00
18″	265.00
22″	275.00
Cinderella, 13″	200.00
18″	300.00
Dr. Defoe, 14″	450.00
Fairy Queen, 15″ ...	225.00
Flora McFlimsey,	
16″	375.00
22″	450.00
Jane Withers, 13″ ..	675.00
18″	675.00
Kate Greenaway, 14″	350.00
Little Colonel, 13″	450.00
Little Women, 9″ ...	200.00
15″	350.00
Margaret O'Brien, 18″	550.00
McGuffey Ana, 13″ .	265.00
25″	365.00
Princess	
Elizabeth, 14″ ...	250.00
24″	400.00
Scarlett O'Hara,	
11″	300.00
21″	550.00
Sonja Henie, 15″ ...	275.00
22″	450.00
Southern Girl, 14″ .	265.00
21″	300.00

Page 22 (Hard Plastics)
Violet/Active Miss, 18″	325.00
Alice, 18″	250.00
Annabelle, 15″	250.00
20″	325.00
Babs Skater, 15″ ...	225.00
21″	375.00
Ballerina, 16½″	225.00
10½″	275.00
Binnie Walker, 15″	165.00
Bride, 17″	265.00
21″	325.00
Cinderella (poor), 14″	385.00
Cynthia, 15″	495.00
23″	650.00
Fairy Queen, 18″ ...	350.00
Flowergirl, 18″	250.00
Godey Lady, 18″ ...	525.00

Groom, 18″	375.00
Hedy LaMarr, 17″ ..	425.00
Lady Churchill, 18″ .	525.00
Little Men, 15″	500.00
Little Women, 14″ ..	250.00
Madelain, 17″	300.00
Maggie, 15″	225.00
Margot Ballerina, 18″	400.00
Mary Martin, 14″ ...	550.00
McGuffey Ana, 14″ .	385.00
Nina Ballerina, 17″ .	300.00
Patty Pigtails, 15″ ..	350.00
Peter Pan, 15″	350.00
Polly Pigtails, 17″ ..	275.00
Prince Charming, 17″	550.00
Prince Phillip, 17″ ..	450.00
Princess Margaret Rose, 14″	250.00
Queen, 18″	425.00
Renoir, 14″	425.00
Sir Winston Churchill, 18″	525.00
Sleeping Beauty, 16½″	400.00
Snow White, 15″ ...	350.00
Story Princess, 15″ .	325.00
Wendy, 15″	275.00
Wendy Ann, 16″ ...	250.00
Winnie Walker, 15″ .	165.00

Page 23 (Cissy)
Cissy in ballgowns ..	250.00 up
Bride	250.00
Bridesmaid........	250.00
Century's of Fashion	350.00
In various street dresses	175.00
Elaine	525.00
Miss Flora McFlimsey	375.00
Flowergirl	200.00
Gainsbourgh	400.00
Garden Party	400.00
Godey............	400.00
Lady Hamilton	500.00
Melanie	475.00
Queen in gold	525.00
in white.........	525.00
Scarlett O'Hara	500.00
Sitting Pretty, 17″ ..	275.00

Page 24 (Portraits)
Agatha, 1967	425.00
1974, 75, 76	325.00
Bride, 1965	650.00
1969	395.00
Cornelia, 1972	425.00
1973	425.00

1974	400.00
1975	350.00
1976	325.00
Gainsbourgh, 1968 .	425.00
1972	425.00
1973	275.00
Godey, 1967	425.00
1969	400.00
1970-71	350.00
Coco Godey, 1966 .	1,500.00 up
Goya, 1968	500.00
Jenny Lind, 1969...	600.00
1970	600.00
Lady Hamilton, 1968	500.00
Lissy Coco, 1966 ...	1,500.00 up
Madame Doll, Coco	
1966	1,500.00 up
Madame Pompadour,	
1970	950.00
Melanie, 1967	550.00
1969	425.00
1970	400.00
1971	400.00
1974	400.00
Melanie, Coco 1966 .	1,500.00 up
Mimi, 1971	400.00
Queen, 1965	575.00
1968	500.00
Renoir, 1965	450.00
1967, 69 & 70....	525.00
1971	450.00
1972	400.00
1973	375.00
Renoir, Coco, 1966..	1,500.00 up
Renoir Mother, 1967	500.00
Scarlett O'Hara, 1965	525.00
1967	500.00
1968	550.00
1969	450.00
1970	450.00
1975-76	375.00
Scarlett, Coco, 1966.	1,500.00 up
Southern Belle, 1965	625.00
1967	450.00

Page 25 (Cissette)

Agatha Portrette,	
1968	425.00
Ballerina, 1957-59 ..	275.00
Barbary Coast,	
1962-63	950.00 up
Bride, 1957	150.00
Bridesmaid........	165.00
Cissette: Various	
street clothes	145.00
In ballgowns	250.00
Gift set with wigs .	450.00 up
Gainsbourgh Por-	
trette, 1957......	300.00
Godey Portrette,	
1968-69	425.00

1970	425.00
Irish, 1963	950.00 up
Jacqueline, 1962 ...	475.00
Klondike Kate, 1963	950.00 up
Lady Hamilton, 1957	450.00
Margot, 1961	300.00
Mealanie Portrette,	
1970	425.00
Melinda Portrette,	
1968	425.00
1969	425.00
Queen, 1957	400.00
1960	400.00
1963	400.00
1972, 73 & 74....	400.00
Renoir Portrette,	
1968-69	425.00
1970	425.00
Sleeping Beauty, 1960	375.00
Scarlett O'Hara Por-	
trette, 1968-1973 .	375.00
Sound of Music, Large	
set: Gretl.......	165.00
Small set: Brigitta,	
Leisel	250.00
Louisa	300.00
Southern Belle,	
1968-73	400.00
Tinkerbelle, 1969...	300.00

Page 26 (Alexanderkins)

Discontinued

African...........	350.00 up
Amish boy & girl ...	350.00 up
Argentine boy	350.00 up
Bolivia	350.00
Ecuador	350.00 up
Eskimo...........	475.00
Hawaiian	350.00 up
Greek boy	350.00 up
Indian boy-Hiawatha	350.00
Indian girl-Pocohantas	350.00
Korea	350.00
Morocco	350.00
Miss U.S.A.	275.00
Peruvian boy	425.00
Spanish boy	350.00 up
Vietnam	400.00
Cowboy & Cowgirl ..	400.00 ea.
English Guard	475.00
McGuffey Ana	300.00
Priscilla	350.00
All bend knee interna-	
tionals, except	
above	125.00
Alexander-kins	
(Wendy-kins) Dress-	
ed in various out	
fits, straight leg,	
non-walker, 7½"	145.00

Straight leg, walker	135.00
Bend knee walker .	125.00
Bend knee, non-	
walker..........	125.00
Add 30-50.00 for un-	
usual outfits like	
nurse, riding	
habit, etc.	
Alice in Wonderland .	300.00
American Girl	425.00
Aunt Agatha	425.00
Ballerina, 1953-54 ..	145.00
Best Man	300.00
Bride	50 to
	225.00
Groom	175.00
Cherry Twins	250.00
Cinderella........	300.00
Cousin Grace or Karen	425.00

Page 27 (Sound of Music)

Large set: Gretl,	
Louisa, Marta,	
Fredrich, Brigitta,	
Liesl.......(each)	165 to
	275.00
Large set: Maria	325.00
Complete large set ..	1,400.00
Small set: Marta,	
Fredrich, Gretl,	
Brigetta, Liesl,	
Louisa..........	175 to
	300.00
Small set: Maria	275.00
Complete small set..	1,200.00

Page 28 (Babies)

Babsie Baby	100.00
Baby Betty........	125.00
Baby Genius,	
Composition	125.00
Hard plastic	150.00
Vinyl	95.00
Baby McGuffey,	
compo.	125.00
Cloth/vinyl	55.00
Baby precious	65.00
Bitsy/Butch, compo..	100.00
Cloth/vinyl	100.00
Cherub, 12"	95.00
26"	125.00
Christening Baby ...	75.00
Honeybea	95.00
Little Genius, compo.	65.00
Littlest Kitten	125.00
Mary Cassatt Baby ..	165.00
Rosebud	95.00
Slumbermate, compo.	150.00
Cloth/vinyl	85.00

Page 29

Bebe Phenix, Closed

mouth 24″ 3,000.00
Open mouth 2,000.00
Page 30
Identified French all-
bisque, 6″ .... 650 to
725.00
8-9″ .... 695 to
950.00
French type, 6″ .... 125 to
475.00
8″ 795.00
Page 31
German swivel head
all-bisques: glass
eyes, 4-6″ .... 200 to
300.00
painted eyes, 4-6″ . 185 to
210.00
glass eyes, 8″ .... 275 to
475.00
One piece body &
heads: glass eyes, 4″ 150.00
6½″ 275.00
8½″ 375.00
One piece body & head
with painted eyes:
4″ 140.00
5½″ .... 140 to
125.00
7½ .... 165 to
185.00
Page 32
Bonn Doll, 7½″ 200.00
Page 33
Babies: Jointed at
necks, 3½-6″ .... 145 to
350.00
Characters: 3½″ .. 100.00
6″ .... 200 to
175.00
Candy babies:
2½-4″ 35.00
5-6″ 65.00
Japan: 3½-5″ .... 15 to
35.00
Bye-lo, swivel head,
7″ 625.00
Marked:
682/14/Germany,
6″ 350.00
Page 34
All bisque from Japan:
Ones of good quali-
ty, 3½-5″ .... 15 to
65.00
All one piece/molded
on clothes: 4″ .... 20 to
45.00
Jointed shoulders
only: 5-6″ ...... 15 to
45.00

8″ .... 25 to
65.00
Marked: Nip-
pon/name of doll:
4″ .... 25 to
50.00
6½″ .... 35 to
65.00
Queue San Baby:
4½″ 100.00
Child/molded on
clothes: 4½″ (legs
together) 22.00
Nodders: 3″ .... 25 to
225.00
Occupied Japan:
3½-5″ ....6 to 15.00
7″ .... 15 to
25.00
Page 35
All bisque: Japan,
4½″ 45.00
All bisque boy, 3½″ . 35.00
Page 36
Grumpy, 4″ 55.00
Marked: 5430/-
Germany, 3½″ ... 22.00
Molded blonde hair, 5″ 60.00
Didi or Mimi....... 1,250.00
Little Imp........ 250.00
Wide a Wake-Germany 250.00
Wide a Wake-Japan . 95.00
Our Fairy 1,250.00
Baby Bud-Germany . 150.00
Baby Bud-Japan 75.00
Peterkin, 9″ 350.00
Baby Darling, 5″ ... 50 to
60.00
Queue San (various
poses), 5″ 100.00
Googly, painted eyes
to side, 6″ .... 165 to
450.00
Googly, glass eyes to
side, 6″ .... 250 to
600.00
Peek-a-Boo by
Drayton, 4″ 100.00
Page 37
A.B.G., 13″ 265.00
19″ 375.00
Composition Bye-lo,
20″ 350.00
Amberg baby, 20″ .. 575.00
Page 38
Betsy McCall, 14″ .. 65.00
Love Me Baby, 16″ . 30.00
Page 39
Toni, 25″ 185.00
Sweet Sue, 25″ 200.00

Toni, 10″ 50.00
Page 40
Toodles, 24″ 95.00
Tiny Betsy McCall,
8″ 57.50
Page 41
Bride, 18″ 100.00
Baby Toodles, 19″ .. 85.00
Jimmy John, 26″ ... 95.00
Page 42
Sweet Susanne, 18″ . 100.00
Betsy McCall/trunk,
14″ 70.00
Butterball, 19″ 85.00
Page 43
A.G.D., 14″ 45.00
Page 44
Special, 25″ 425.00
390 Walker, 24″ ... 400.00
Page 45
Floradora, 27″ 465.00
323 Googly, 7½″ ... 600.00
12″ 850.00
Page 46
Googly 200, 9″ 700.00
9″ 995.00
Just Me, 12″ 1,200.00
8″ 900.00
Painted Bisque, 8″ .. 375.00
995 baby, 17″ 365.00
Page 47
351, 16″ 450.00
7″ 150.00
1776, 21″ 425.00
327, 18″ 375.00
990, 18″ 375.00
Page 48
550, 10″ 795.00
16″ 1,600.00
Black 518, 20″ 600.00
Baby Betty, 17″ 350.00
20″ 400.00
Page 49
310, 16″ 235.00
10″ 125.00
2000, 14″ 285.00
21″ 450.00
390, 30″ 475.00
36″ 900.00
40″ 1,200.00
Page 50
390, 19″ 235.00
30″ 475.00
My Dearie, 23″ 450.00
27″ 525.00
Page 51
7″ 100.00
390, 10½″ 125.00
Floradora, 9″ 150.00
21″ 350.00

8

Page 52

1894, 5½"	100.00
1894, 18"	375.00
Original	425.00
1894 in box, 16"	235.00
Original	300.00

Page 53

200 Welsch, 23"	400.00

Page 54

Snuggle-doll, 16"	30.00
Nancy Lee (Nanette), 14"	95.00
Snuggle doll, 17"	30.00

Page 55

Boy, 14"	75.00
Juliana, 17"	100.00
Nancy Lee, 17"	110.00

Page 56

My Angel, 36"	95.00
Raving Beauty, 18"	100.00
Little Miss Gadabout, 18"	100.00

Page 57

Lyf-lke Baby, 23"	120.00
Googly Indian, 9"	165.00

Page 58

Bonnie Babe, 12"	675.00
General Walking Doll, 9"	16.00
Babs Walker, 28"	135.00

Page 59

Karl Baumann baby, 8"	165.00
Belton, 26"	2,400.00

Page 60

Socket head, 19"	185.00
Socket head, 22½"	425.00
Babies First Doll	6.00

Page 61

Boudoir, 32"	120.00
Gypsy, 29"	70.00

Page 62

Bebe Bru Marchant, 13"	2,400.00

Page 63

Socket head, 21"	3,300.00
Bebe Bru, 17"	8,400.00

Page 64

Bebe Teteur, 14"	6,400.00
Circle Dot, 17"	7,500.00

Page 65

Kid body Bru, 14"	5,500.00
Giggles, 14"	385.00
Kewpie Cuddles, 14"	110.00

Page 66

Jeff, 5½"	70.00
Cookie, 2¾"	35.00
Skippy, 5"	60.00

Page 67

Smitty, 10"	65.00

Skeezix, 13"	65.00
Mammy, 20"	125.00
Pappy, 21"	150.00

Page 68

Dagwood, 14"	125.00
Alexander, 12"	125.00
Celluloid, 9"	12.00

Page 69

Christmas Tree doll, 8"	16.00
Celluloid, 2½"	10.00
Celluloid, 15"	145.00

Page 70

Celluloid, 15"	100.00
Celluloid, 12"	22.00
Celluloid, 6"	10.00

Page 71

Celluloid, 13½"	60.00
Celluloid Kewpie, 6½"	60.00

Page 72

Celluloid, 6"	8.00
Celluloid, 6"	12.00
Late Chase Girl, 16"	185.00

Page 73

China, 12"	325.00

Page 74

China with head band, 6"	350.00
China boy, 10"	85.00
Black china, 9½"	325.00

Page 75

Black china, 18"	600.00
Covered wagon, 18"	475.00
Flat top, 36"	750.00

Page 76

Boudoir Pet, 12½"	4.00
Boy, 15"	15.00
Burlap, 21"	6.00

Page 77

Eden toy, 10"	5.00
DQ kid, 14"	8.00
Amy, 11"	3.00
Little Sister, 10½"	12.00

Page 78

Happy face, 12"	5.00
Jack, 12" & Jill, 11"	7.00 ea.
Mollye, 12"	40.00

Page 79

Mid-1930's, 19"	95.00
Charlie Chaplain, 17"	365.00
Little Bo Peep, 15"	20.00

Page 80

Googly, 23"	10.00
Pied Piper, 21"	6.00
Lucy Arnez, 27"	75.00

Page 81

Crib Pal, 11"	3.00
Golden Bear, 7"	6.00
Cinderella, 8"	25.00

Page 82

Little Red Riding Hood, 8"	20.00
Girl, 16"	45.00
Creche, 11"	375.00

Page 83

Emily, 25"	55.00
Terri Tricycle, 4"	5.00
Bunny Baby, 20"	18.00

Page 84

Peachy Pet, 24"	125.00
E.D., Open mouth, 17"	1,400.00

Page 85

E.D. Closed mouth, 20"	2,600.00
E.D. Open mouth, 9½"	625.00
Diamond Baby, 13"	125.00

Page 86

Bashful, 9"	85.00
Snow White, 21"	65.00
Dopey, 11"	135.00

Page 87

Small World, 8"	20.00
Doll House Doll, 6"	185.00
Doll House Dolls, 5"	22.00

Page 88

All bisque, 4"	165.00
Polly Dolly, 11"	165.00
Betty Marie, 23"	135.00

Page 89

Bride, 11"	35.00
Lady Marion, 11"	35.00
Jutta, 22"	475.00

Page 90

Socket head, 28"	525.00
Shoulder head, 12"	165.00
Shoulder head, 13"	200.00

Page 91

1780's, 15"	1,795.00
Sylvia Flowergirl, 7½"	3.00
Carmen, 7"	4.00

Page 92

Country Picnic, 7½"	3.00
Mash figure, 3½"	4.00
Honore, 7"	95.00

Page 93

Susan Stroller, 13"	32.00
Musical Linda, 17"	10.00
Annette, 29"	40.00

Page 94

Tandy Talks, 21"	60.00
Rosemary, 20"	185.00

Page 95

Baby Bubbles, 26"	235.00
Black, 26"	425.00
Patsy Ruth, 27"	425.00
Mae Starr, 30"	425.00

Page 96

Patsy with wig, 14"	185.00
Skippy, 15"	225.00

Patsy Ann, 19" 225.00
Page 97
Patsy Ann, 19" 225.00
Patsy Lou, 22" 275.00
Patsy Baby, 10" 125.00
Patsy Ann boy, 19" . 225.00
Page 98
Wee Patsy, 5" 200.00
Baby Tinyette, 8" ... 135.00
Button Nose, 8" 125.00
Ann Shirley/painted
  eyes, 14" 135.00
Page 99
Black Ann Shirley,
  21" 300.00
Ann Shirley, 21" ... 225.00
Little Lady Bride, 18" 150.00
Little Lady, 16" 125.00
Page 100
Little Lady, 28" 325.00
Portrait, 12" 150.00
Page 101
HP/Vinyl Little Lady,
  15" 95.00
Vinyl Patsy Ann, 15" 95.00
DyDee Baby, 22" ... 95.00
Dy-Dee Baby, 11" .. 45.00
Plastic/vinyl Patsy,
  15" 225.00
Page 102
My Fair Baby, 18" .. 45.00
Black Suzie Sunshine,
  18" 75.00
Gumdrop, 16" 45.00
Page 103
My Fair Baby, 12" .. 20.00
Pumpkin, 11" 45.00
Bridal set 250.00
Pumpkin, 10½" 45.00
Page 104
Expression doll, 9½" 35.00
B.F., 15" 2,600.00
Page 105
B.F., 16" 2,700.00
BiBye Baby, 16" ... 30.00
Fethalite, 11" 8.00
Page 106
Little Girl, 29" 145.00
Page 107
103/16/X, 26" 2,300.00
Frozen Charlotte, 7" 135.00
Page 108
Sister, 16" 40.00
Brother, 16" 40.00
Page 109
Vanessa, 28" 45.00
Azores, 10" 14.00
Bindi, 13" 95.00
Page 110
Brazil, 14" 25.00

Indian boy, 12½" ... 35.00
Page 111
R.A.F., 18" 95.00
Indian boy, 12" 27.00
Shirley Temple
  (Canada), 13" 175.00
Page 112
Barbara Ann Scott,
  14" 225.00
Tak-Uki, 30" 200.00
Chinese, 6" 35.00
Page 113
American Indian, 11" 65.00
Canadian Mountie, 9" 35.00
Tak-Uki, 13" 35.00
Page 114
Lisa-Bella, 24" 22.00
  Talker 28.00
Black Forest, 16" ... 20.00
  8" 12.00
Mascot Doll, 5" 4.00
Page 115
Ratti, 18" 125.00
AntiBellum, 16" 95.00
Page 116
Little One, 12" 65.00
Plastic & vinyl, 16" . 15.00
Furina, 11" 85.00
Page 117
Kitty Bonomi, 15" .. 25.00
Vanessa, 15" 15.00
Mereleita, 11½" 15.00
Page 118
Sweet Adriana, 14" . 85.00
Nippon, 18½" 165.00
Tomi, 14" 18.00
Page 119
Japan, Pouty, 13" .. 650.00
  Crawler, 14" 20.00
Page 120
Wedding Doll, 5½" .. 18.00
Japanese, 12" 35.00
Japanese, 11½" 45.00
Page 121
Naughty Weepy, 7½" 8.00
Baby, 5½" 25.00
Black girl, 4½" 25.00
Page 122
Barbara Streisand,
  14" 125.00
Page 123
Wind Song, 19" 45.00
Charlene, 19" 45.00
Eskimo, 14" 40.00
Page 124
Composition, 6" 6.00
Composition, 19" ... 65.00
Composition, 8½" .. 8.00
Page 125
Sambo, 5", Tiger,

4½" ......(pair) 10.00
Swinger, 5¼" 20.00
Composition, 13" ... 45.00
Page 126
Fulper, 20" 465.00
Fulper, 26" 695.00
Page 127
Camille, 8" 4.00
Terrific Tracy, 8" .. 3.00
Sandy Sweet, 7" ... 4.00
Page 128
F.G., 25" 3,6000.00
F.G., 16" 2,600.00
Page 129
Honey West, 11½" .. 35.00
P.G., 18" 2,400.00
Page 130
749 Half Doll, 5½" . 625.00
Page 131
Pillow Doll, 4" 45.00
FY Half Doll, 3½" .. 12.00
Japan, 8" 15.00
Page 132
Half doll, 3½" 45.00
8030, 3¾" 25.00
Made in Japan, 3¼" 22.00
Page 133
Telephone doll, 18" . 385.00
Bathing Beauty, 2" . 40.00
Bonnet dolls, 2½" .. 65.00
Page 134
Ball head, 3" 95.00
25071, 2¾" 50.00
Bald head, 3" 95.00
Molded hair, 3" 60.00
Page 135
Perfume Bottle, 3½" 55.00
Germany, 3½" 50.00
Yellow, 2½" 40.00
White, 3" 40.00
Page 136
18" 350.00
109, 30" 695.00
Page 137
Oriental, 17" 895.00
1200, 14½" 260.00
24" 450.00
Page 138
Indian, 9" 365.00
  Compo. body 300.00
Page 139
250, 29" 775.00
Page 140
300, 25" 700.00
15" 795.00
Page 141
8192, 11" 365.00
Sweetie-kins, 29" ... 45.00
8192, 24" 750.00

10

Page 142

Ruthie Walker, 22″ .	35.00
Bye Bye Baby, 12″ . .	45.00

Page 143

Peggy, 25″	135.00
Cindy Kay, 15″	50.00
Baby Tweaks, 20″ . . .	28.50

Page 144

Chubby, 20″	20.00
Walking Ruthie, 13″ .	10.00
Teesie Tot, 10″	8.00

Page 145

Mary Poppins, 12″ . .	35.00
Teenie Bopper, 11″ .	12.00
Pippi, 11″	22.50

Page 146

Betty, 14½″	8.00
Black Bye-lo	20.00
Betsy McCall, 29″ . .	85.00

Page 147

Grown Up Miss, 18″	50.00
Gold Medal Doll, 26″	150.00

Page 148

Sleepy Baby, 24″ . . .	35.00
Mary Hoyer girl, 14″	110.00
Mary Hoyer boy, 14″	125.00
May Belle, 14″	125.00

Page 149

My Fair Lady	650.00
Zodiac, 24″	500.00

Page 150

Shirley Temple, 11″ .	650.00
Flirty eyes, 13″	475.00

Page 151

Deanna Durbin, 21″ .	400.00
Shirley Temple, 17″ .	525.00
Gulliver, 21″	475.00

Page 152

Judy Garland, 21″ . .	300.00
Plassie, 17½″	60.00
Judy Garland, 15″ . .	750.00
Wardrobe doll, 16″ .	65.00

Page 153

Miss Curity, 16″ . . .	95.00
Toni, 18″	85.00
Mary Hartline, 16″ .	100.00

Page 154

Betsy Wetsy, 12″ . . .	30.00
Bonnie Braids, 13″ .	42.50

Page 155

Peter Pan, 18″	185.00
Betsy McCall, 14″ . .	125.00
Bozo, 18″	20.00

Page 156

Harriet H. Ayers, 15″	95.00
Baby Big Eyes, 21″ .	45.00
Betsy Wetsy, 23″ . . .	30.00

Page 157

Betsy Wetsy/case, 12″	48.00
Magic Lips, 24″	55.00

Page 158

Mia	28.50
Talking Crissy	20.00
Talking Velvet	18.00
White Velvet	18.00
Black Velvet	50.00
Movin' Grovin' Crissy	20.00
Tara	20.00
Kerry	35.00
Cricket	50.00
White Tressy	28.50
Black Tressy	50.00

Page 159

White Crissy/Braids .	20.00
Black Velvet/Swirley	35.00
Black Swirley Curler	
Crissy	35.00
Look Around Crissy .	18.00
Look Around Velvet .	18.00
Black Look Around	
Crissy	50.00
Black Cinnamon	85.00
White Cinnamon . . .	45.00
Cricket	50.00
Movin' Grovin' Velvet	18.00
Black Movin' Grovin'	
Velvet	50.00

Page 160

Tubsy, 18″	22.50
Shirley Temple, 1972,	
17″	150.00
Tiny Thumbelina, 10″	10.00

Page 161

Tressy	28.50
White Crissy	20.00
Black Crissy	50.00
Dianna Ross, 18″ . . .	125.00

Page 162

Shirley Temple, 36″ .	1,300.00 up
National Velvet, 38″	750.00

Page 163

Dew Drop, 20″	12.00
Bam Bam, 16″	15.00
Tiny Kissey, 16″ . . .	42.00

Page 164

Miss Revlon, 18″ . . .	70.00
Miss Revlon, 10½″ .	45.00
Miss Revlon, 15″ . . .	60.00
Miss Revlon, 20″ . . .	80.00
Miss Revlon, 22″ . . .	95.00

Page 165

Miss Revlon, 17″ . . .	65.00
Shirley Temple	
Cinderella, 15″ . . .	175.00
Shirley in short	
dresses, 15″	150.00
Peter Playpal, 36″ . .	185.00

Page 166

Dina	45.00
Brandi	45.00

Swirlee Curler Crissy	20.00
Black Movin' Grovin'	
Crissy	20.00
Walker, 7″	10.00

Page 167

Cutie, 14″	14.00
Pixie, 16″	14.00
Jullien, 21″	1,800.00

Page 168

Jumeau, 11″	995.00

Page 169

#14, 23″	1,800.00
306, 22″	2,600.00
Depose, 17″	3,600.00

Page 170

Tete, 26″	2,500.00

Page 171

Closed mouth, 20″ . .	3,500.00
Closed mouth, 13″ . .	2,400.00
Tete/box, 18″	1,800.00

Page 172

149, 20″	850.00
Tete, 13″	2,400.00
K & K, 17″	325.00

Page 173

Kennedy, 13″	65.00
Devil, 8″	4.00

Page 174

117n, 18″	1,000.00
128, 18″	850.00
126, 29″	1,700.00

Page 175

126, 18″	725.00
126, 10″	350.00
116a, 13″	1,700.00
17″	2,200.00

Page 176

36, 14″	345.00
154, 16″	500.00
Black 100, 18″	1,600.00

Page 177

109, 23″	500.00
Kaysam, 15″	35.00
Meadow, 7″	8.00

Page 178

121, 15″	450.00

Page 179

Hilda, 14″	1,850.00
20″	3,200.00
1070, 16″	2,700.00
21″	3,400.00
260, 15″	450.00
145, 10½″	275.00

Page 180

151, 12″	400.00
128, 24″	2,200.00
148, 18″	525.00
152, 17″	500.00

Page 181

167	475.00

27"	450.00

Page 226

Airline, 14"	125.00
Terry-kins	65.00

Page 227

Swedish, 15"	22.00
Perky, 10"	18.00

Page 228

Monica, 20"	250.00
Debbie Lou, 14"	30.00

Page 229

Orsini, 18"	1,000.00

Page 231

Mitzi, 15½"	165.00
Painted bisque, 16" .	165.00
Black, 15"	450.00
Black Baby........	300.00

Page 232

SPS, 23"	550.00
Santa Claus, 26" ...	400.00
Paper Mache, 9" ...	60.00

Page 233

German Mache, 12" .	145.00
Black Mache, 6"	235.00
Celluloid Mache, 32"	125.00

Page 234

Unica, 18"	100.00
Paper Mache, 11" ..	25.00
Paper Mache, 8" ...	25.00

Page 235

Uncle Rollie, 3"	5.00
Playmate, 12"	3.00
Baby, 13"	7.00

Page 236

Pray N' Play, 11½" .	30.00

Page 237

Vanity Girl, 5½" ...	3.00
Anniversary, 7½" ..	3.00
Cowboy, 7"	5.00
Lady Hershel, 6" ...	3.00

Page 238

Bridesmaid, 7"	3.00
Dutch Girl, 7½"	3.00
Little Bo Peep, 7½" .	5.00
Bride, 7½"	3.00

Page 239

Charlie McCarthy, 18"	65.00
Bugs Bunny, 10" ...	4.00
Road Runner, 10" ..	4.00

Page 240

Popeye, 12"	6.00
Tom, 12"	4.00
Villian, 12"	5.00
Olive Oyl, 10"	6.00

Page 241

Cat/Gladiator, 11" ..	1.00
Mohawk/Pirate, 11" .	1.00
Fingerding, 5"	2.00

Page 242

Puppets, 2"	1.00

Page 243

Pullian, 15"	15.00
Bye-lo, 12½"	485.00
Timmy, 28"	16.00

Page 244

R.D., 20"	1,900.00
R.D., 17"	2,000.00

Page 245

Junior Miss, 7"	4.00
R.A., 22"	345.00
Spunky, 5½"	7.00

Page 246

Barry Goldwater, 5½"	45.00
Pip, 3"	6.00
Baby Laugh A Lot, 16"	15.00

Page 247

Hayley Mills, 11" ...	45.00
Sandra Sue, 8"	35.00
Sweet April, 5½" ...	6.00

Page 248

Boy, 26"	12.00
Granny, 19"	45.00

Page 249

Joy Bride, 12"	25.00
Baldy, 7"	25.00
Joy, 12"	25.00

Page 250

Nipple Doll, 4"	22.00
All rubber, 8"	12.00
Skater, 6"	6.00

Page 251

BSW, 29"	950.00
BSW, 16"	365.00
2048, 17"	900.00

Page 252

P.S., 10"	225.00
1899, 15"	295.00

Page 253

1285, 16"	1,000.00

Page 254

Schimitt body, 20" .	1,400.00
Socket head, 18" ...	4,500.00

Page 255

914, 26"	550.00
Oriental, 17½"	1,100.00
S.P.B.H., 22"	425.00

Page 256

Girl, 14½"	325.00
Baby, 14"	425.00
Boy, 19"	1,200.00

Page 257

Baby Jane, 13"	16.00
Baby Zuri	14.00
Flip Wilson, 16" ...	10.00

Page 258

S & H, 22"	1,900.00

Page 259

Shoulder head, 25" .	650.00
550, 21"	500.00
Socket head, 21" ...	500.00

Page 260

570, 21½"	500.00
1010, 19"	475.00
Dep 7½, 16"	385.00

Page 261

1079, 22"	895.00
1079, 20"	725.00
1079, 25"	1,000.00

Page 262

1159, 12½"	675.00
1250, 22"	525.00

Page 263

1039, 13½"	375.00
Santa, 20"	695.00
1260, 16"	425.00
Sweetie Pie, 10" ...	8.00
242, 17"	3,200.00

Page 265

236, 12½"	900.00
236, 26"	2,400.00
60, 11½"	225.00

Page 266

60, 24"	895.00
Brown bisque, 10½"	600.00

Page 267

A7, 14"	1,600.00
FRI, 10½"	1,400.00

Page 268

Two rows teeth, 14"	1,500.00

Page 269

A9, 18"	2,700.00
Sun Rubber, 13" ...	45.00
200, 10"	125.00

Page 270

SD, 14"	6.00
Talking Terri Lee, 16"	125.00
Terri Lee, 16"	95.00 up

Page 271

Brown Terri Lee, 16"	325.00 up
Brown Jerri Lee, 16"	325.00 up
Linda Baby........	175.00
Connie Lynn, 19"..	275.00
Tiny Terri Lee, 10½"	87.50

Page 272

Brownie, 7½"	25.00
Two Head Troll, 3" .	11.00
Troll, 3"..........	7.00

Page 273

Troll, 3"	9.00
Chunk-a-Luk, 8½" ..	7.00
Troll, 5½"	14.00

Page 274

Surprise Doll, 16" ..	30.00
Baby Sweetums, 20"	6.00
Pollyana, 31"	70.00

Page 275

Debteen, 21"	30.00
Impish Elfy, 11" ...	6.00
Bare Bottom Baby, 12"	14.00

REVISED PRICES VOLUME II

Page 26
All bisque, 11" 1,400.00
French: 4½" 650.00
  5½", bare feet .. 675.-725.00
  5½", molded shoes .. 675.00
  6½", jointed elbows
    & knees .. 1,200.-1,450.00
Page 27
German all bisque,
  swivel neck, 4" 200.00
  5" 225.00
  7"-8" 425.-550.00
  9"-10" 475.00
  Not jointed at neck,
    4½" 150.00
    5½" 175.00
    7" 275.00
    8"-9" 375.00
    10"-11" 600.00
Page 28
9", all bisque 475.00
6", all bisque 185.00
4½", all bisque 150.00
Page 29
7" 275.00
4½", Campbell Kid.... 135.00
4", Tommy Peterkin .. 150.00
4½", molded clothes ... 85.00
Page 30
4½", Bunny 125.00
3¼", Molded ribbon bow 65.00
Page 31
6½", Dutch Boy 25.00
3½", U.S.N. 40.00
Figurine, 3½"-5" ... 15.-40.00
Figurine, 6½"-7½" . 45.-65.00
Page 32
6", Nodder 48.50
5½" All bisque 45.00
German nodders:
  4½"-5½" 55.-75.00
Japan/Nippon:
  4½"-5½" 25.-35.00
Comic Characters:
  German, 3½"-4½" . 55.-75.00
Santa Claus: 6" 100.00
Animals, 3½"-5" ... 30.-65.00
Page 33
With bonnet, 4" 30.00
Occupied Japan, 5" 20.00
Baby, Japan, 5" 65.00
Page 34
Germany, 4½" 60.00
Bye-lo Salt, 2" 325.00
10½", Piano baby 225.00
  Original 225.00
  Reproduction 75.00

5½", Piano baby 95.00
6"-8", With animal ... 195.00
With doll/Teddy bear,
  6"-8" 400.00
Page 35
Amberg, 14" 145.00
Newborn Babe, 12" ... 350.00
Page 36
A.M. googly, 6½" 495.00
  258 googly, 12" ... 1,100.00
253/258, 8" 650.00
  12" 1,100.00
#200, 8" 500.00
  12" 750.00
#323, 8" 600.00
  12" 850.00
#310, 8" 900.00
  12" 1,200.00
#310, Painted bisque,
  8" 385.00
Page 37
My Dream Baby, 6½" . 150.00
  9" 200.00
  12" 250.00
  16" 450.00
  19" 600.00
  23" 750.00
  26" 800.00
Black or Brown:
  6½" 200.00
  12" 425.00
  16" 495.00
  19" 600.00
  23" 700.00
  26" 995.00
Baby Gloria, 16" 600.00
Page 38
1894, 11½" 250.00
  22" 450.00
Talking doll, 17" 475.00
Page 39
990, 25" 625.00
980, 11" 265.00
Mold numbers 370-390:
  10", Crude body 100.00
  10", Good body 125.00
  14" 165.00
  16" 235.00
  18" 275.00
  20" 300.00
  24" 375.00
  26" 400.00
  29" 465.00
  32" 500.00
  36" 900.00
  38" 1,000.00
  40" 1,200.00

  42" 1,500.00
Marked: 1890, 1897, 1914, etc:
  12" 250.00
  15" 300.00
  18" 375.00
  20" 425.00
  26" 500.00
  30" 575.00
  36" 1,000.00
  40" 1,300.00
Page 40
Baby Betty, 17" 400.00
400-401:
  10" 550.00
  16" 1,200.00
  18" 1,400.00
  21" 1,700.00
500: 10" 345.00
  14" 500.00
  16" 695.00
  20" 1,000.00
550: 12" 895.00
  14" 1,200.00
  16" 1,600.00
  20" 2,000.00
560: Baby, 9½" 375.00
  12" 425.00
  14" 500.00
  16" 575.00
590: 12" 850.00
  15" 1,200.00
  18" 1,500.00
  20" 1,800.00
600: 12" 900.00
  15" 1,400.00
  18" 1,600.00
  20" 1,900.00
Fany, 231: 14" 2,100.00
  18" 3,000.00
  20" 3,400.00
Page 41
Floradora: 9"-10" 150.00
  14" 200.00
  16" 275.00
  18" 300.00
  22" 375.00
  25" 425.00
  28" 475.00
  32" 550.00
Page 42
Queen Louise: 10" 165.00
  14" 325.00
  16" 350.00
  18" 375.00
  20" 400.00
  24" 450.00
  28" 500.00

32″ 600.00
9″, 390 . . . . 125.00
22″, 390 . . . . 345.00
Page 43
18″, A.7 M. 495.00
Page 44
13½″, Painted bisque
514 . . . . 165.00
17″, Painted bisque
2966 . . . . 185.00
Page 45
32″, Bed doll 90.00
Page 46
Belton: 12″ 900.00
15″ 1,200.00
20″ 1,850.00
23″ 2,100.00
26″ 2,400.00
Page 47
11″, Black
Heubach 1,400.00
Page 48
16″, Brown Germany . . 785.00
10½″, Black Germany . 250.00
12″, Brown
Jumeau 1,400.00
Page 49
11″, Brown 1909 . . . . . 385.00
16″, Black
Germany 1,000.00
12″, Black/White
Topsy-Turvy 250.00
Page 50
18″, Mammy doll 450.00
Page 51
11″, Black Papier
mache 325.00
10″, Black-Germany . . . 300.00
7″, Brown papier
mache 125.00
Page 52
9″, 399 . . . . 375.00
Page 53
10″, Black papier
mache 295.00
15½″, Brown papier
mache 85.00
Page 54
Scowling Indian,
14″ 275.00
20″, China 385.00
8½″, Indian 150.00
16″, Indian 125.00
Page 55
Bonnet doll, 5½″ 185.00
13″ 400.00
12″ 385.00
Page 56
Bonnet doll, 13″ 365.00

13½″ 300.00
11″ 265.00
8″ 200.00
Page 57
Bru Jne. Closed mouth:
16″, All kid bodies . . 6,500.00
18″ 7,400.00
21″ 8,300.00
26″ 9,500.00
Bru Jne. Bisque lower arms:
12″ 5,000.00
14″ 6,600.00
16″ 8,500.00
20″ 10,000.00
25″ 14,500.00
32″ 17,500.00
36″ 20,000.00
Bru: Composition body:
14″ 3,400.00
17″ 4,000.00
25″ 5,600.00
28″ 6,200.00
Circle Dot Bru: 16″ . . . .
19″ 11,500.00
23″ 14,500.00
28″ 17,300.00
Bru/open mouth: Compo.
body: 14″ 2,200.00
17″ 2,900.00
22″ 3,400.00
25″ 4,000.00
28″ 5,200.00
32″ 5,700.00
Walker body: 18″ . . . .
22″ 3,000.00
26″ 3,600.00
Nursing Bru: 12′″ 3,400.00
15″ 6,500.00
18″ 7,200.00
12″, not good
quality 2,100.00
15″ 3,700.00
18″ 4,700.00
S.F.B.J.: 12″ 1,200.00
15″ 2,200.00
18″ 2,800.00
Page 58
3½″, Celluloid boy 12.00
12″, Sailor 15.00
8″, Orphan Annie 85.00
Page 59
17″, Celluloid head
bear 100.00
14″, Chalk lamp 35.00
Page 60
Bald China: 12″ 500.00
16″ 650.00
20″ 800.00
Bang/black hair, 12″ . . 135.00

16″ 250.00
20″ 400.00
26″ 650.00
Bangs, blonde hair: 12″ 150.00
16″ 285.00
20″ 450.00
26″ 700.00
Brush strokes: 14″ . . . 400.00
18″ 650.00
Brown eyes, 12″ 325.00
16″ 500.00
20″ 595.00
25″ 895.00
28″ 1,000.00
Covered wagon, 12″ . . . 165.00
16″ 425.00
20″ 595.00
Exposed ears, 14″ 300.00
18″ 450.00
22″ 550.00
26″ 700.00
Flat top, 14″ 125.00
17″ 200.00
24″ 325.00
Glass eyes: 14″ 995.00
18″ 2,000.00
22″ 2,400.00
26″ 2,800.00
Man or boy: 14″ 500.00
16″ 750.00
20″ 900.00
Pierced ears: 14″ 400.00
18″ 650.00
22″ 795.00
Snoods, combs, etc.: 14″ 400.00
17″ 600.00
20″ 800.00
25″ 1,200.00
Spill curls: 14″ 300.00
18″ 585.00
22″ 650.00
Page 61
With flowers: 13″ . . . 1,450.00
23″ 995.00
15″ 950.00
Page 62
20″ 500.00
23″ 1,400.00
19½″ 425.00
Page 63
25½″ 650.00
24½″ 365.00
17½″ 450.00
Page 64
8″, Common hair
china 45.00
12″ 65.00
16″ 100.00
19″ 145.00

23" 165.00
27" 200.00
12", Pet name china .. 135.00
14" 145.00
17" 175.00
20" 200.00
24" 265.00

Page 65
12½" 350.00
19" 750.00
8" 65.00

Page 66
5½" 85.00
6" 95.00
5" 145.00
4½" 110.00
5" .. Common hairdo .. 18.00
5½" 20.00
4½" 85.00

Page 67
3½", Doll house doll ... 90.00
6¾", Brownie......... 75.00

Page 68
17" 85.00
8½" 22.00

Page 69
20" 100.00
18" 40.00
15" 125.00

Page 70
10", Clown........ 425.00
11" 600.00
14" 650.00

Page 71
8½" 600.00
12" 125.00
12", Germany 175.00

Page 72
20", 1880's 375.00
11", 1920's 75.00

Page 73
20", Dressel........ 475.00
25" 550.00
12", J.D........... 1,200.00

Page 74
7", Effanbee......... 65.00
12", Grumpy 150.00
20"Bubbles 185.00

Page 75
19", Uncle Sam 450.00
11", Baby Bud 140.00
5½", Frozen
    Charlotte......... 135.00

Page 76
17", Fulper 450.00
21", Gobel 425.00

Page 77
5½", Half doll 265.00
18", H........... 14,000.00

4", Half doll 65.00
Page 78
9", 10044 .... 125.00
9", Mimi 125.00
3" 85.00
Page 79
5" 55.00
4", Germany 85.00
4", With legs 50.00
3½", 16924 .... 45.00
Page 80
3" 45.00
4", Lamp cover 85.00
5" 48.50
4" 27.50
Page 81
17", Handwerck 325.00
24" 450.00
30" 695.00
Page 82
14", Hendren 185.00
15" 195.00
Page 83
15", Koppelsdorf 265.00
19" 325.00
23" 365.00
15", Compo. body 265.00
19" 325.00
23" 365.00
28" 700.00
20" 350.00
Page 84
19", Dolly
    Dimples 1,800.00
17" 1,400.00
Page 85
13" 1,400.00
11" 650.00
11", 192 .... 345.00
Page 86
15½", Horsman 550.00
Page 87
15", Campbell Kid 150.00
13½"Peterkin 145.00
Page 88
19½", Sally 125.00
26" 145.00
10" 100.00
Page 89
19", A.B.W. 385.00
Page 90
15", Ideal........... 95.00
20", Jumeau 2,000.00
Page 91
10", Closed mouth .. 2,200.00
14" 2,600.00
16" 2,800.00
19" 3,300.00
21" 3,600.00

23" 3,700.00
25" 4,100.00
28" 5,200.00
30" 5,500.00
10", Open mouth 995.00
14" 1,400.00
16" 1,600.00
19" 1,900.00
21" 2,100.00
23" 2,300.00
25" 2,500.00
28" 2,800.00
30" 3,000.00
14", 1907 .... 1,000.00
17" 1,300.00
20" 1,600.00
25" 2,100.00
28" 2,700.00
32" 3,200.00
10", Closed mouth,
    E.J. 3,000.00
14" 4,000.00
16" 4,500.00
19" 5,000.00
21" 5,600.00
21", Long face .... 10,000 up
25" .... 12,000 up
30" .... 12,000 up
16", Portrait 4,500
20" 5,400.00
20", Phonograph.... 2,400.00
25" 2,900.00
19", 200 Series
    incised .... 10,000 up
16", S.F.B.J. or Unis .. 650.00
20" 850.00
16", Closed mouth .. 1,400.00
20" 1,800.00
14½", Tete Jumeau . 1,400.00
Page 92
20", 192 .... 3,000.00
25", 1907 .... 2,100.00
22", E.D........... 1,800.00
Page 93
32", 14 .... 3,200.00
20", DEP 850.00
Page 94
9", 101 .... 1,000.00
12" 1,600.00
16" 2,900.00
20" 3,200.00
15", 115 .... 2,500.00
18" 2,700.00
22" 3,200.00
15", 115 or
    115a/open mouth ... 500.00
18" 700.00
22" 1,200.00
15", 116 or 116a ... 2,000.00

18″ 2,300.00
22″ 2,900.00
15″, 116 or
  116a/open mouth . . . 450.00
18″ 650.00
22″ 1,000.00
117 or 117a-18″ 3,800.00
24″ 5,000.00
30″ 5,700.00
15″, 109 . . . . 7,000.00
18″ 8,200.00
15″, 112 . . . . 7,000.00
18″ 8,200.00
15″, 114 . . . . 2,700.00
18″ 4,000.00
28″, 70 . . . . 700.00
15″, 122 . . . . 850.00

Page 95
19½″, 114 . . . . 4,200.00

Page 96
25″ 750.00
10½″, 121 . . . . 450.00
16″, 126 . . . . 500.00

Page 97
16″, With three
  heads 4,800.00
16″, 172 . . . . 1,600.00

Page 98
10″, 221 . . . . 3,700.00
163, 168, 173,
  221 . . . .
12″ 4,000.00
15″ 4,700.00
17″ 5,000.00
20″ 5,400.00
13½″, 216 . . . . 465.00
23″, 162 . . . . 625.00
15″, Closed mouths . 1,300.00
18″ 1,600.00
22″ 2,000.00
26″ 2,400.00
Turned head/closed
  mouths, 15″ 500.00
18″ 995.00
24″ 1,400.00
Turned heads/open
  mouth, 15″ 300.00
18″ 425.00
24″ 575.00
22″, 129 . . . . 625.00
13½″, 639 . . . . 495.00
14½″, 128 . . . . 1,300.00

Page 100
Open mouths: 129, 143,
  145, 147, 148, 162,
  164, 166, 167, 168,
  192, 195, 196, 215,
  264, 14″ 375.00
17″ 500.00

20″ 575.00
26″ 695.00
30″ 1,100.00
36″ 1,500.00
40″ 1,800.00
19½″, D 575.00
34″, 146 . . . . 1,300.00

Page 101
26″, 171 . . . . 600.00

Page 102
Open mouths: 121, 132,
  142, 150, 151: 12″ . . 400.00
16″ 500.00
18″ 675.00
24″ 800.00
152, 211: 12″ 400.00
16″ 500.00
18″ 650.00
24″ 875.00
Hilda: 12″ 1,700.00
16″ 2,700.00
18″ 3,000.00
24″ 4,000.00
226, 227, 260: 12″ . . . 225.00
16″ 575.00
18″ 650.00
24″ 850.00
17″ 595.00
12″ 395.00

Page 103
Kewpies: 4″ 100.00
6″ 200.00
8″ 350.00
10″ 425.00
12″ 625.00
Jointed shoulders and
  hips: 6″ 450.00
8″ 750.00
12″ 1,000.00
Glass eyes: 12″ 4,600.00
16″ 6,500.00
Action: 4″ 225.-400.00
7½″, Shoulder head . . . 600.00
10″ 895.00
Dog: Large 350.00
Small 225.00

Page 104
Celluloid: 2″-3″ 35.00
6″ 50.00
8″ 60.00
10″ 75.00
12″ 95.00
Compo: 12″ 100.00
Jointed: 12″ 145.00
Vinyl/jointed: 12″ 75.00
Hard plastic: 9″ 120.00
12″ 175.00
22″ 200.00
13″ 85.00

6″ 25.00

Page 105
9″, G.K. 135.00
14″, K.W.G. 200.00

Page 106
14½″ 525.00
18″, F.G. 2,500.00

Page 107
18″ 3,500.00

Page 108
30″ 4,000.00

Page 109
11″ 995.00
24″ 3,500.00
17½″ 1,800.00

Page 110
14″ 3,700.00
13″ 2,200.00
19″ 1,600.00

Page 111
15″ 700.00
17″ 675.00
19″ 800.00

Page 112
Lenci child: 16″ 575.00
22″ 895.00
Golfer: 16″ 800.00
22″ 1,200.00
Indian boy: 16″ 900.00
Indian Chief: 22″ . . . 1,200.00
Shirley Temple type:
  30″ 1,200.00
Oriental: 16″ 900.00
22″ 1,300.00

Page 113
22″ 1,200.00
20″ 175.00

Page 114
25″ 725.00

Page 115
30″ 725.00
25″ 900.00
10″ 225.00
7½″ 135.00

Page 116
19″ 350.00
18″ 245.00

Page 117
11½″ 85.00
25″, Mache 1,100.00
18½″, Limoges 625.00

Page 118
23″, B.D. 75.00
19″, 224 . . . . 500.00

Page 119
8″ 495.00
5½″ 145.00
5½″, Undressed 85.00
5¾″ 135.00

Page 120
16½", P.G. 1,800.00
5" 110.00
9" 115.00
Page 121
28", 12 . . . . 2,400.00
21" 2,800.00
Page 122
24", 136 . . . . 495.00
17½" 425.00
Page 123
20" 450.00
12" 145.00
Page 124
29", M 1,600.00
14½", 2015 . . . . 300.00
14" 795.00
Page 125
11" 265.00
23" 750.00
24" 475.00
Page 126
11", Denny 145.00
13", Our Pet 135.00
Page 127
18", Santa 400.00
Page 128
20" 75.00
20", Baby 195.00
Page 129
14", Melba 375.00
20", Baby Peggy 850.00
20", Bisque 2,800.00
Page 130
18" 115.00
Page 131
21½" 125.00
18", F.Y. 275.00
12", 76018 . . . . 150.00
Page 132
23", Wellings 325.00
Page 133
16" 350.00
20" 450.00
Page 134
30" 1,300.00
4½" 325.00
8" 395.00
Page 135
11½" 625.00
18" 850.00
19" 795.00
Page 136
20" 265.00
14½" 145.00
18" 325.00
Page 137
10½" 110.00
12" 225.00

10" 300.00
Page 138
24" 225.00
18", Parian 650.00
Page 139
21" 995.00
15" 1,200.00
16" 995.00
Page 140
24", Tanagra 850.00
11½", Bye-lo 395.00
10½" 300.00
16", Compo 300.00
Page 141
13½", Raleigh 275.00
6½", Googly 600.00
Page 142
16", Goodyear 1,400.00
15", 1930 . . . . 500.00
Page 143
Molded hair, ribbon,
    etc.: 14" 1,000.00
16" 1,150.00
Pouty, 16" 500.00
19" 675.00
Baby: 16" 525.00
17" 595.00
"Dolly" face: 16" . . . 375.00
19" 400.00
Sleep eyes: 16" 475.00
19" 600.00
Page 144
Mold #130, 550,
    1009, etc.: 15" 385.00
18" 495.00
22" 525.00
26" 675.00
Closed mouths, 718, 719,
    939, etc.: 16" 1,800.00
20" 2,200.00
25" 2,600.00
28" 2,900.00
Characters, open
    mouth: 16" 750.00
20" 950.00
25" 1,200.00
28" 1,600.00
1160: 6" 300.00
9" 375.00
1159: 18" 1,200.00
22" 1,300.00
25" 1,600.00
Babies: 1294, etc.: 15" 525.00
20" 700.00
25", 62 . . . . 675.00
24", S.G. 600.00
Page 145
24", 11½" 600.00
Page 146

26", 1078 . . . . 675.00
25", 1079 . . . . 950.00
8", 1078 . . . . 200.00
Page 147
20", P.D. Smith 1,400.00
Page 148
3", Snow Baby 75.00
4½" 85.00
Jointed: 4" 165.00
Poor quality, 3" 25.00
4½" 35.00
30"S.F.B.J. 1,100.00
8½", 60 . . . . 195.00
3¼", Snow Bear 95.00
Page 149
18½", Mechanical . . . 1,600.00
12", Wire eye 2,495.00
22", Mache 1,250.00
Page 150
26", A Series 4,400.00
Page 151
19½", Lori Baby 1,10.00
14½", Superior 325.00
Page 152
9" 110.00
11", 1840's 1,695.00
17½", Creche 475.00
Page 153
25", Wax 365.00
20" 185.00
26", English 375.00
Page 154
28" 345.00
20" 250.00
10" 185.00
Page 155
26", Webber 1,250.00
19", 200 . . . . 375.00
9", MOA 185.00
Page 156
10½" 165.00
16" 87.50
16" 425.00
Page 160
7½", Alice 9.00
8", Bride 3.00
Page 161
8", Alexanderkin 145.00
Mint-short dress . . 125.-145.00
Mint-Ballgown . . 145.-175.00
Played with-street dress 100.00
Played with-ballgown . . 120.00
Clothes washed-short
    dress 85.00
Clothes washed-ballgown 100.00
Not original-short dress . 70.00
Not original-ballgown . . . 90.00
Nude-short dress 50.00
Nude ballgown 60.00

African . . . . 350.00 up
Amish Boy or Girl . . . . 350.00 up
Argentine boy . . . . 400.00 up
Bolivia 350.00
Ecuador . . . . 350.00 up
Eskimo 475.00
Hawaiian . . . . 350.00 up
Greek Boy . . . . 350.00 up
Indian boy or girl 425.00
Korea 350.00
Morocco 350.00
Miss USA 275.00
Peruvian boy 425.00
Spanish boy . . . . 350.00 up
Vietnam 400.00

Page 162
20", Little Genius 85.00
20", Baby McGuffey . . . 200.00
23", Pinky 85.00
12", Precious 85.00
12", Slumbermate 150.00
19", Cookie 125.00
24", Princess 125.00
16", Sunbeam . . . 95.-145.00
23", Honeybun 65.-95.00
19", Bonnie 100.00
15", Kathy 75.00
25", Huggums 85.00
8", Kitten 125.00
20", Happy 200.00
10", Cissette 145.00
In street dress-mint . . . 145.00
Ballgown-mint 300.00
Played with street dress . 95.00
Played with ballgown . . 125.00
Queen-mint 400.00
Queen played with 250.00
Southern Belle Mint . . . 400.00
Played with 200.00
Scarlett Mint 375.00
Played with 175.00
Jacqueline mint 475.00
Played with 200.00

Page 163
10", Gold Rush . . . . . . 950.00 up
15", Cynthia 495.00
17", Dionne Quints
Mint each 385.00
Mint set 2,300.00
8", Toddlers mint 135.00
Played with 50.00
Set 900.00
11", baby mint 225.00
Played with 85.00
Set 1,600.00
11", Toddler Mint 225.00
Played with 85.00
Set 1,600.00
14", Mint 300.00

Played with 100.00
Set 1,800.00
19", Mint 400.00
Played with 175.00
Set 2,400.00

Page 164
Elise Street dress-Mint . 185.00 up
Played with 85.00
Ballgown, Mint . . . . . . 200.00 up
Played with 85.00
Mary-bel head, Mint . . . 185.00 up
Played with 95.00
Ballerina Mint 225.00
Played with 85.00
Bride Mint 225.00
Played with 85.00
7", "Fisher" Quints,
Set 325.00

Page 165
17", Flora McFlimsey . . 375.00
22" 450.00
15" 300.00
12" 200.00
15", 1953 . . . . 375.00
18", Godey 525.00

Page 166
17", Leslie ballgown . . 225.00
Bride 225.00
Ballerina 185.00
Street dress 225.00
12", Lissy #1161 . . . . 350.00
Bride 200.00
Street dress 275.00
Ballerina 295.00
Ball gown 350.00
14", Little Colonel 365.00
9" 175.00
11"-13" 350.00
18" 450.00
23" 575.00
27" 695.00

Page 167
8", Little Lady . . . . 450.00 up
15", Little Women 250.00
Set 1,325.00
Amy, loop curls 350.00
8", Straight leg,
walkers, each 125.00
12", Lissy, each 275.00
7", Composition, each . 165.00
9", each 200.00
13"-15", each 200.00
8", Maggie Mixup 275.00
18", Margaret O'Brien . 400.00
14½" 300.00
21" 650.00
18", Hard plastic 500.00
17", Polly, #1751 . . . . 250.00
Bride 185.00

Ballgown 250.00
Street dress 225.00
Ballerina 185.00
7", Scarlett 200.00
9"-11" 225.-300.00
13"-14" 350.00
16"-17" 350.-450.00
18"-19" 550.00
21" 550.00

Page 170
14", Sonja Henie 275.00
18" 395.00
21" 450.00
Small Set 1,200.00
Fredrich 175.00
Gretl 175.00
Marta 175.00
Brigitta 175.00
Louisa 300.00
Liesl 250.00
Maria 275.00
Large set 1,400.00
Fredrich 225.00
Gretl 165.00
Marta 165.00
Brigitta 225.00
Louisa 275.00
Liesl 225.00
Maria 365.00

Page 171
16", Lucy Baby Mint . . 100.00
Nude 65.00

Page 172
14", Sweet Sue 75.00
18" 100.00
14", Hard plastic/vinyl . 60.00
10½", All vinyl 50.00
17" 75.00
21" 125.00
25" 175.00
18", Godey Lady 100.00
30", Miss Echo 110.00

Page 173
24", Babie Babbles 85.00
19", Sally Says 85.00
19", Pittie Pat 85.00

Page 174
14", Sweet Sue 75.00
23", Toodles 85.00

Page 175
19", Butterball 85.00
18", Toodle-Loo 95.00
12", Nancy 90.00
17" 140.00
19" 165.00
23" 195.00

Page 176
21", Sonja Henie 175.00
18" 140.00

Page 177
11", Nurse 65.00
19", Dream Baby 85.00
23", Angel Face 42.00
Page 178
14", Nancy Lee 95.00
24", Emmett Kelly 95.00
17", Charlie Chaplin . . . 55.00
Page 179
12", Kewpie 150.00
4"-5", One piece body . 125.00
7"-8" 200.00
6", Jointed 500.00
Action Kewpies . . 250.-450.00
With dog 550.00
Dog alone 265.00
Soldier/vase 375.00
With table and tea
 service 1,200.00
Bee on foot . . . .
On sled 575.00
With Teddy Bear 425.00
Bisque shoulder head: 7" 500.00
9" 700.00
12" 1,500.00
Shoulder head with glass
 eyes: 9" 2,800.00
12" 3,600.00
15" 4,800.00
Socket head/glass
 eyes: 12" 3,600.00
15" 400.00
Celluloid: 2½" 30.00
3½" 45.00
5½" 55.00
8" 90.00
10" 100.00
12" 125.00
Composition: 12" 95.00
Jointed, 12" 150.00
Page 180
All cloth, 12" 110.00
14" 145.00
Hard plastic: 9" 60.00
Jointed: 9" 150.00
12" 200.00
15" 275.00
Vinyl: 7" 12.00
12" 25.00
Jointed: 8" 35.00
9" 50.00
12" 85.00
20½", Sally Lou 100.00
15", Miss Peep 45.00
Page 181
Betty Boop: 12" 375.00
24", Cloth 145.00
Page 182
12", Lady 100.00

Page 183
23" 28.00
20" 75.00
15" 12.00
Page 184
14" 60.00
20" 95.00
Page 185
25" 45.00
14", each 50.00
Page 186
20" 30.00
16" 22.00
16", Alice 55.00
Page 187
15" 45.00
12" 50.00
21" 35.00
Page 188
7", Ben Franklin 32.00
7", Betsy Ross 65.00
7", George Washington . 32.00
7", Martha Washington . 32.00
Page 189
27", New Lenci . . 250.-375.00
6½", Comet 10.00
15", Superman 65.00
Page 190
8", Ginger 15.00
24", Lucy Mae 25.00
5", Smokey Bear 10.00
Page 191
Flower Fantasy 12.00
11½", Pinocchio 175.00
18", Mickey Mouse 85.00
12", Tinkerbell 35.00
Page 192
Clear with combs, scarfs,
 etc: 18" 250.00
Glass eyes, 18" . . . . 350.00 up
China, 18" . . . . 225.00 up
23" . . . . 300.00 up
Men, 18" . . . . 275.00 up
23" . . . . 350.00 up
Washingtons, 20" 325.00
Set 800.00
21", China 250.00
Page 193
28" 325.00
20" . . . . unknown
Pennydoll 185.00
Page 194
17", Gigi Perreaux 125.00
16", Flowerkins 45.00
20", Ballerina 28.00
12", Baby Luv 40.00
17", Miss Sunbeam 28.00
14", Granny 85.00
10½", Lil' Susan 15.00

15", Grumpy 165.00
Page 195
15", First Patsy 185.00
Page 196
Patsy and family: see
 section in this book.
Page 197
9", Patsyette 150.00
8", Babyette 150.00
20", Lovums 175.00
22", Lovums 185.00
Page 198
15", Patricia 185.00
19", Patsy Ann 225.00
Page 199
17", Barbara Lou 675.00
14", Baby 85.00
12", Portrait 150.00
Page 200
24", Honey Ann 150.00
14", Honey 75.00
10", Mickey 95.00
Page 201
10½", Mickey 95.00
18" 125.00
30" 165.00
24", Baby 65.00
26" 65.00
12", Butterball 25.00
18", Susie Sunshine 60.00
Page 203
Sleeping Beauty 125.00
Alice 125.00
Cinderella 125.00
Snow White 125.00
Mary Poppins 25.00
Children, each 28.00
6", Can Can 12.00
6", Geisha 15.00
Page 204
15", Jamaica 30.00
15" 42.00
22 French 125.00
Page 205
18", Bella 50.00
10½" 38.00
13½", Celluloid 42.00
Page 206
12" 22.00
19" 50.00
6½", Lilli . . . . 250.00 up
11½", #1 Barbie . . . . . 750.00 up
Page 207
14" 80.00
24" 65.00
Page 208
8" 30.00
4" 10.00
7½", Japan Quints,

each 75.00
Page 209
12", Wood 4.00
15", Korea 12.00
8", Let's Pretend 7.00
Page 210
12", Gay Bob 35.00
Page 211
10½", Gerber white 20.00
  Black 45.00
8", Dennis 22.00
21½", Clown 45.00
Page 212
22", Dimples 175.00
15", Betty 85.00
12", Chubby 40.00
Page 213
18", Cynthia 100.00
12", Campbell Kid 95.00
18", Chubby 48.00
Page 214
12", Campbell 40.00
27", Cindy 85.00
18", Cindy Ruth 65.00
Page 215
26", Ruth's Sister 65.00
16" 20.00
14", 1977 .... 15.00
Page 216
14", Mary Hoyer . 115.-135.00
Page 217
8", Boy 85.00
8", Girl 85.00
12" 22.00
Page 218
18" & 21" .... 400.00 up
Page 219
24" .... 500.00 up
Page 220
Shirley Temple: See section
  in this volume.
Page 221
1973 .... 65.00
16" 95.00
Page 222
25" 165.00
Page 223
18", Miss Charming ... 180.00
28", Miss Charming ... 300.00
19" 110.00
Page 224
12", Fannie Brice 200.00
15", Judy Garland .... 750.00 up
21", Backward 21 .... 185.00
14", Toni 75.00
18" 85.00
21", Toni 95.00
14", Miss Curity 95.00
14", Mary Hartline 100.00

15", Honey Baby 65.00
19", Flossie Flirt 95.00
Page 226
21", Toni 95.00
16", Baby Jo Anne..... 28.00
23", Posie 50.00
Page 227
18", Miss Revelon 60.00
30", Baby Coo's 85.00
7½", Campbell, each ... 15.00
Page 228
42", Daddy's Girl .... 750.00 up
25", Bye Bye Baby 175.00
29", Miss Ideal........ 95.00
Page 229
36", Patti Playpal 135.00
34", Patti Playpal 125.00
15½", Carole Brent 35.00
Page 230
22", Kissy 50.00
Tammy.............. 20.00
20" 28.00
Page 231
9", Betsy 16.00
11½"-12", Super Women,
  each 65.00
10½", New born....... 12.00
Page 232
17", Baby Dreams 40.00
20", Mary Jo 35.00
Bendables, set 45.00
Page 233
11" 27.00
14", Miss Teenage 50.00
Page 234
Dusty 14.00
Horse 10.00
Skye 16.00
Page 235
4", Bisque 18.00
10", Kruse 125.00
10½", Our Girl 45.00
Page 236
17", Our Girl 45.00
17½" 50.00
19" 75.00
Page 237
4", Head 50.00
3", set 50.00
17" 48.00
Page 238
18" 45.00
13" 38.00
15" 45.00
Page 239
3" 15.00
10" 9.00
28" 65.00

Page 240
23" 55.00
18", Girl 42.00
18", Boy 42.00
Page 241
21" 65.00
19", Nun 60.00
Page 242
17", Miss America 35.00
36", Jodi 48.00
Page 243
25" 25.00
22" 35.00
5½" 25.00
Page 244
Barbie, 1965 .... 50.00
Page 245
Bubble Cut 55.00
Molded hair, set 150.00
Swirl bang 75.00
Herman Munster 25.00
Peter Paniddle 20.00
10", Valerie 9.00
Page 247
11", Cinderella 12.00
Kiddle Kone 9.00
6½", Lori 22.00
Set 35.00
Page 248
1972 Barbie 40.00
12", Boone 10.00
19", Spiderman 20.00
Page 249
6", Mickey 25.00
12", Nubia 25.00
Page 250
12", Queen........... 20.00
12", Steve 15.00
8", Captain 18.00
8", Huggee Bear 18.00
Page 251
18", Baby 40.00
Cher outfit 14.00
22" 20.00
Page 252
17", Mollye 170.00
Page 253
8", Muffie 75.00
5", #186 .... 35.00
5", #180 .... 35.00
5", #181 .... 35.00
Page 254
5", #182 .... 35.00
#183 .... 35.00
#184 .... 35.00
#185 .... 35.00
Page 255
5", Spring 35.00
5", Summer 35.00

ALL BISQUE FRENCH

French all bisques generally have longer, thinner legs than the German made ones. They will be jointed at the neck, shoulders and hips with the arms being longer looking, and more slender than German dolls. Also, they generally have glass eyes and very few have open mouths. The painting of the bisque is better than the German dolls, and the eyebrows will be feathered, the lashes painted well, and the mouths will generally be outlined. The French all bisque can be bare footed or have modeled on shoes, boots with painted socks to the knees or the entire leg will be painted (high socks). There are dolls that have jointed knees, and/or elbows, and these are the most sought after by the collectors. If original or nicely dressed, and in excellent condition the following are prices: 4½", Swivel neck, molded shoes –$650.00; 5½", Bare feet – $675.-725.00; 5½", Molded shoes – $675.00; 6½", Also jointed at elbows and knees – $1,200.-1,450.00. French *types*: 5½" – $325.00; French *types* with swivel necks: 5½" – $475.00; Later French such as SFBJ, 5" – $300.00, 7" – $400.00.

7" French all bisque jointed at neck, shoulders and hips. Painted on high laced boots and white ribbed socks. Bent left arm with excellent modeling to hands. Set glass paperweight eyes, feathered brows and open/closed mouth with outlined lips. Looks very much as a miniature Bru. Marks: 132. Shown in two separate wigs. Courtesy Jane Walker.

ALL BISQUE GERMAN

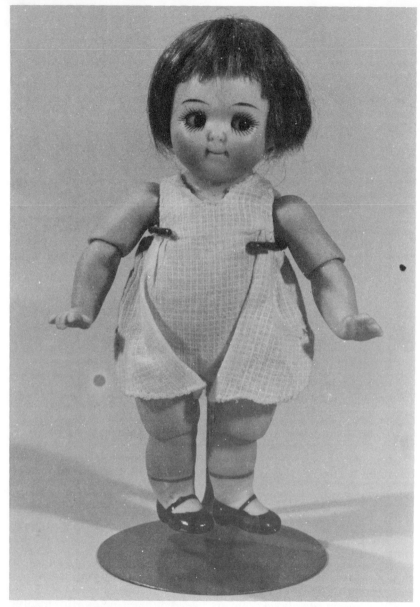

6'' All bisque googlie with set glass eyes to sides, closed "watermelon" mouth, and has original wig and clothes. Multi jointed arms and legs and painted on white socks and black Mary Jane shoes. Marks: 111/3, on head, and 3, on arms and legs. Courtesy Virginia Jones.

7½" All bisque with blue sleep eyes, open mouth with four teeth. Label on chest: Princess/Made in Germany. Head is incised 150, arms: 83 over 150 and legs: 150. Has large feet with painted shoes and socks. This could either be a Kestner or a Bonn doll. Jointed at shoulders and hips. Courtesy Louise Benfatti.

10" All bisque with large set eyes, open mouth and four teeth. Jointed at shoulders and hips. Marks: #30 over 10. Painted on shoes and socks. Courtesy Sylvia Bryant.

German all bisques jointed at shoulders, hips and neck, with glass eyes, open or closed mouths, nicely dressed or original and with good wig, most will have molded on shoes and socks: 4" – $200.00; 5" – $225.00; 6" – $300.00; 7"-8" – $425.-550.00; 9"-10" – $675.00; 12" – $800.00. Same, but with painted eyes: 4" – $125.00; 5" – $150.00; 6" – $200.00; 7"-8" – $275.00; 9"-10" – $475.00. German all bisques jointed and shoulders and hips only with glass, open or closed mouth, with good wig and nicely dressed: 4½"-5½" – $150.-175.00; 7" – $275.00; 8"-9" – $375.00; 10"-11" – $600.00. Same but with painted eyes: 4½"-5½" – $140.00; 7" – $165.00; 8"-9" – $185.-200.00; 10"-11" – $250.-350.00.

All prices on the above dolls are based on the fine *quality* bisque and painting of the bisque. The later all bisque dolls have far less quality, and lower prices.

Kestner was the major maker of all bisques from Germany, and some of their mold numbers are: 112, 130, 150 (most common), X150, 151, 152, 164, 192, 208, 257, 307, 310, 314, 600 & 620.

German all bisques with molded on clothes, jointed at shoulders and hips only, or at shoulders only: 4½" – $75.-85.00; 5½" – $125.00; 6"-7" – $150.-185.00.

ALL BISQUE CHARACTERS

All bisque dolls with character faces, stances, or names were made both in Germany and in Japan. The German models have finer bisque, and painting of the bisque. Most will be jointed at the shoulders only, or the shoulders and the hips, with few being jointed at the neck. They can be bare footed, or have modeled on shoes and socks. It must be remembered that a lot of these character dolls made in Japan were taken directly from the German molds: Baby Bo Kaye, 6½" – $1,300.00; Baby Bud, Germany, 5" – $150.00; Baby Bud, Japan, 5" – $75.00; Baby Darling, 5" – $50.-60.00; Baby Peggy Montgomery, 6" – $300.00; Bonnie Babe, 5" – $725.00; Bye-Lo, 6", jointed neck, glass eyes – $600.00; Campbell Kid, molded clothes, 4½" – $135.00; Chin Chin by Heubach, 5" – $275.00; Didi by Orsini, 6" – $1,250.00; Googly, glass eyes, 6" – $250.-600.00; Googly, painted eyes, 6" – $165.-450.00; Grumpy boy, Germany, 4" – $100.00; Grumpy boy, Japan, 4" – $55.00; Heubach, molded hair, 6½" – $375.00; Heubach, molded ribbon, 6½" – $485.00; Heubach, wigged, 7" – $450.00; Heubach, Bunny boy, 4½" – $100.00; Little Imp, (Hoofed feet), 6½" – $250.00; MIBS by Amberg, 3½" – $175.-200.00; Mimi by Orsini, 6" – $1,250.00; Our Fairy, 8" – $1,250.00; Peek-a-Boo by Drayton, 4" $100.00; Peterkin, 9" – $350.00; Painted eyes, 6" – $365.00; Queue San Baby, various poses, 5" – $100.00; Sonny by Averill, 5" – $450.00; Tommy Peterkin, German for Horsman, 4" – $150.00; Wide Awake Doll, Germany, 7½" – $250.00; Wide Awake Doll, Japan, 7½" – $95.00.

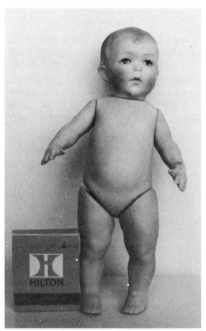

5" "Sonny" all bisque. Excellent quality with modeled and painted hair, beautifully painted eyes, and detail of mouth. Jointed at neck, shoulders and hips. Marks: Sonny/Copr. by/Georgene Averill/Germany. Courtesy Virginia Travis.

6" All bisque googly marked: 200 A 10/0 M/Germany/ DRGM 243. Closed "watermelon" mouth, painted on shoes and socks and jointed at neck, shoulders and hips. Made by Armand Marseille. Courtesy Jane Walker.

4½" All bisque baby that is all in one piece. Bent right arm with closed fist, and very bent legs. Fits into the original box as shown. Original clothes. Painted hair and features. Unmarked. Courtesy Marcia Piecewicz.

2" & 1¼" Snow Babies all bisque. No joints, and have a "pebbled" covering to clothes. Well painted, but unmarked. Courtesy Penny Pendlebury.

BABIES: All bisque babies of good and bad quality were made in both Germany and Japan. They were made, good and bad, all during the production span, but the poor ones are generally from a later date. "Babies" have bent baby limbs, at least the legs are in a bent position. Ones that are jointed at the neck, shoulders and hips are the most desirable. They would be priced: 3½" – $145.00 to 6" – $350.00. The tiny 6"-7" Bye-lo would be – $450.00-650.00. (See Putnam Section for full price ranges). The babies jointed at neck can have sleep or inset glass eyes and bring higher prices than painted eyes. They may have wigs or painted hair.

All bisque babies with extremely well painted features, character faces, jointed shoulders and hips, and details such as free form thumbs, molded bottles in hand, or molded clothes would cost: 3½" – $100.00; 6" – $200.00.

Babies sold or given away at candy counters were called "Candy Babies", and are generally poorly painted and have high color bisque cost: 2½" – $20.00; 4" – $35.00; 5"-6" – $65.00.

Babies made in Japan can be good or poor quality. A poor to medium quality: 3½" to 5" – $5.-40.00. A really nicely done of the same size would be: 3½" to 5" – $15.-65.00. SNOW BABIES: Made both in Germany and Japan, these can also be good or poor quality from both countries. 1½" single – $55.00; 1½", two together – $125.00; 1½", three together – $175.00; 5" with jointed hips and shoulders – $300.00; 7"-9" pebbled shoulder head doll on cloth bodies with china limbs – $350.00. Rare and priced very high. Snow Babies are: On sled in glass "snow scene" – $145.00; 3½" with bear – $165.00; 3" with snowman – $150.00; 3" laughing child – $95.00; Snow bear with Santa – $250.00; Three on a sled – $125.00.

NODDERS
ALL BISQUE
JAPAN FIGURINES

"Knotters" are called "Nodders" and are jointed at the neck only, and when their heads are touched they "nod". The reason the correct term is "Knotters" is due to the way they are generally strung, with the stringing tied in a knot through the head. They can also be made with cutouts on the bodies to take tiny rods out the side of the necks. Both styles were made in Germany and Japan. Santa Claus, 6" – $100.00; Teddy Bear, 6" – $100.00; Other animals (rabbit, dog, etc.), 3½"-5" – $30.-65.00; Comic characters, Germany, 3½"-5" – $55.-75.00; Others made in Germany, 4½"-5½" – $55.-75.00; Those made in Japan/Nippon, 4½"-5½" – $25.-35.00; Sitting position, excellent quality man or woman (may be orientals) 6½"-8" – $225.00.

All bisque dolls from Japan vary a great deal on quality. There are some very nicely painted ones, and others are very poorly painted, or the paint is chipped off. The following are prices for various qualities. *All these are at least jointed at the shoulders.* Nice painted dolls with good quality bisque: 3½" – $10.-15.00; 5" – $25.00; 6" – $45.00; 7" – $65.00. Marked "Nippon" with name - Baby Darling, etc., 4" – $30.00; 6½" – $75.00. Child with molded on clothes: 4½" – $20.00; 6" – $45.00. Nodders (elastic strung): 3" – $15.-20.00. Comic Characters: 4" – $20.00 up. Comic Characters: See comic section of All Bisque. The late Occupied Japan (1940): 3½" – $6.00; 5" – $10.00; 7" – $15.00.

There were a great many figurines that became popular in the 1920's and 1930's that are placed for sale with dolls. To be a real doll, the item must have moving parts, even if it only has shoulder joints, or neck jointed. The all bisque figures have molded, painted on clothes and painted features. Generally these items are just painted, and the colors are not fired into the bisque/ceramic and the paint chips easily over the years. A sample of values are: Indians, Dutch Children, 2½" – $15.00; Teddy Bears – $20.-45.00; Santa Claus – $20.00; Adults – $25.00; Children, 3" – $10.-15.00.

2" All bisque with molded hair, painted eyes and jointed at the shoulders only. Incised: Japan. Courtesy Florence Black Musich.

4½" All bisque bear incised Made in Japan #113. 3½" bear incised Made in Japan #114 and 2½" bear incised Made in Japan #115. Not jointed. Courtesy Florence Black Musich.

5" Painted all bisque that is jointed at shoulders and hips. Molded blonde hair, painted features. No marks. Shoes are painted on, and wears original clothes. (Author).

5" All bisque Minnie Mouse and incised on front of skirt: Minnie Mouse. Marked on back: Walt E. Disney. The other object is a frosted ceiling light shade that is 7" in diameter marked WDP. Courtesy Florence Black Musich.

CARTOON AND ADVERTISING ALL BISQUE: 2½", Mickey McGuire, Copyright by Fontaine Fox, Germany – $55.00; 2½", Herby #C82, Japan – $35.00; Nodder – $45.00; 4", Mr. Peanut, Japan – $35.00; 5", Johnny-Call For Phillip Morris, Germany – $45.00; 5", Mickey Mouse, Walt Disney – $60.00; 3", Mickey Mouse with musical instrument – $45.00; 5", Minnie Mouse, Walt Disney – $60.00; 3½", Betty Boop, Fleischer Studios, Japan – $25.-35.00; 3½", Betty Boop with musical instrument – $25.-35.00; Baby Tarzan and Mother Gorilla – $35.00; 3½", Orphan Annie – $45.00; Nodder – $55.00; 3½", Seven Dwarfs, each – $25.00; 3", Popeye – $45.00; 7", Annie Rooney, Germany – $125.00; 3½", Winnie Walker, Branner, Germany – $65.00; 3½", Skeezic – $45.00; 4", Dick Tracy, Germany – $55.00; 3½", Mary Ann Jackson (Our Gang) – $50.00; 3½", Our Gang Boys, each – $50.00; 4", Moon Mullins and Kayo – $45.00; 4", Lady Plush Bottom, Germany – $45.00; 4", Mr. Bailey The Boss, Germany – $45.00; 3½", Aunty Blossom, Germany – $45.00.

AMBERG, LOUIS & SONS

LOUIS AMBERG, AND SONS
Doll Makers, and Importers

Baby Peggy Montgomery: Mold #973, 982, 983, 2" – $2,600.00; 22" – $3,000.00. All bisque with closed smiling mouth, molded hair with full bangs and "Dutch" bob hairdo. One piece body and head, painted on Mary Jane shoes and white socks. 6" – $300.00.

Mibs: Marks: L.A. & S. 1921/Germany: can have two different paper labels with one reading - Amberg Dolls/Please Love Me/I'm Mibs, and some without the Amberg Dolls. Molded hair with long strand on forehead. Mibs of all bisque: One piece body and head, jointed at shoulders and hips - 3" – $175.00; 6" – $285.00. Mibs-composition with molded hair with long strand on forehead. Painted on Mary Jane shoes and white socks. Cloth body with composition limbs. Painted blue eyes, 12" – $275.00; 16" – $375.00.

New Born Babe: Mold #G45520. Marks: L.A. & S. 1914/G45520 Germany and some have "heads copyrighted by Louis Amberg". Cloth bodies and can have composition, celluloid or rubber hands. Bisque heads with painted hair, sleep eyes and closed mouth with protruding upper lip. 9" – $300.00; 14" – $475.00; 18" – $750.00.

New Born Babe: Open mouth version. Marks: L.A. & S. 371. 9" – $225.00; 14" – $400.00; 18" – $550.00.

Charlie Chaplin: Composition head and hands. Eyes painted to side, cloth body and legs. Black suit and white shirt. 13"-14" – $300.00.

Vanta Baby: Marks: Vanta Baby-Amberg. Cloth body with composition head and limbs and has fat legs. Spring strung, sleep eyes, open/closed mouth with two teeth. Made to advertise Vanta Baby Garments. Bisque head, 18" – $500.00. Composition head, 18" – $135.00.

22" Baby Peggy Montgomery. Closed smiling mouth with dimples, sleep brown eyes, original full bang wig. Bisque shoulder head on kid body with bisque lower arms. Marks: 1924/L.A. & S. N.Y./Germany. 50-983/2. Courtesy Elizabeth Burke.

14" Marked: Amberg/Pat. Pend./L.A. & S./1928. All composition with swivel waist, beautifully molded hair, and painted features. Courtesy Sally Swain.

32

ARMAND MARSEILLES (A.M.)

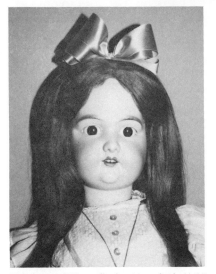

11" marked: "Germany/258/A O M. One of the "Cheer-Up" googlies of 1916. Courtesy Magda Byfield, Surry, England.

32" Armand Marseille that is marked: A. 15 M. Brown sleep eyes, open mouth with four teeth. She is on a fully jointed composition body. Courtesy Glorya Woods.

The Armand Marseille firm has more examples of their dolls around than any other company due to the fact that they just made, and imported more. They also filled the replacement head market by supplying large quantities of heads to dealers and wholesalers. The Armand Marseille firm began in 1865, but the vast amount of their dolls were made in the 1890's and into 1920's. This firm was always extremely proud of their work and the vast majority of their dolls are fully marked.

The mold number "370" just means that the doll has a shoulder plate, or is a shoulder head (swivel). Mold number "390" means that it is a socket head to be used on a composition/mache body.

There are collectors that look just for the "name" Armand Marseille dolls. Some of these incised name dolls are: Alma, Baby Betty, Baby Gloria, Baby Phyllis, Beauty, Columbia, Darling Baby, Dutchess, Fany, Floradora, Incidein, Heredera, Just Me, Kiddiejoy, Lilly, Lissy, Mabel, Melita, Majestic, My Companion, My Dearie, My Playmate, Nobbikid, Queen Louise, Rosebud, Roseland, Sadie, Special, Dollar Princess.

Armand Marseille dolls can be very poor in quality, or they can compare with the finest German dolls. The finer the bisque (pale, not high color or "smeared looking"), and the finer painted features will bring higher prices.

370 and 390 mold number dolls; 10" with crude five piece body – $100.00; 10" on good quality, fully jointed body – $125.00; 14" – $165.00; 16" – $235.00; 18" – $275.00; 22" – $325.00; 24" – $375.00; 26" – $400.00; 28" – $450.00; 32" – $500.00; 36" – $900.00; 38" – $1,000.00; 40" – $1,200.00; 42" – $1,500.00.

Dolls marked with 1890, 1894, 1897, 1914, etc: 12" – $250.00; 15" – $300.00; 18" – $375.00; 20" – $425.00; 22" – $450.00; 26" – $500.00; 30" – $575.00; 36" – $1,000.00; 40" – $1,300.00.

ARMAND MARSEILLES (A.M.)

Queen Louise: 10" – $165.00; 14" – $325.00; 16" – $350.00; 18" – $375.00; 20" – $400.00; 24" – $450.00; 28" – $500.00; 32" – $600.00.

Floradora: 9" – $150.00; 14" – $200.00; 16" – $275.00; 18" – $300.00; 22" – $375.00; 25" – $425.00; 28" – $475.00; 32" – $550.00.

Babies: Can be on composition, bent leg baby bodies, or on cloth bodies: Mold numbers 341, with closed mouth or 351, with open mouths are *My Dream Baby* made for the Arranbee Doll Company. There will be babies with mold number 345-*Kiddiejoy* that is same as the 351 mold: 6"-7" – $150.00; 9" – $200.00; 12" – $250.00; 14" – $325.00; 16" – $450.00; 20" – $600.00; 24" – $795.00; 28" – $850.00. These same mold numbered babies with brown or black bisque (fired in) are: 6½" – $200.00; 9" – $265.00; 12" – $425.00; 16" – $495.00; 19" – $600.00; 23" – $700.00; 26" – $995.00. Babies with character mold numbers: 327, 971, 985, 990, 992, 995 & 996 will be found most often: 10" – $250.00; 14" – $275.00; 16" – $325.00; 18" – $375.00; 22" – $475.00; 26" – $695.00. If these baby heads are on toddler bodies the cost will average $100.00 more.

Babies with more uncommon mold numbers such as: 328, 329, 352, & 560a: 10" – $225.00; 14" – $300.00; 18" – $400.00; 22" – $500.00. Allow $100.00 more for toddler bodies. Baby Gloria: 14" – $475.00; 18" – $700.00; 24" – $950.00; 28" – $1,300.00. Fany-Mold number 230 & 231: 14" – $2,100.00; 18" – $3,000.00; 24" – $5,000.00; 28" – $6,200.00. Baby, toddler or child. Googlys: Mold 310-Just Me fired in color: 9" – $900.00; 12" – $1,200.00. Painted bisque: 9" – $385.00; 12" – $595.00. Mold numbers 254, 320, 210 and others with intaglio eyes: 7" – $495.00; 12" – $1,100.00. Most common is the mold number 323 with glass eyes: 7" – $600.00; 12" – $850.00.

Armand Marseille made some very interesting character molds, and these are fairly rare and most are excellent quality. They may be wigged, or have molded hair, some have glass eyes while others have intaglio painted eyes, and some will have fully closed mouths, and others have open/closed mouths: *248:* 10" – $600.00; 14" – $800.00; 17" – $1,100.00. *372:* Kiddijoy: 14" – $500.00; 17" – $795.00. *360:* 14" – $325.00; 18" – $575.00. *500:* 10" – $345.00; 16" – $695.00; 20" – $1,000.00. *550:* 10" – $795.00; 16" – $1,600.00; 20" – $2,000.00. *560a:* 10" – $375.00; 16" – $575.00; 20" – $700.00. *590:* 10" – $495.00; 16" – $1,300.00; 20" – $1,800.00. *600:* 10" – $695.00; 16" – $1,500.00; 20" – $1,900.00. Adult face mold numbers 400 and 401 have long thin jointed limbs with knee joints above knee, 14" – $750.00; 16" – $1,200.00. With painted bisque: 14" – $350.00; 16" – $600.00.

ARMAND MARSEILLES (A.M.)

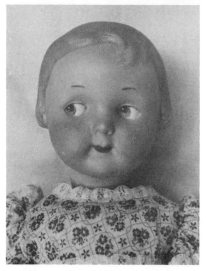

12" with 9" head circumference with very nice bisque, molded hair and blue intaglio eyes to the side. Comes on a five piece mache body as well as a fully jointed composition body. (This one on a replaced body) The mouth is closed. Marks 210/A.O.M./Germany/D.R.G.M. Courtesy Sylvia Bryant.

20" Mold number 231/Fany, in script/A.7 M. Can be on baby body, toddler body and on a fully jointed child body. Can either blue or brown sleep eyes. Has closed mouth and a very character face. Courtesy Elizabeth Burke.

14" Marked: A.M. 251/G.B./Germany/A.O.M./D.R.G.M. 248. Toddler body with full joints, sleep eyes and open/closed mouth with molded tongue. Excellent bisque. Courtesy "Tete" Cook.

10" "Just Me" mold number 310 with painted bisque. Eyes to side and closed mouth. Five piece body with bent right arm. Replaced clothes and wig. Courtesy Diane Hoffman.

ARMAND MARSEILLES (A.M.)

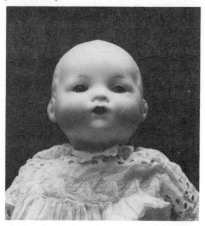

20" Socket head in shoulder plate on cloth body, sleep eyes and open mouth with teeth. Marks: A.M./Germany/342/4. Courtesy Lois Miluis.

14" "My Dream Baby" twins marked: A.M./Germany/341. The mouths are closed and they have blue sleep eyes. Cloth body and limbs. Old organdy gowns and lace caps, old wicker buggy. Courtesy Gloria Woods.

Character child that is marked: Armand Marseille/360a/A.8/0 M./D.R.G.M. R. 232. Bisque socket head on bisque shoulder plate with kid body, and bisque lower arms. Open mouth. Courtesy Sylvia Bryant.

22" Marked 370/A.M./3 DEP. kid body with bisque lower arms. Open mouth. Courtesy Diane Hoffman.

36

26" Marked 370/A.M. 5 DEP./Made in Germany. Kid body with green paper label: Floradora/½ cork stuffed. Blonde mohair wig, blue sleep eyes and inset fur eyebrows. Courtesy Louise Benfatti, costumed by Sally Freeman.

Right: 12" All original boy marked Germany/390/A.5/0 M. Blue sleep eyes, open mouth on composition body with stick arms and legs. Left: 12" girl marked 1894/A.M. 5/0 DEP/Germany. Brown set eyes, open mouth and on composition body with stick arms and legs. Courtesy Marcia Piecewicz.

390 Armand Marseille in a state of restoration. Shows the "stick" legs (long upper legs), and how the original long hose-socks were stapled to the wooden upper leg. Courtesy Diane Hoffman.

24" Marked A.M. 390 with brown sleep eyes, mohair wig and on composition body with stick legs. Factory original costume of red cotton sateen dress and hat, off white cotton lace trim, three piece satin underwear, black stockings and shoes. Courtesy Sally Freeman.

ARMAND MARSEILLES (A.M.)

10'' All original, in original box and marked A.M. 390. Open mouth and on five piece mache body with painted on shoes and socks. (Author).

11'' Mint in the box marked A.M. 390. Open mouth, fired in color and on a five piece mache body with painted on boots and socks. All original. Card in box says Canada, with a British flag. Courtesy "Tete" Cook.

12'' Marked Made in Germany/ Armand Marseille/390/D.R.G.M. 246/1/A. 6/0 M. Brown sleep eyes, blonde hair, open mouth on five piece mache body. Lavender organdy original dress trimmed in white lace and tatting, and blouse under dress appears to be cheese cloth. Long white hose, white slip and panties with white shoes and black design for a buckle. The hat is white trimmed with lavender organdy. Courtesy Eloise Godfrey.

7'' Marked Germany/390/A. 3/0 M. twins with sleep eyes, open mouths and mohair wigs. Well molded bodies with painted on long hose and brown heeled shoes. Dressed by Sally Freeman. Courtesy Dorothy Mulholland.

ARMAND MARSEILLES (A.M.)

14" Marked Armand Marseilles/Germany/401/A. 5/0 M. Flapper. Has adult flapper body with bust line, jointed at the knees and elbows. Closed mouth. The body is stamped "Germany", on the back. Very pointed chin. Courtesy Elizabeth Burke.

18" Marked A.M. 500 Germany. Cloth body, jointed and with stitched fingers. The head is painted mache with sleep eyes and a full closed mouth. All original. (Author).

17" Marked Germany/550/A.3 M./-D.R.G.M. Character doll with full closed mouth and protruding upper lip, brown sleep eyes and mohair wig. Excellent quality bisque. Courtesy Jane Walker.

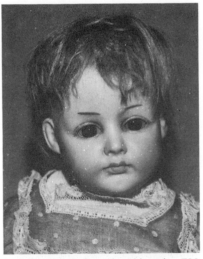

16" Character baby with mold number 700. Will be found on both toddler bodies and bent leg baby bodies. Courtesy Magda Byfield, Surry, England.

ARMAND MARSEILLES (A.M.)

19" Character Armand Marseille mold number 800. Large brown eyes and wide open/closed mouth with molded gum and tongue. Large cheek dimples and excellent quality bisque. Courtesy Barbara Earnshaw.

Large character boy marked A.M. 990 Germany. Excellent bisque with well painted brows. Brown sleep eyes with lashes, open mouth and dimple in chin. Courtesy Barbara Earnshaw.

19" Marked Baby Betty/A.M./Made in Germany/D.R.G.M. Brown set eyes, bisque shoulder plate, kid body with pin joints at elbows and knees and has bisque lower arms. The lower legs are composition, open mouth, four teeth and dimple in chin. Courtesy Gloyra Woods.

21" Marked Floradora, on paper label on body and marked 275. 4/0/ Germany, on head. Almond shaped blue sleep eyes, bisque shoulder plate on kid body with bisque lower arms. Cloth lower legs and feet. Open mouth and dimple in chin. Courtesy Glorya Woods.

23½'' Marked A. 9 T. with open mouth. Composition jointed body. Has two rows of teeth in open mouth. Courtesy Kimport Dolls.

13'' Small open mouth marked A.T. with two rows of teeth. Composition jointed body. Mark: A.4 T. Courtesy Kimport Dolls.

A. Thuillier made dolls in Paris from 1875 to 1890, and may be the makers of the dolls marked with "A.T.". The marked A.T. bisque heads have been found on wooden, composition and kid bodies, and it is known that A. Thuillier made dolls with these combinations of bodies during the short fifteen years he was in business. A.T. dolls can have closed mouths, or open mouths (with two rows teeth). This company made dolls that were sold dressed and undressed, and can come in sizes from 12" up to 30". The quality of A.T. dolls is no different from any other firm, they can be exquisite quality, or poor quality. Only the most beautiful bisque, eyes and correct bodies will command the high prices placed on these scarce dolls of today. The dolls will be marked with A, followed by a number, which denotes size (example 6), then the letter T. Closed mouth: 14" – $11,000.00; 18" – $14,000.00; 26" – $18,000.00. Open mouth (two rows teeth): 14" – $10,000.00; 18" – $12,000.00; 26" – $16,000.00.

BABY SANDY

19" and 11" Baby Sandy. All composition with molded hair. The large one has sleep eyes and smaller one painted eyes. The large one is in copy of original dress and small one is all original. Made by Ralph Freundlich. Marks: Baby Sandy, on head. Courtesy Martha Sweeney. 8" - $115.00; 11" - $145.00; 14" - $215.00; 19" - $300.00.

BELTON

"Belton" dolls are marked with a number, or nothing. They come on French bodies, both very crude and very fine ones. Many have almost white bisque with a pink wash blending over the eyes. They can have wide open/closed mouths, or lips almost together, but the majority have the area between the lips left white.

"Dome", "Bald", and "Ball" heads are different, and are German. These heads are solid shaped and completely round without the concave; although some will have one or two holes for stringing or wigs.

Prices for dolls with the French bodies and *concave* heads with two or three stringing and wig holes that are nicely dressed and wigged: 10" – $750.00; 12" – $900.00; 15" – $1,200.00; 18" – $1,550.00; 20" – $1,850.00; 23" – $2,100.00; 26" – $2,400.00.

17" "Belton" with concave flat head with three holes, open/closed mouth and set paperweight eyes. On French fully jointed body. No marks. (Author).

16" "Belton" marked 106, at base of crown and has an .8, on neck. Concave head with three holes. French body with straight wrists. Pierced ears. Closed mouth. Courtesy Betty Shelly.

14½" Belton type with concave top to head and three holes. Closed mouth and on French jointed body. Courtesy Kimport Dolls.

24", 20", and 10" "Beltons". All are on French bodies and all have concave heads with holes. Open/closed mouths and pierced ears. Courtesy Barbara Earnshaw.

24" Belton-type with concave dome to head and three holes in the concave part. Set paperweight eyes, and an open closed mouth with part between lips painted white. French style body with straight wrists. No marks. Courtesy Barbara Earnshaw.

13" "Belton" marked 137. Concave head with two holes. Open/closed mouth with white painted in-between lips. Pierced ears and on French body with straight wrists. Courtesy Trudy Shelley.

17" "Belton-Type" that is marked 289 / DEP. Concave head with three holes. Pierced ears and on nice French body. Closed mouth. Courtesy Betty Shelley.

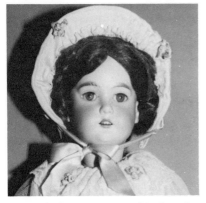

24" Marked C.M. Bergmann/Made in Germany. Bisque head on composition jointed body. Light brown feathered, molded brows, blue sleep eyes, open mouth with four teeth. Courtesy Glorya Woods.

22" Bed-Boudoir Doll that is all original with painted features. The eyes are narrow and painted to the side. Tuffs of human hair are sewn to the skull cap, which is glued to the head. Face mask on cloth body and legs, but the arms are jointed at elbows and wrists with finely detailed wooden hands. (Author).

C.M. Bergmann dolls with open mouths, ball jointed bodies, nicely dressed and good wigs: 18" – $300.00; 21" – $365.00; 24" – $450.00; 27" – $550.00; 30" – $695.00; 34" – $1,000.00.

C.M. Bergmann dolls may have other makers names along with their own on the dolls, such as Simon & Halbig or Armand Marseille. Prices are determined by the quality of the bisque.

Bed-Boudoir Dolls that are excellent quality with finely painted features and excellent quality clothes: 28" – $95.00; 32" – $120.00. Dolls with composition heads, stapled on wigs, and composition limbs; 28" – $70.00; 32" – $90.00. Men or children of any materials: 24" – $85.00; 28" – $110.00.

Three bed-boudoir dolls of the 1920's. Left has red yarn hair and is a molded mask "stockenette" type with oil painted features. Center is a red head, has inset eyelashes, is composition with painted features. Right is blonde with painted features. Courtesy Mary Sweeney.

BOUDOIR DOLLS

30'' French Bed-Boudoir Doll with silk face, suede cloth arms and cotton sateen body. Beautiful detail clothes and hair. Painted features. Courtesy Nancy Lucas.

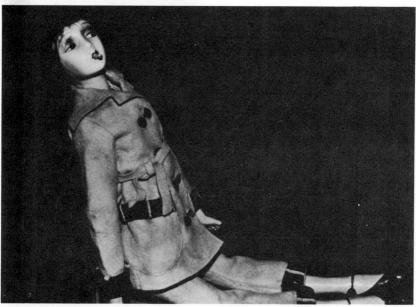

29'' Cigarette Smoker. All composition with pin joints at elbows and knees, long thin neck and has hole in mouth for cigarette. Molded, painted on shoes with heels, adult body with thin waist and original felt clothes. Wig, and painted features with eyes to the side. Unmarked. Courtesy Mary Sweeney.

24" Open mouth marked Bru Jne R. 11. Pierced ears. Full jointed composition body. Courtesy Kimport Dolls.

30" Marked Circle and dot Bru. (⊙) Bisque lower arms, open/closed mouth and large paperweight eyes. Courtesy Mary McGinty.

Bru dolls will be marked with the name Bru, Bru Jne, Bru Jne R, and sometimes with a circle-dot (⊙), or a half circle and dot. (◠). Bru dolls are found on kid bodies, kid over wood, all wood, or on all composition bodies. When there is a bisque shoulder plate, it too will be marked with Bru and a number over the edge of the shoulder.

Closed mouth dolls. Bru: All kid body with bisque lower arms: 16" – $6,500.00; 18" – $7,400.00; 21" – $8,300.00; 26" – $9,500.00. Bru Jne: Kid over wood, wood legs, bisque lower arms: 12" – $5,000.00; 14" – $6,600.00; 16" – $8,500.00; 20" – $10,000.00; 25" – $14,500.00; 28" – $15,500.00; 32" – $17,500.00; 36" – $20,000.00. Bru Jne: All wood body: 16" – $7,800.00; 20" – $8,800.00. Bru: Marked: Bru Jne R. All composition body: 14" – $3,400.00; 17" – $4,000.00; 22" – $4,800.00; 25" – $5,600.00; 28" – $6,200.00. Bru: Circle-dot: 16" – $7,400.00; 19" – $11,500.00; 23" – $14,500.00; 26" – $16,000.00; 28" – $17,300.00. Brevete Bebe: 17" – $7,200.00; 20" – $8,500.00.

Open mouth dolls: Bru: Marked: Bru Jne R. All compositon body: 14"2,200.00; 17" – $2,900.00; 22" – $3,400.00; 25" – $4,000.00; 28" – $5,200.00; 32" – $5,700.00. Composition walker body, throws kisses: 18" – $2,400.00; 22" – $3,000.00. Nursing Bru (Bebe). Operates by turning key in back of head: 12" early, excellent quality – $3,400.00; 15" – $6,500.00; 18" – $7,200.00; 12", not as good quality – $2,100.00; 15" – $3,700.00; 18" – $4,700.00; 12" High color, late S.F.B.J. type – $1,200.00; 15" – $2,200.00; 18" – $2,800.00.

BRU
CELLULOID

22½'' Brevette Bru with paper label on chest of kid body. Bisque lower arms. Closed mouth. Swivel head on bisque shoulder plate. Courtesy Kimport Dolls.

24½'' Marked Bru Jne. Wood lower legs, kid body, kid over wood upper arms and bisque Bru hands. Closed mouth, pierced ears. Courtesy Kimport Dolls.

12'' Celluloid boy with inset blue eyes/lashes, an open/closed mouth with two upper modeled teeth, molded, painted hair and jointed at neck, shoulders and hips. Marks: Minerva/Germany/32 and a helmet, on head. Box: No. 3882/AW/32-4.50. Redressed. Courtesy Virginia Jones.

16'' Heavy celluloid with set blue eyes, open mouth, open dome with mohair wig. Five piece celluloid body. Marks: s Ⓐ s . Shown with 18'' Shirley Temple in an original Ideal dress. Courtesy Glorya Woods.

Celluloid dolls were made in Germany, Japan, France, U.S.A. and Italy. They date from the 1880's into the 1940's when they were made illegal due to the fact they can burn/explode if placed near an open flame/heat. Some are all celluloid, or can have celluloid heads on kid, cloth or ball jointed bodies. Some major German makers were Kammer & Rheinhardt, Kestner, Kathe Kruse, and Bruno Schmidt. These companies often ordered the heads from both Buschow & Beck and Rheinische Gummi und Celluloid Fabrik Co. Germany: All celluloid baby: Inset or painted eyes: 14" – $95.00; 16" – $125.00; 19" – $165.00; 22" – $185.00; 26" – $225.00. All celluloid dolls-Germany: Jointed at neck, shoulders and hips. 5" – $18.00; 9" – $25.00; 12" – $42.00; 16" – $85.00; 18" – $100.00. All celluloid-Germany. Jointed only at shoulders, or at shoulders and neck only: 5" – $15.00; 7" – $18.00; 9" – $22.00. Celluloid shoulder heads-Germany. Molded or wigged hair, glass or painted eyes, open or closed mouths. Kid or kidaleen bodies, cloth bodies and can have any materials for arms. Nicely dressed: 14" – $100.00; 17" – $145.00; 20" – $175.00; 24" – $225.00. Celluloid socket heads-Germany. Glass eyes (allow more for flirty eyes), ball jointed or five piece bodies. Open or closed mouths: 15" – $200.00; 18" – $265.00; 22" – $300.00; 25" – $365.00. All celluloids-Japan: 5" – $10.00; 8" – $20.00; 12" – $27.50; 16" – $85.00; 19" – $135.00; 22" – $165.00; 26" – $175.00.

22" Large celluloid Kewpie with head and body, legs in one piece and jointed only at the shoulders. Marks: Made in Japan. 9" hard plastic Kewpie with one piece body, legs and head, and has jointed shoulders. Marked: Kewpie/Rose O'Neill. 2½" Celluloid Kewpie marked: 10/0 Germany. Paper sticker on back: Rose O'Neill-/1913/Kewpie Reg. US Pat.Off./Des.Pat. 1114-1913/Germany. 5" Celluloid Kewpie: Kewpie/Rose O'Neill/1913. Courtesy Glorya Woods.

Back side of the 22" celluloid Kewpie marked: Made in Japan. Courtesy Glorya Woods.

CELLULOID

Left: 19" All celluloid with 14" head circumference. Ca. 1925. Marked with four circles/Made in Japan. Center: 26" All celluloid. Ca. 1920. Marked with symbol that looks like a house with an S.M. inside/Made in Japan/26. Right: 22" All celluloid marked with a K in a diamond/Made in Japan. Ca. 1925. All have set in blue glass eyes, closed mouths and molded hair. All came from Australia. Courtesy Jessie Smith (Canada).

Body on right inserts into the dolls head to control the movement. Fingers also fit into the arms of the celluloid and cloth baby. Courtesy Sheryl Schmidt.

Tiny 12"-13" celluloid puppet doll marked with the turtle mark of Rheinische Gummi und Celluloid Fabrik Co. of Mannheim-Neckarau, Bavaria Germany. Also had celluloid hands. Blue set eyes and closed mouth. Courtesy Sheryl Schmidt.

Close up of the detail of the face on the celluloid puppet baby. Courtesy Sheryl Schmidt.

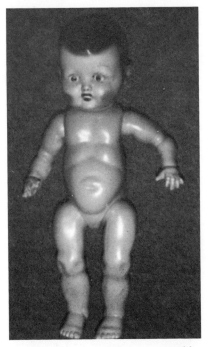

5½" All celluloid doll shown with photo of owner holding the same doll. 1928. The doll is marked with Japan and cross bars in a circle. Courtesy Theo. Lindley.

18" All celluloid, set blue eyes, open/closed mouth and much body and limb detail. Hair is painted dark brown. Marks: Turtle in a diamond, on back. Courtesy Jeanne Mauldin.

5½" All celluloid doll with one piece head, body and limbs. Jointed at shoulders only. Painted features and hair. Shown with metal kitchen set of about same time as doll. Ca. 1928. Childhood items of Theo. Lindley.

CHASE, MARTHA

Martha Jenks Chase of Pawtucket, Rhode Island began making the Chase dolls in 1893 and they are still being made by the members of her family. They all have oil painted features and are made of stockinet and cloth. They will be marked "Chase Stockinet" on the left leg, or under the left arm. There is a paper label (often gone) on the backs with a drawn head with the Chase at the top and Hospital Doll formed inside a hat brim, plus the "Pawtucket, R.I./Made in USA."

The older Chase dolls are "jointed" at the shoulders, hips, knees and elbows, where the later ones are only jointed at the shoulders and hips. Older dolls: Babies: 16" − $395.00; 20" − $465.00; 24" − $525.00. Child: 12" − $250.00; 16" − $650.00; 20" − $795.00. Lady: 16" − $995.00; 24" − $1,600.00. Life size: $2,000.00. Man: 16" − $1,050.00; 24" − $1,695.00. Life size: $2,100.00. Black: 24" − $2,000.00; 28" − $2,600.00. Newer Chase dolls. Jointed at shoulders and hips only: Babies: 14" − $145.00; 16" − $185.00. Child-boy or girl: 14" − $145.00; 16" − $185.00. 25" Portrait of George Washington: $2,300.00. 22"-25" Women Portraits: $1,500.-2,000.00.

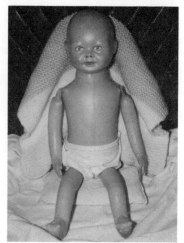

24" Chase Baby, American cloth doll, oil painted fabric head, hard mask pressed features, painted short brown impasto hair, painted brown eyes and painted upper curly lashes. Closed mouth, all cloth body and has inset thumbs. Is holding 12" "common hairdo" china doll. Courtesy Margaret Mandel.

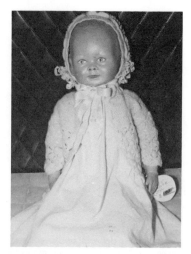

21" Chase Hospital Infant. Blonde with molded hair, pierced nostrils and ears. Closed mouth. Painted features in oils. Made of waterproof materials and is a heavy life size infant. Used in Nurses training. Ca. 1945. Courtesy Glorya Woods.

CHINA DOLLS

Early china glaze dolls are rare and high priced. These extremely rare dolls have long necks, "pink-flesh luster" tint, very deep shoulders, their faces, and the hairdos are very adult.

Almost all china dolls have black hair, but during the 1880's blondes became more popular and by 1900 one out of three of the "common" type chinas had blonde hair.

Adelina Patti: 1860's. Center part, roll curl from forehead to back on each side and "spit" curls at temples and above partly exposed ears: 14″ − $300.00; 18″ − $425.00.

Biedermeir or Bald head china. Ca. 1840. Has bald head, some with top of head glazed black. Takes wigs. 14″ − $425.00; 20″ − $800.00.

Bangs full across forehead. 1870's Black hair: 16″ − $250.00; 20″ − $400.00; 26″ − $650.00. Blondes: 16″ − $285.00; 20″ − $450.00; 26″ − $700.00.

Brown eyes (painted). Can be any hairstyle and any date. 16″ − $500.00; 20″ − $595.00; 25″ − $895.00.

Common hairdo, called "lowbrow" or "butterfly". After 1905. Black and blondes. Wavy hairdo, center part, with hair that comes down low on forehead. 8″ − $45.00; 12″ − $65.00; 16″ − $100.00; 19″ − $145.00; 23″ − $165.00; 27″ − $200.00.

Covered Wagon. 1840's to 1870's. Hair parted in middle with flat hair style and has "sausage" curls around head. 16″ − $425.00; 20″ − $595.00.

Curly Top. 1845-1860's. Ringlet curls that are loose and over entire head. 16″ − $425.00; 20″ − $595.00.

Dolly Madison. 1870's-1880's. Loose curly hairdo with modeled ribbon bow in center of the top of the hairdo. Few curls on forehead. 14″ − $250.00; 18″ − $325.00; 21″ − $375.00.

Flat Top. 1850's-1870's. Black hair parted in middle, smooth on top with short curls around head. 17″ − $200.00; 20″ − $285.00; 24″ − $325.00.

Glass eyes. Can have a variety of hair styles. 1840's-1870's. 14″ − $995.00; 18″ − $2,000.00; 22″ − $2,400.00; 26″ − $2,800.00.

Japanese. 1910's-1920's. Can be marked or unmarked. Black hair or blondes. Can have "common" hairdo, or have much more adult faces and hairdos. 14″ − $100.00; 17″ − $145.00.

Man or Boy. Can be any date. 14″ − $500.00; 16″ − $750.00; 20″ − $900.00.

Pet Name Chinas. 1905. Same as "common", "lowbrow". Molded shirtwaist with name on front. Names are: Agnes, Bertha, Daisy, Dorothy, Edith, Esther, Ethel, Florence, Helen, Mabel, Marion, Pauline. 8″ − $95.00; 12″ − $135.00; 16″ − $165.00; 19″ − $200.00; 23″ − $245.00; 27″ − $285.00.

Pierced ears. Can be a variety of hair styles. 14″ − $400.00; 18″ − $650.00. More must be allowed for rarity of hairdo.

Snood, combs, any applied hair decoration. 14″ − $400.00; 17″ − $600.00.

Spill Curls. With, or without head band. Many individual curls across forehead and over shoulders with forehead curls continued to above ears. 14″ − $300.00; 18″ − $585.00; 22″ − $650.00.

Wood body. Articulated with slim hips, china lower limbs. 1850's. 12″ − $850.00; 15″ − $2,400.00.

CHINA

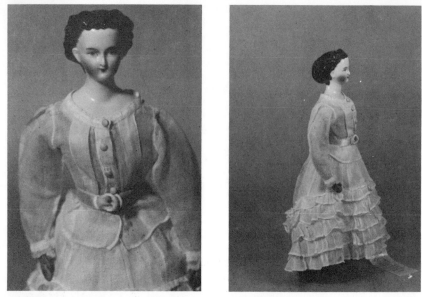

18" China with full exposed ears and brush strokes over the ears. The hairdo is pulled into large bun in back which has a modeled band holding it in place. Thin neck and adult features. All original with kid body and limbs. Courtesy Barbara Earnshaw.

25" China with hairdo pulled back into a "page boy" style with braids coming out from under the back hair, up the front and over the top. She also has two smaller braids that are "V"d near the center of the back of the hairdo. Kid body and limbs. Courtesy Barbara Earnshaw.

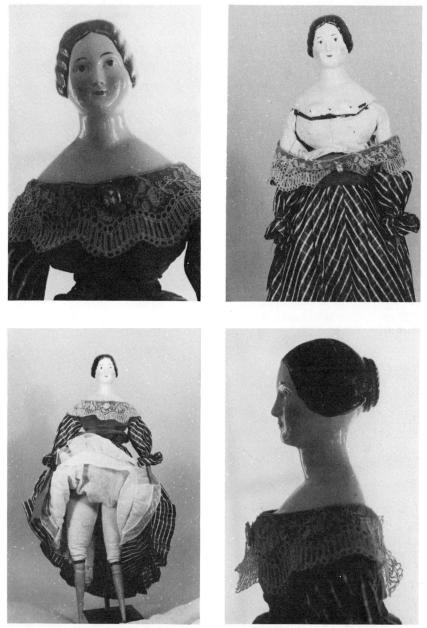

Large china of the 1840's and 1850's with sausage curls, loosely modeled all around head. She has pink luster skin tones and three sew holes front and back. Cloth body and upper arms and legs with china limbs. Courtesy Barbara Earnshaw.

CHINA

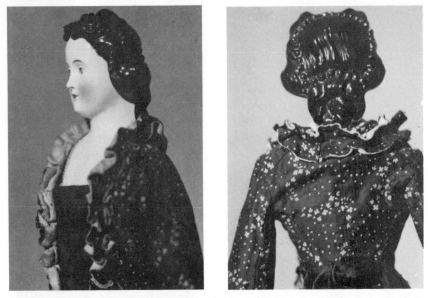

21" China with hairdo that is at the sides and has modeled beads around hairdo. The hair is pulled into a bun at the nape of the neck. She has a kid body and limbs and is all original. (Author).

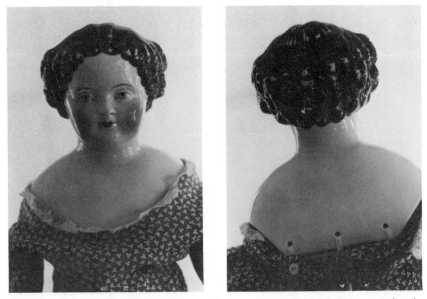

30" Very tall brown eyes china with long neck, deep shoulders, modeled bosom and early hairdo. Kid body with wooden arms and legs. Ca. 1820's. Courtesy Barbara Earnshaw.

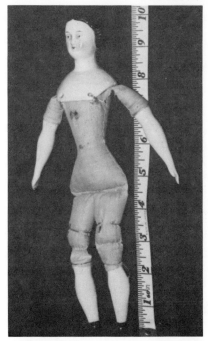

10" China head with thin neck and deep shoulders. Pale pink luster with hairdo that has brush strokes on the sides, three waves on each side, pulled back into a braided bun with a bow on the bun. Hair on the neck extends ¼" below the trailing ribbon ends. Cloth body with china "spoon" hands, china feet with flat sole shoes. Dates from 1860's, and called "Inaugural" china. Courtesy Anita Belew.

21" Snood china with gold luster trim. Cloth body with leather lower arms and stipple brush marks around face. Courtesy Kimport Dolls.

19" China with wide puffs of hair that stand out on each side of the head. She has fully exposed ears. Cloth body with leather arms and sewn on boots. Ca. 1850's. All original "Little Bo Peep" style gown. (Author).

CHINA

5" Tall head of man with glass eyes, modeled on shirt and tie, as well as, rolled high curls and side part. Courtesy Barbara Earnshaw.

16" Common china called "lowbrow" or "butterfly" hairdo. The short lower legs, as well as being quite fat, with high heels dates after 1900. Courtesy Diane Hoffman.

19" Brown glass eyes, ears exposed.

19" Pink luster with brown painted eyes.

13" Molded scarf and grapes.

Puffs over ears, bun in back.

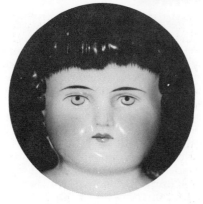

20'' Full bangs with brush marks.

Mold used both for ''parian'' and china.

25'' High peak and white hairpart.

29'' Boy or girl with exposed ears.

16'' Light brown ''Curly Top''.

CLOTH

CLOTH DOLLS

Arnold Print Works. "Brownie" dolls designed by Palmer Cox. Copyrighted in 1892. Printed on cloth and sold by the yard in stores by Arnold Print Works. Twelve dolls per yard: Canadian, Chinaman, Dude, German, Highlander, Indian, Irishman, John Bull, Policeman, Sailor, Soldier, and Uncle Sam. & Made up. 8" – $80.00. Yard-uncut – $225.00.

Art Fabric Mills. Marked on foot: Art Fabric Mills/New York/Pat. Feb. 13th 1900. Underclothes and features are printed on cloth. 1899-1923. 12" – $50.00; 18" – $125.00; 26" – $175.00.

Babyland made by E.I. Horsman from 1904 to 1920. Marked on torso, or bottom of foot. With oil painted features or printed features. With and without wig. All cloth, jointed at shoulders and hips. 12" – $200.00; 18" – $325.00; 24" – $475.00; 30" – $650.00. Black dolls: 12" – $300.00; 18" – $425.00; 26" – $575.00.

Bruckner Cloth Dolls: Neck band label: Bruckner Doll/Made in U.S.A., or on shoulder: Pat'd. July 8th 1901. Stiffened mask face with oil painted features. Cloth body and limbs. Child doll: 12" – $125.00; 16" – $200.00. Black doll: 12" – $175.00; 16" – $375.00. Two heads-Black and White (Topsy-Turvy), 12"-12½" – $200.00.

Charlie Chaplin: Made by Amberg & Sons, and marked on bottom of feet. 17" – $365.00.

Chad Valley: Label or paper tag: Chad Valley-Made in England. All cloth, with velvet body, jointed neck, shoulders and hips. Painted or glass eyes, mohair wigs. Child with painted eyes: 12" – $75.00; 16" – $200.00; 18" – $275.00. With glass eyes: 14" – $175.00; 16" – $275.00; 18" – $375.00. Child representing Royal Family (four in set: Princess Elizabeth, Princess Margaret Rose, Prince Edward, Princess Alexandria, have glass eyes, and were made in 1941. Prince Edward as Duke of Kent: 15" – $550.00. As Duke of Windsor: 15" – $550.00.

Columbian Doll: Marked from 1891 to 1888: Columbian Doll/Emma E. Adams, and after 1905: The Columbian Doll/Marietta Adams Ruttan. All cloth with hand painted features. 19" – $895.00.

Drayton, Grace. Dolly Dingle. 1923 by Averill Manufacturing Co. Cloth with painted features. Marked on torso. 11" – $185.00; 14" – $235.00. Chocolate Drop: 1923 by Averill Mfg. Co. Brown cloth with painted features and three tufts of yarn hair. Stamped on torso: 11" – $235.00; 14" – $295.00. Hug-Me-Tight: By Colonial Toy Mfg. Co. in 1916. One piece printed cloth: 11" – $95.00; 14" – $165.00.

Farnell's Alpha Toys: Marked with label on foot: Farnell's Alpha Toys/Made in England. Child: 14" – $185.00; 16" – $235.00. King George VI: 16" – $295.00. Palace Guard/Beefeater: 16" – $235.00.

Georgene Novelties: Marked with paper tag, and were both Georgene Averill and Madame Hendren. All cloth with mask face and painted features. Yarn hair. Foreign Costume dolls: 13" – $55.00; 18" – $100.00; 24" – $150.00. Children: 13" – $85.00; 17" – $135.00. Tear Drop Baby. Has one tear drop painted on cheek: 16" – $165.00.

Kewpie Cuddles: Marked with cloth label sewn to seam: Made by Kreuger, Inc. Pat. number 1785800: Fat all cloth body, painted mask face. Has tiny wings. 10" – $100.00; 13" – $145.00.

Liberty of London Royal Dolls: Marked with cloth or paper tag. Flesh colored cloth faces with stitched in and painted features. All cloth bodies. 1939 Royal portrait dolls that are 8" to 10". Included Queen

Elizabeth, Queen Mary, Queen Victoria and King George VI, $95.00. Other Historical dolls: 10" — $85.00.

Kamkins. By Louise Kampes. 1928 to 1934. Marked on back of head or on foot, also has paper label, heart shaped, on chest. All cloth with molded face mask and painted features, wigs and as boy or girl: 19" — $500.00; 24" — $625.00.

Kathe Kruse. Made in Germany from 1910. Modeled muslin heads hand painted in oils and all on jointed cloth bodies which are marked: Kathe Kruse on the sole of foot, and may also have the word Germany or a number. Later Kruse dolls also will have a paper tag attached by a string. Early cloth dolls: 15"-16" — $650.00. Later (1930's) with wigs: 15"-16" — $350.00.

Mollye: Made from 1920 into 1950's. Designed and made by Mollye Goldman, International Dolls Co. Marked with paper tag. Babies: All cloth, painted face mask, mohair or yarn wigs. 13" — $65.00; 17"-18" — $85.00; 24" — $100.00. Internationals: All cloth. 13" — $65.00; 17" — $85.00; 20" — $100.00. Philadelphia Baby: Also called "Sheppard Doll" as was made by J.B. Sheppard in late 1890's and early 1900's. Stockinet covered body with painted cloth arms and legs. Head is modeled and painted cloth. 21"-22" — $950.00. Printed Cloth dolls: Advertising dolls to be cut out and stuffed, such as: Rastus, The Cream of Wheat Chef: 18" — $. Aunt Jemima set of four dolls: $70.00 each. Dolls with printed underwear: Cut: 6" — $45.00; 15" — $75.00; 18" — $100.00. Uncut: 6" — $65.00; 15" — $95.00; 18" — $125.00. Girls and boys with printed outer clothes: 6" — $55.00; 15" — $85.00; 18" — $125.00. Uncut: 6" — $75.00; 15" — $100.00; 18" — $150.00.

Smith, Mrs. S.S.: Called the "Alabama" doll. Made in 1907. Marked on lower torso: No. 1 Patented Dec. 1907, and on body: Mrs. S.S. Smith/Manufacturer/Roanoke Ala. All cloth with modeled painted head, molded hair and painted on shoes. 17" — $750.00. Marked with same makers name, but with: Patented Sept. 26,1905: Wigged child: 17" — $650.00. Black Doll, 17" — $1,400.00.

Steiff: Made in Germany early 1900's. All felt with jointed neck, shoulders and hips. Head seam runs straight down center of the face. Can have glass or painted eyes. Painted hair or wigged. Metal button in ear and printed on body: Steiff-trademark Made in Germany. 14" — $375.00; 18" — $565.00.

Walker, Izannah: Made in 1870's and 1880's. Modeled head with painted features in oils. Ears are applied. Cloth body and limbs. Hands and feet may be stitched, or can have painted boots. Marked: Patented Nov.4,1873. Brushstroke hairdo: 16" — $2,500.00. With two vertical curls painted in front of ears: 18" — $3,600.00; 24" — $4,200.00.

CLOTH

17" Columbian type doll made of muslin, hand painted face in oils, brown eyes, apple cheeks and face stiffened with sizing. Head is in three pieces, five fingers indicated with stitching, rigid arms, stitch jointed hips and knees, pointed toes with sewn on black fine cotton stockings. Original dress. Ca. 1900. Unmarked. Courtesy Margaret Mandel.

19" Homemade rag doll, muslin body sawdust stuffed, separate thumbs, facial features deliniated by red. Black fabric snood, black velvet choker, red stroud cloth stockings, brown calico dress, quilted petticoat. Card with doll reads "Rag doll" Bettydear' made by 'loving hands' about 1850. Courtesy Margaret Mandel.

13½" Early 20th Century advertising doll of Buster Brown shoes. Ca. 1920. The 18" Teddy Bear is of yellow mohair, has glass eyes, felt pads and American made. Ca. 1920's. Courtesy Margaret Mandel.

20" Marked: Bruckner/Pat'd July 8th 1901. Stiffened mask face with oil painted features, cloth body. Old clothes. Made in U.S.A. by Albert Bruckner. Courtesy Diane Hoffman.

18" Lithographed sailor boy of cotton sateen, showing fine detail. Ca. 1910. The early terrier is 17" long, probably English made and has glass eyes. Courtesy Margaret Mandel.

17" Raggedy Ann with wooden heart, brown yarn hair, and stamped on the back: Patented/Sept. 7, 1915. Shoe button eyes. Original. All cloth body and limbs. Courtesy Nancy Lucas.

18" All cotton sateen, fully jointed with painted face, apple cheeks, dots for eyebrows, rosebud lips, mohair wig stitched to head and original plaid dress and felt coat, 25" green tin car and trailer, precursor to the 'Jet Stream'. 1930's 25" Steiff tiger with ear clip. All straw stuffed and glass eyes. Courtesy Margaret Mandel.

CLOTH

7" Tall all felt dolls made in England by Norah Wellings. During the 1920's and 1930's these dolls were sold aboard the ocean liners traveling between England and United States. Courtesy Irene Brown.

30" "Golliwog". All cloth with lamb's wool hair. This one came from Australia. Maker unknown. Courtesy Jessie Smith.

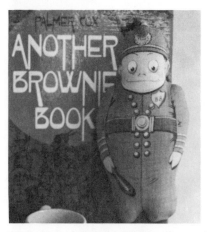

7" Brownie designed by Palmer Cox and made of cloth that is printed. Made by the Arnold Prints Works and dates from 1892 to 1907. Will be marked on foot: Copyrighted. 1892 by Palmer Cox. This is "Policeman", and there were twelve in set: Uncle Sam, Canadian, Dude, Highlander, Irishman, John Bull, Indian, Sailor, Soldier, Chinaman and German. Courtesy Sally Freeman.

20" Character Matador. Oil painted mask face, elaborate outfit, stitched fingers and body molded to show muscles in legs. Unmarked. Courtesy Diane Hoffman.

16" Green velvet monkey that is all excellent quality. Sewn on shoes, non-removable vest and jacket. Very detailed and modeled face. Unmarked. Courtesy Jayn Allen.

13" Marked: C.O.D. 93 4/0. Made by Cuno and Otto Dressel. Brown set eyes, open mouth with four teeth, mohair wig, and on all kid body with bisque lower arms. Courtesy Sylvia Bryant.

20" Marked: Jutta Baby/Dressel. He is on a toddler body, with original short boy wig, blue sleep eyes and open mouth. Costumed by owner. Courtesy Glorya Woods.

CUNO AND OTTO DRESSEL

The Dressel firm was founded in 1700, but very little is known of them until 1863. The firm was located in Sonneberg, Thuringia, Ger-

DRESSEL
CUNO & OTTO
FLEISCHMANN & BLOEDEL

many and Cuno & Otto were the sons of the founder. The Dressel firm was listed as dollmakers in 1873. They made bisque head dolls with jointed kid, or cloth bodies as well as the ball jointed composition/mache body. By 1906 they had registered the trademark for "Jutta", and by 1911 they were also making celluloid dolls. Sample marks from this company are:

       C.O.D.
                GERMANY   ◄·►   ✦

Child dolls with bisque heads, composition, or kid bodies and open mouths: 15" – $265.00; 18" – $300.00; 22" – $365.00; 25" – $425.00. Character dolls with closed mouths and painted intaglio eyes: 12" – $1,200.00; 14" – $1,800.00; 17" – $2,600.00. Lady dolls of the 1920's with adult face, closed mouth, marked 1469 and with adult five piece composition body. High heel feet and thin limbs: 14" – $975.00; 16" – $1,200.00. Marked "Jutta" baby with open mouth and five piece bent limb baby body: 14" – $300.00; 17" – $395.00; 20" – $425.00; 24" – $495.00; 26" – $550.00. Jutta on toddler body: 14" – $395.00; 17" – $485.00; 20" – $525.00; 25" – $625.00. Child doll "Jutta" marked with or without the S & H #'s 1914, 1348, etc: 17" – $395.00; 20" – $425.00; 24" – $495.00; 27" – $695.00; 30" – $775.00.

20" Marked Eden Bebe/Paris. Large paperweight eyes, open mouth and pierced ears. Heavy feathered eyebrows. (Author).

Fleischmann & Bloedel of Paris, Furth & Bavaria. Founded in 1873 and joined S.F.B.J. in 1899. Marks: Eden BeBe/Paris. Closed mouth: 15" – $1,500.00; 18" – $2,200.00; 22" – $2,800.00. Open mouth: 15" – $1,000.00; 18" – $1,500.00; 22" – $1,950.00.

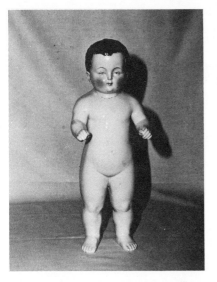

18½" Frozen Charlie. China glaze finish. Excellent detail to hair, molded eyelids and hands and feet. Marked on bottom of foot: 4/0 ⅜ . Made by the Kling Company of Germany. Courtesy Jo Fasnatch.

3" "Frozen Charlotte", all china finish, unjointed with black molded hair. In original sacque and wood Hope Chest. (Author).

FROZEN CHARLOTTE-CHARLIE

The name "Frozen Charlotte" for girls and "Frozen Charlie" for boys is used for figures of dolls that have the arms to the front with hands usually modeled as if holding the edge of a slay. The Ballad of "Young Charlotte" is shown on page 107 of *Antique Collector's Dolls*, Vol. I. These figures date from the 1850's into the 1900's, and are also known as "Pillar" dolls. Two uses for the figures, besides a play thing, were that of a tea cup cooler, and often they were baked into party cakes as tiny gifts for children.

Frozen Charlottes can be all china, partly china, such as the hair, stone bisque and a fine quality of porcelain. They can have molded hair, painted bald heads, or wigged. The majority have no joints, with hands extended and legs separate, but unjointed. They generally came without any clothes, and they can have painted on boots, shoes and socks, or be bare footed.

It must be noted that in 1976 a large amount of the 15½"-16" "Charlies" were reproduced in Germany, and are excellent quality. It is almost impossible to tell these are reproductions. All china with molded black hair and unjointed, 1"-2" – $20.00; 4"-6" – $50.00; 8"-10" – $95.00; 12" – $115.00. Molded blonde hair and unjointed: 3"-4" – $60.00; 6"-8" – $85.00. Wigged: 7" – $175.00; 15½", BOY – $350.00. Stone bisque: 4" – $22.00; 8" – $48.00. Stone bisque, jointed at shoulders: 4" – $30.00; 8" – $55.00. China or "Parian"-jointed at shoulders: 4" – $110.00; 8" – $250.00. Black Charlottes or Charlie, unjointed: 3" – $50.00; 6" – $70.00; 8" – $85.00. Molded on clothes, 6" – $85.00; 9" – $100.00.

FULPER

The Fulper Pottery Co. began in 1805, but only made doll heads for a short time between 1918 and 1921. The heads were developed for the Horsman Doll Co. Since the Fulper dolls are all American made with American materials they are sought after by collectors of Americana, even if the quality of the heads does not match the dolls made in France or Germany. Sample marks are:

Made in
U.S.A.

Child: 16" – $435.00; 21" – $525.00. Baby: 18" – $525.00; 25" – $825.00. Toddler: 18" – $575.00; 25" – $895.00.

19" Marked Fulper/Made in USA. (see drawing). Open mouth with two teeth, set brown eyes, pale bisque and on five piece bent leg baby body. Courtesy Glorya Woods.

22" Bisque head is marked: Fulper/ Made in USA/Horsman/Doll/1918 (see drawing). Open mouth, two teeth and on ball jointed body. Courtesy Glorya Woods.

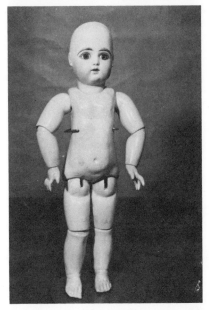

17" Bisque head on French jointed body with straight wrists. Closed mouth, paperweight eyes and all original clothes and wig. Marks: F.G. in scroll. (See drawing). Courtesy Barbara Earnshaw.

16" Marked F.G., in scroll with closed mouth and paperweight eyes. Shows typical French body. The knee joints on the French dolls is plain, and flush with the lower legs where the German dolls have knee details, such a dimples and indentations. (Author).

GAULTIER, FERNAND

Fernand Gaultier is accepted, by collectors, as the maker of dolls marked with F.G., and these dolls are often found on the cloth covered, or all composition marked GESLAND bodies. The Gesland Freres firm was operated by two brothers with one of them having the initial F. The dolls will be marked with an F.G., along with a number, or the F.G. in scroll: F.G. Any dolls marked: **F. + G.** are reproductions made in the 1960's. F.G. dolls: Closed mouths and good bisque: 14" – $2,300.00; 16" – $2,600.00; 19" – $2,900.00; 22" – $3,200.00. Open mouth, good bisque: 14" – $995.00; 16" – $1,200.00; 19" – $1,600.00; 22" – $1,800.00. Marked F.G. Fashion doll: All kid body and limbs, or kid with bisque lower arms. Closed mouth and bisque swivel head on shoulder plate: 12" – $1,100.00; 14" – $1,295.00; 17" – $1,500.00; 20" – $1,800.00; 24" – $2,400.00; 28" – $3,300.00. F.G. marked heads on marked Gesland bodies: Bisque head on stockinet over wire frame with composition or bisque lower limbs: Child dolls, closed mouth: 15"-16" – $2,500.00; 18"-19" – $3,400.00; 24"-25" – $4,400.00. Child Gesland with open mouth: 15" – $1,200.00; 19" – $1,900.00; 25" – $2,200.00. Gesland Fashion doll with bisque lower limbs: 15" – $2,500.00; 18" – $3,200.00; 22" – $3,600.00.

GLADDIE

18" Bisque head with modeled hair, laughing half closed eyes and wide open/closed mouth with modeled upper teeth. Cloth body with composition limbs. Redressed. Courtesy Shirley Bertrand.

"GLADDIE", THE LAUGHING CHILD

The May, 1957 issue of Coronet magazine carries an article by Holger Jensen, the husband of Helen Jensen who designed the "Laughing Child." Mr. Jensen relates the story of this charming child who was "the guardian angel of our family for 30 years. It's come to our rescue when we've been hungry, cheered us when we've been depressed and from time to time doubled as a rich uncle." He tells how his wife was modeling portrait heads in Miami, Florida and was given a show by a leading art gallery. She had 23 works to display, and to even out the number Helen Jensen modeled their two year old little girl Janet. This first head was cast in bronze.

An executive of a doll firm made arrangements to make the "Laughing Child" into a doll, but the Jensens found it would be a year or more before they began to collect royalties, so with ten copies of the head the Jensen's set out for Texas. They sold a "Laughing Child" to a Dallas art gallery, and headed West.

The day before Christmas, in Deming, New Mexico, with one of their old car's tires flat for the third time that day, and with a couple days rent paid at an auto-court, they had $2.00 left.

The Jensens made a Christmas tree out of sage brush, and hung the two children's stockings on the front bumper of the car. Helen Jensen slipped out and bought toys for the children and their $2.00 was gone. The Christmas dinner consisted of oatmeal.

They could not go forward, but had enough gas in the tired car to go back to El Paso where they sold one of the heads of the "Laughing Child" in a gift shop. They then sent a telegram to the doll company asking for an advance, and were sent $100.00 by return wire.

The Jensens made it to California the day before New Years, and in Los Angeles the little heads did very well.

Holger Jensen finishes his article with 'The "Laughing Child's" special attraction must lie in the fact that it was modeled by a mother of her own much-loved child, with the result that, like Pygmalion's Galatea, it almost came alive. Little wonder that it became, too, our guardian angel'.

GLADDIE
GOEBEL

"Gladdie" the "Laughing Child" was designed in 1927, and on the market in 1928-1929. It can be made of a ceramic material head, which is painted, or of fired bisque. The body is cloth and limbs are composition, and will be marked: Gladdie/copyright by/Helen W. Jensen. Modeled from a two year old girl, the doll is mostly found dressed as a boy. 17"-18" - with painted ceramic head – $875.00. 17"-18" - with fired bisque head – $1,600.00.

17" Bisque head with walker body that is wood and mache. Straight legs. Set eyes and open mouth with teeth. Marks: (see drawing), on one side and R/13/0/Germany on the other side. Courtesy Pauline Hoch.

6" Bisque head on five piece mache body with molded on shoes and socks. Molded hairdo with one flower on one side and two flowers on the other side. Painted eyes, open/closed smiling mouth with painted upper teeth. Marks: heart/interwound W G. Courtesy Pauline Hoch.

The Goebel factory has been in operation since 1879 and located in Oeslau, Thur. Germany. The interwoven W.G. mark has been used since 1879. William Gobel inherited the factory from his father, Franz Detley Gobel. About 1900 is when this factory only made dolls, doll's heads and porcelain figures. They worked in both bisque and china glazed items.

The Gobel marks are:

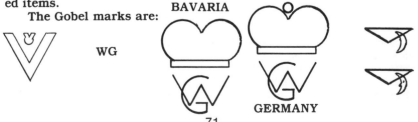

BAVARIA

WG

GERMANY

71

GOEBEL
H

Painted eye googly with five piece mache body with molded on shoes and socks: 6½" – $625.00; 10" – $850.00. Bisque head girl with flowers on sides of molded hairdo, on five piece mache body with molded on shoes and socks: 6" – $325.00; 10" – $495.00. "Dolly" faced bisque with open mouth, fully jointed composition body: 12" – $145.00; 16" – $285.00; 20" – $375.00; 24" – $465.00.

21½" Marked "H", on head, ball jointed French body. Closed mouth. Courtesy Kimport Dolls.

The maker of the dolls marked with an "H" is not known. They were made about 1880, and are found on a combination of wood and composition bodies. The quality can differ greatly with the "H" marked dolls, and the highest prices are for perfect, beautiful examples. Closed mouth: 16" – $12,500.00; 20" – $16,000.00; 25" – $19,000.00.

HALF DOLLS

Half Dolls or pincushion dolls can be of china, bisque, composition, papier mache or terra cotta. Not all were used as pincushion dolls, but for such other items as lamps, tea cozies, candy boxes, powder boxes and perfume bottles.

Most date from 1900 on into the 1930's with the majority made in Germany, but with many made in Japan. Generally they will only carry the mark of country and/or a number. The most desirable will be marked with the company, such as William Goebel: ♡ or Dressel, Kister & Company: ♩

The most desirable are half dolls that have the arms and hands molded away from the body, jointed shoulders, bald heads with wigs and children or men. Arms/hands completely away from figure. 5″ – $95.00 up; 8″ – $150.00 up; 12″ – $400.00 up. Arms extended but hands attached to figure, 3″ – $65.00 up. Common figures with arms and hands attached to figure, 3″ – $22.50 up. Japan: 3″ – $15.00 up.

7″ Art Deco Flapper half doll. Painted bisque, mohair wig, painted eyes with long lashes and eye shadow. Bisque arms with corks and was originally for a lamp. Marked: Keloid, on front and Holland, on back. The original box is stamped: The Roman Chariot Co. Overschie, Rotterdam. Made in Holland. Courtesy Glorya Woods.

5″ Half doll that is wax over composition, mohair wig and a closed smiling mouth. Arms are attached with wires into small corks in arm ends. Large cork in base. Marks: Courtesy Theo Lindley.

4″ Half doll that is wax over composition. Red mohair wig. Delicate bisque arms and hands attached with wire. Courtesy Lenora Schweitzberger.

HALF DOLLS

3" Half doll attached to pincushion base with china legs sewn to same base. Green dress, blonde hair. Made in Japan. Courtesy Lenora Schweitzberger.

3" Half doll on top of brush. Arms up and has blue ribbon in hair. Marks: 6102 Germany. Courtesy Lenora Schweitzberger.

3½" Half doll on top of brush. Original. Blue hat ties in front. Made in Japan. Courtesy Lenora Schweitzberger.

4" Half doll set into pincushion base with china legs sewn on base. Both arms and hands are away from the body. Molded short hair. Made in Germany. Courtesy Lenora Schweitzberger.

HANCOCK
HANDWERCK

Hancock and Sons made dolls from the 1890's into the 1930's. They were located in Cauldon, Staffordshire, England. The dolls will be marked: NTI England, or NTI Hancock. Closed mouth boy: 16" – $525.00; 20" – $700.00. Closed mouth girl: 16" – $525.00; 20" – $700.00.

12" Boy and 18" Girl marked: NTI England (boy), and NTI Hancock's (girl). Both have cauldon pottery heads and shoulder plates, glass eyes and closed mouths. Both have stuffed cloth bodies and unglazed bisque arms and legs. Courtesy Lorraine Hancock Weston.

23" Marked: Handwerck. 109-12/H. Blue sleep eyes, heavy brows, open mouth and on stamped Handwerck body. Courtesy Glorya Woods.

HANDWERCK

30" Marked: Handwerck/109-15. Composition and wood body, open mouth, blonde mohair wig and brown sleep eyes with painted lashes. Courtesy Glorya Woods.

20" Marked: Germany/Handwerck/2½. Large brown sleep eyes with painted lashes, feathered brows, open mouth, blonde mohair wig and on composition jointed body. Original white dress with eyelette collar, and blue silk ribbon trim. Has pale blue cotton crepe undies (Teddies). Courtesy Glorya Woods.

31" Marked: Handwerck/109/15½. Blue sleep eyes, open mouth, and on composition and wood jointed body. Courtesy Glorya Woods.

33" Marked: Heinrich Handwerck/Simon & Halbig 7. Open mouth, sleep eyes and on jointed composition body. Courtesy Penny Pendleberry.

HANDWERCK, HEINRICH

Heinrich Handwerck started making dolls in 1876 and was located at Gotha, near Walterhausen, Germany. They made entire dolls and doll's bodies, but a great many of their heads were made by other companies, especially Simon & Halbig.

Some of the mold numbers from this company are: 12X, 19, 23, 69, 79, 89, 99, 100, 109, 119, 124, 125, 139, 152, 189, 199, 1200, 1290. A large number of their dolls will only have the maker's name, and no mold numbers. Marks used by the Heinrich Handwerck firm are:

Marked Heinrich Handwerck child: 16" – $300.00; 19" – $365.00; 23" – $425.00; 27" – $600.00; 30" – $695.00; 36" – $1,200.00; 40" – $1,500.00.

12" Happyfat. Composition head and lower arms. The body and large feet are tightly stuffed cloth. All original with original tag on overalls. Painted features and hair. (Author). 11"-12" Composition $450.00. All bisques boy or girl, with jointed arms, painted features, hair, and molded clothes: 4½"-5" Germany - $325.00, 4½"-5" Japan - Nippon - $150.00. Happyfats were designed by Kate Jordon, and made for and registered by George Borgfeldt. 1913 to 1922.

GEBRUDER HEUBACH

21" Marked with 8 and the Heubach sunburst incised beneath. Sleep eyes, composition jointed body, plaster pate and original wig. Open mouth with five teeth and excellent modeling around the mouth and lips. Courtesy Sheryl Schmidt.

12" marked with: 7307/1/sunburst mark with cheek dimples, open mouth, glass eyes and on jointed body. Holds a tiny 6" marked: 7345/14/0/Heubach, in square/ Germany. The 6" is a doll house size. Courtesy Jane Walker.

Close up of the 6" tall doll house Heubach marked with the 7345 mold number. Courtesy Jane Walker.

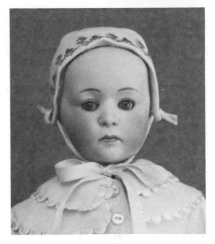

15" "Stuart" toddler with porcelain bonnet, glass sleep eyes and closed mouth. Painted flowers over top of bonnet. Appears to have original clothing. Unusual in size. Courtesy Anne Rankin.

15" "Stuart" toddler with porcelain bonnet, apparently has original clothing. Courtesy Anne Rankin.

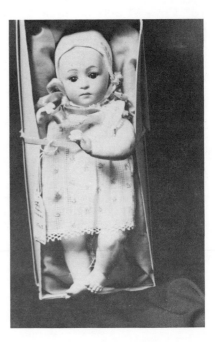

Rare 12", glass eyes (sleep) "Stuart" baby in original box. The box is yellowed, but plain with no label. Very sweet expression. Has removable bonnet with design of flowers across the top, holes in sides for ribbon ties. In great many cases these porcelain bonnets are permanently attached by the original owners, as they have a tendency to be heavy and will chip. Five piece bent leg baby body with very good modeling. Courtesy Anne Rankin.

GEBRUDER HEUBACH

GEBRUDER HEUBACH

The Heubach Brothers (Gebruder) factory was located at Lichte, Thur, Germany. The factory ran from 1863 into the 1930's. It is not known at what date they began making dolls, but they were known for fine porcelain bisque pieces, and it is known that they began to produce character dolls in 1909 or 1910. Sample marks Gebruder Heubach dolls are:

The following are some of the mold numbers from this firm: 28, 30, 37, 43, 45, 56, 58, 60, 63, 66, 68N, 69, 70, 71, 73, 74, 76, 77, 77G, 78, 79, 81, 83, 86, 87, 90, 91, 93, 94, 95, 101, 119, 122, 165, 750, 892, 0716, 0746, 1063, 1602, 3774, 4660, 5636, 5777, 6662, 6692, 6736, 6773, 6789, 6836, 6894, 6969, 6970, 7043, 7054, 7066, 7072, 7118, 7143, 7246, 7345, 7602, 7604, 7622, 7650, 7788, 7802, 7856, 7977, 8004, 8192, 8193, 8232, 8306, 8578, 8774, 9355, 9558, 9573, 10542, 10633, 96643. Santa. Character dolls with bisque heads, open/closed or closed mouths, intaglio painted eyes on kid or jointed composition bodies. Molded hair or wigs. ALLOW MORE FOR GLASS EYES. 5636 - laughing child: 10"-12" – $1,000.-1,200.00; 17" – $1,850.00. 5777 & 9355 - "Dolly Dimples": 16" – $1,200.00; 22" – $2,200.00. 5730 - "Santa", 20" – $1,800.00. 6736 - laughing child, wide open/closed mouth, modeled lower teeth: 10"-12" – $695.00; 16"-17" – $1,300.00. 6969, 6970, 7246, 7407, 8017, etc: boy or girl pouty. (Allow more for glass eyes): 12" – $1,400.00; 16" – $1,700.00; 20" – $2,500.00. 7604: Laughing child: 10"-12" – $325.00; 14"-15" – $595.00; 18" – $695.00. 7622: Molded hair pouty: 10"-12" – $650.00; 15"-16" – $1,100.00. 7788: "Coquette" tilted head, molded hair, can have modeled ribbon in hairdo: 12" – $700.00; 16" – $1,600.00. 7977: "Stuart Baby": Modeled bisque bonnet: 10"-12" – $1,000.00; 14"-16" – $1,500.00; Glass eyes: 10"-12" – $1,500.00; 16" – $1,900.00. 8192: 14" – $495.00; 17" – $545.00; 20" – $625.00. 8774: "Whistling Jim". Eyes to side, and mouth modeled open in whistling: 12" – $750.00; 16" – $1,000.00.

Infants or babies: Bisque heads, wigs or molded hair, bent limb bodies and open/closed pouty mouths. Can have intaglio or sleep eyes: 8" – $275.00; 10" – $325.00. Portrait Indian man or woman: 13" – $2,400.00. 119 marked (along with 1867): Braids coiled around ears: 16" – $1,400.00. "Dolly" faced dolls, glass eyes and open mouths: 16" – $425.00; 19" – $550.00; 24" – $675.00. 10633: "Dainty Dorothy". Open mouth: 16" 450.00; 20" – $575.00; 25" – $695.00. Heubach googly: 8" – $825.00; 12" – $1,250.00.

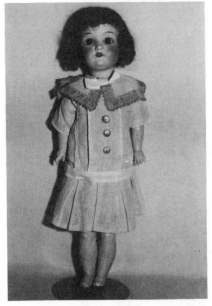

18" Marked: Heubach Kopplsdorf/300-4 baby with five piece bent leg baby body. Brown human hair wig and brown sleep eyes. Open mouth with four teeth, cheek dimples and movable tongue. Courtesy Glorya Woods.

15" Marked: Heubach/250. 6/0/ Koppelsdorf/Germany. This doll is all original with dark brown mohair wig, and dark brown sleep eyes. Ball jointed body with straight wrists. Courtesy Pat Timmons.

ERNST HEUBACH OF KOPPLSDORF

This company began in 1887 and by 1895 had over 100 people working for it. Ernst Heubach was the brother-in-law of Armand Marseille, and it is suspected that he was the cousin of the Heubach Brothers (Gebruder). Some Heubach dolls will be marked with the full name and the mold number, others may have the following marks:

These are some of the Heubach mold numbers: 27X, 99, 230, 235, 236, 237, 238, 242, 250, 251, 262, 267, 271, 273, 275, 277, 283, 300, 302, 312, 317, 320, 321, 338, 342, 349, 367, 399, 407, 410, 438, 444, 450, 452, 458, 616, 1310, 1900, 1901, 1902, 1906, 1909, 2504, 2671, 2757, 3027, 3412, 3423, 3427, 7118, 32144.

Character babies, bent leg baby bodies. Toddler bodies will be more. Mold numbers 300, 320, (White), etc. 12" – $325.00; 16" – $400.00; 20" – $500.00; 26" – $750.00.

Black or brown mold numbers 320 and 399: 10" – $325.00; 12" – $395.00; 16" – $525.00; 20" – $650.00.

Character infant, mold number 339, or tan fired bisque head toddler, mold number 452: 12" – $395.00; 15" – $500.00. Child, often with mold number 250: 10" – $145.00; 14" – $245.00; 20" – $345.00; 24" – $375.00; 30" – $800.00. Child character with molded hair and painted eyes: 12" – $400.00; 16" – $695.00. Baby with closed mouth, mold number 349: 10" – $295.00; 14" – $350.00.

HEUBACH KOPPELSDORF

12" Marked: Heubach Koppelsdorf/312 5/0/ Germany. Open mouth, and on fully jointed composition body. Courtesy Beres Lindus, South Australia.

22" Marked: Heubach Koppelsdorf/ 342-6½. Flirty brown eyes, open mouth with movable tongue and has original light brown human hair wig. Is on chubby ball jointed body. Courtesy Glorya Woods. Costumed by owner.

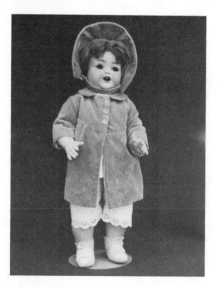

23" Marked Heubach Koppelsdorf 342-6. Sleep eyes, open mouth and on chubby toddler body. Courtesy Yesterday's Child.

33" "Long Face-Cody" Jumeau with closed mouth, applied ears and ball jointed body with straight wrists. Original clothes. Courtesy Barbara Earnshaw.

21" Incised: E 8 J. Closed mouth, applied ears, dark brown paperweight eyes. (Author).

Tete Jumeau: closed mouth: 10" – $2,200.00; 14" – $2,600.00; 16" – $2,800.00; 19" – $3,300.00; 21" – $3,600.00; 23" – $3,700.00; 25" – $4,100.00; 28" – $5,200.00; 30" – $5,500.00. Tete Jumeau: open mouth: 10" – $995.00; 14" – $1,400.00; 16" – $1,600.00; 21" – $2,100.00; 23" – $2,300.00; 25" – $2,500.00; 28" – $2,800.00; 30" – $3,000.00. 1907 Jumeau: open mouth: 14" – $1,000.00; 17" – $1,300.00; 20" – $1,600.00; 25" – $2,100.00; 28" – $2,700.00; 32" – $3,200.00. E.J. (incised) Jumeau: closed mouth: 10" – $3,000.00; 14" – $4,000.00; 16" – $4,500.00; 19" – $5,000.00; 21" – $5,600.00. Incised: Depose-Jumeau: closed mouth: 15" – $2,900.00; 18" – $3,700.00; 22" – $4,300.00; 25" – $5,000.00. Long Face: closed mouth: 21" – $10,000.00 up; 25"-30" – $12,000.00 up. "Portrait" Jumeau: closed mouth: 16" – $4,500.00; 20" – $5,400.00. Phonograph in body Jumeau: open mouth: 20" – $2,400.00; 25" – $2,900.00. 200 series character (marked) Jumeau: 19" – $10,000.00 up. Wire eye (Flirty): open mouth: 20" – $5,200.00; 24" – $5,600.00. Celluloid head, incised Jumeau: 14" – $495.00. S.F.B.J. marked, or Unis marked Jumeaus: open mouth: 16" – $650.00; 20" – $850.00. Closed mouth: 16" – $1,400.00; 20" – $1,800.00. Composition lady body. Tete Jumeau head: 18" – $4,700.00.

JUMEAU

21" "Long Face or Cody" Jumeau with applied ears, closed mouth and marked 10, on head. Jumeau marked composition body. Courtesy Kimport Dolls.

26" Incised: Tete Jumeau. Open mouth with upper teeth. Original dress. Ball jointed body. Lever in back of head operates the eyes. Courtesy Barbara Earnshaw.

16" Marked: Depose/Tete Jumeau/Bte/-S.G.D.G., on head. Paper label on lower back: Bebe Jumeau/Diploma D'Honneur. Original caracul wig and cork pate. Closed mouth. French ball jointed body. Courtesy "Tete" Cook.

20" Marked: Tete Jumeau. Blue paperweight eyes, open mouth and pierced ears. Ball jointed body. Courtesy Glorya Woods.

8" Marked: K star R/21. Painted bisque head, human hair wig, blue sleep eyes with no lashes and open mouth with two teeth. Slender mache five piece body with painted on brown shoes (heels) and white hose. Body stamped on shoulder: Made in Germany. 5" Marked K star R with blonde mohair wig, brown sleep eyes, open mouth with two teeth. Slender body with painted on shoes and hose. Shown also is 8" marked S.F.B.J./60/Paris/12/0. Painted on tan shoes and black hose. Mohair wig, set glass eyes and tan mache body and limbs. Courtesy Glorya Woods.

14" Celluloid head incised: Jumeau with set blue eyes/lashes. Closed mouth and on jointed composition body. Courtesy Sylvia Bryant.

KAMMER AND RINEHARDT

Kammer and Rinehardt dolls often have the Simon and Halbig name or initials along with their own mark, as a great number of heads were made for them. They were located in Waltershausen, Thur, Germany, and began in 1895 although their first models were not on the market until 1896. The trademark of the company was registered in 1895. Marks:

SIMON & HALBIG
116

Character boy or girl. Closed mouth. Add $400.00 for glass eyes. Mold number: 101: 9" – $1,000.00; 14" – $1,800.00; 17" – $3,000.00. 114: 9" – $1,200.00; 14" – $2,600.00; 17" – $3,900.00. 117-117a: 16" – $3,200.00; 18" – $3,800.00; 24" – $5,000.00. 102, 107, 109, 112: 16" – $7,500.00 up; 20" – $9,000.00 up. 118a: 18" – $1,600.00; 22" – $1,800.00. 123, 124: 16" – $6.500.00; 20" – $10,000.00 up. Mold 118, open mouth: 16" – $650.00; 20" – $1,000.00. 117n, open mouth: 16" – $600.00; 20" – $1,200.00.

KAMMER & RINEHARDT

Character Babies. Closed or open/closed mouths. Mold number: 115-115a: 15" – $2,500.00; 18" – $2,700.00; 22" – $3,200.00. 116, 116a: 15" – $2,000.00; 18" – $2,300.0; 22" – $2,900.00. 100, "Kaiser": 10" – $475.00; 16" – $650.00; 18" – $900.00. 100, Black or Tan: 10" – $900.00; 16" – $1,200.00.

Character Babies. Open mouths: Mold number: 121, 122, 128: 14" – $600.00; 18" – $850.00; 22" – $995.00. 121, 122, 128 Toddlers: 14" – $850.00; 18" – $1,100.00; 22" – $1,500.00. 126: 12" – $400.00; 15" – $475.00; 20" – $650.00. 126 Toddler: 16" – $625.00; 20" – $785.00; 24" – $900.00; 28" – $1,200.00; 127 Toddler: 16" – $800.00; 20" – $1,500.00. (add more for flirty eyes)

Molded hair boy. (Mark: K star R-S & H-36). Open mouth: 15" – $450.00; 22" – $795.00. Same with open/closed mouth: 15" – $995.00; 22" – $1,350.00. Small child dolls. Open mouth. Five piece bodies: 5" – $200.00; 8" – $275.00.

Child dolls. Open mouth. Often mold numbers 400, 403, 109, etc. Add more for flirty eyes: 16" – $425.00; 18" – $475.00; 22" – $500.00; 26" – $650.00; 30" – $800.00; 36" – $1,450.00; 40" – $2,000.00. Googly. Mold number 131: 12" – $3,900.00; 15" – $6,500.00; 17" – $7,000.00. Celluloid dolls. Babies with Kid, Kidelen or cloth bodies. Open mouth. 15" – $250.00; 20" – $325.00. Celluloid child. Open mouth. Mold numbers such as 225, 255, 321, 406, 717, 826, 828, etc. Composition jointed bodies: 16" – $450.00; 20" – $575.00.

18" Marked: Simon & Halbig/K star R/46. Blue sleep eyes, open mouth and on fully jointed body. Original shoes, but costumed by owner. Courtesy Glorya Woods.

21" Marked: Simon & Halbig/K star R/53. Brown flirty eyes, brown long hair wig, open mouth and on fully jointed composition body. Courtesy Glorya Woods.

21" Marked: Simon & Halbig/K star R/Germany/55. Original reddish brown wig, brown sleep eyes, open mouth and on fully jointed composition body, but has hard rubber hands. Costumed by owner. Courtesy Glorya Woods.

26" Marked: Simon & Halbig K star R/66. Open mouth and on fully jointed composition body. Courtesy Penny Pendlebury.

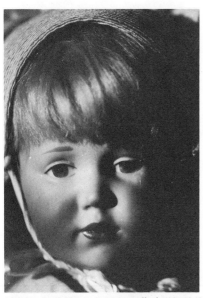

19" Marked: K star R 101. Called "Marie" (boy version is "Peter"). Painted eyes and closed pouty mouth. On fully jointed composition body. Courtesy Jane Walker.

15" Marked: K star R/Simon & Halbig/122/32. Toddler body. Blonde mohair wig, blue sleep eyes with painted lashes upper and lower. Open mouth with two upper teeth and faint cheek dimples. Movable tongue. Holds 5" marked K star R. Both dolls costumed by owner. Courtesy Glorya Woods.

KAMMER & RINEHARDT
KESTNER

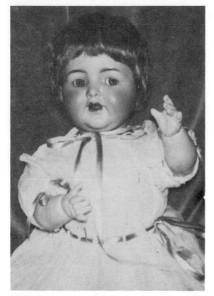

17" Marked: K star R/Simon & Halbig 126 on bent leg baby body. Sleep eyes and open mouth with upper teeth. Courtesy Jessie Smith (Canada).

16" Marked: Simon & Halbig/K star R 403/48. Walker legs, head turns. Open mouth. Composition body with jointed arms and wrists. Courtesy Penny Pendlebury.

16" Marked: Made in/C Germany 7/152. Blonde mohair wig, brown sleep eyes, open mouth and on fully jointed composition body. Costumed by owner. Courtesy Glorya Woods.

Life size "Hilda" that is fully incised. Open crown with original baby wig. Sleep brown eyes and open mouth and on five piece bent leg baby body. Courtesy Cynthia Orgeron.

30" Girl is marked mold number 171. The boy is 24" and marked: J.D.K. 214. Brown sleep eyes, open mouth and on fully jointed composition body. Costumed by owner. Courtesy Glorya Woods.

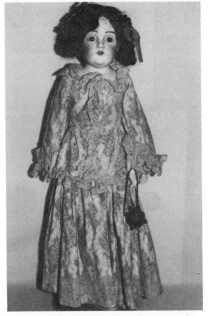

28" Marked: 195/ Made in Germany. Bisque shoulder head, with fur eyebrows, kid body with bisque lower arms. Has original plaster pate and wig, brown sleep eyes and brown wig. Courtesy Pat Timmons.

20" Kestner type (unmarked) with closed mouth and set eyes. Original caracul wig and all original clothes. On fully jointed composition body. Courtesy Barbara Earnshaw.

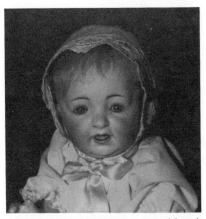

11" Marked: J.D.K./211. Open/closed mouth with molded tongue, sleep blue eyes and mohair baby wig. On five piece bent leg baby body. Courtesy Lorraine Weston.

KESTNER

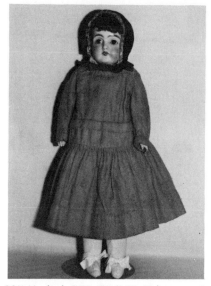

8" Marked: 154 dep 3/0, on head and has Crown Kestner stamp on body. Bisque shoulder head on kid body with bisque lower arms. Courtesy Penny Pendlebury.

20" Marked: DEP. 7½/157. Kid stamped "Kestner" body with bisque lower arms. Brown sleep eyes and brown wig. She wears original undies that are stamped across the back, in blue: The Munsing Underwear. For sale by The Annex. Courtesy Pat Timmons.

19" Girl is marked JDK 166 and has blue set eyes and is a bisque shoulder head on a pin jointed kid body, cloth lower legs and bisque lower arms. Open mouth and on fully jointed composition body. The boy is also 19" and marked JDK 167. Brown sleep eyes, open mouth and on fully jointed composition body. Costumed by owner. Courtesy Glorya Woods.

16" Marked: Made in/C Germany 7/164. Blue sleep eyes, open mouth with three tiny teeth, dimple in chin, and on fully jointed body. Courtesy Glorya Woods.

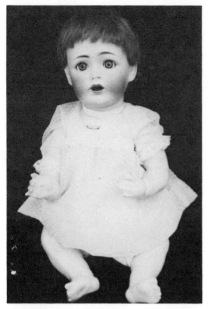

Large baby marked: Germany/J.D.K./257. Bisque head with sleep eyes and open mouth. Five piece bent baby leg body. Courtesy Edith Evans.

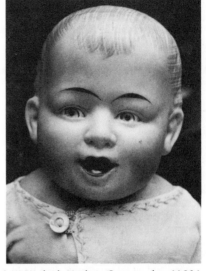

14" Marked: Made in Germany/ges V 216 gesch. Shoulder head on kid body with bisque lower arms. Wide open/closed mouth with two modeled lower teeth. Brush stroke hair that is lightly modeled over ears. Ca. 1912. Intaglio blue eyes. Courtesy Jane Walker.

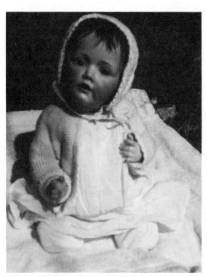

21" Marked: Germany/245/J.D.K./.1914/-Hilda/ges gesch N 1070. On five piece bent leg baby body. Open mouth and sleep brown eyes. Open crown with wig. Courtesy Pauline Hoch.

Very large 36" marked: Made in Germany/J.D.K./260. On fully jointed composition body. Large brown sleep eyes, lashes painted top and bottom, feathered brows and open mouth with four teeth. Brown mohair wig with side part and dressed in owner's mother's dress of 1902. Courtesy Margaret Mandel.

KESTNER

KESTNER

Child with closed mouth. Kid or composition body. Mold number X, and other pouties: 14" – $1,400.00; 17" – $1,700.00; 20" – $1,900.00; 24" – $2,400.00.

Closed mouth marked XI. Composition body, straight wrists: 14" – $1,550.00; 17" – $1,800.00; 20" – $2,000.00; 24" – $2,400.00.

Closed mouth marked with size number only: 14" – $1,200.00; 17" – $1,500.00; 20" – $1,800.00; 24" – $2,200.00.

Turned shoulder head. Closed mouth: Mold numbers such as 169, 639, 698, 969, etc.: 17" – $950.00; 20" – $1,100.00; 24" – $1,400.00. Turned shoulder head. Open mouth: 17" – $375.00; 20" – $475.00; 24" – $575.00. Character Children. Closed mouth, or open/closed: Mold number 208-painted eyes: 17" – $2,700.00; 22" – $3,200.00. 212, Glass eyes: 14" – $2,000.00; 17" – $3,100.00; 20" – $3,600.00. Open mouth, 224, 16" – $495.00. 241, glass eyes: 16" – $1,900.00; 20" – $2,800.00. 249: 20" – $1,000.00. 260-257 child or toddler: 16" – $650.00; 20" – $850.00.

Boxed set-complete doll and three extra heads: $4,800.00. Extra heads from set on old bodies. Allow $400.00 more for glass eyes. Mold numbers 175, 176, 177, 178, 179, 182, 184, 185, 186, 190, 212, etc.: 12" – $1,600.00; 16" – $2,300.00. Larger size of same mold numbers: 18" – $2,900.00; 22" – $3,400.00. Adult mold number 162: 17" – $950.00. Gibson Girl. Mold number 172, or marked on body: 12" – $1,200.00; 17" – $1,700.00; 21" – $2,850.00. Character babies. Open mouth. Wigged or molded hair: 142, 150, 151: 12" – $400.00; 16" – $500.00; 20" – $700.00. 152: 12" – $400.00; 16" – $500.00; 20" – $700.00. 211, 226: 14" – $475.00; 20" – $700.00. 237, 245, 1070 Hilda: 12" – $1,700.00; 16" – $2,700.00; 20" – $3,200.00. Toddler: 16" – $3,300.00; 20" – $3,700.00; 23" – $4,200.00. 239: 12" – $450.00; 16" – $575.00. 243 Oriental: 14" – $2,200.00; 18" – $2,800.00. 247: 12" – $625.00; 16" – $1,200.00. 257: 12" – $450.00; 16" – $500.00; 20" – $700.00; 26" – $900.00. Century Baby for Century Doll Co. Closed mouth, cloth body with composition arms: 14" – $550.00; 18" – $750.00; 24" – $1,200.00. Googly. Mold number 221: 12" – $4,000.00; 14" – $4,800.00. Child with open mouth, composition or kid body, may have fur eyebrows: Mold numbers: 129, 143, 145, 146, 147, 159, 162, 164, 166, 167, 168, 192, 195, 196, 215, 264, etc.: 14" – $375.00; 17" – $500.00; 20" – $575.00; 26" – $695.00; 30" – $1,100.00; 36" – $1,500.00; 40" – $1,800.00. Often found mold numbers: 154, 171, 174: 15" – $375.00; 18" – $450.00; 22" – $495.00; 27" – $700.00. Any in trunks with wardrobes: 9" – $550.00; 12" – $750.00; 14" – $950.00. Tiny dolls with above mold numbers. Open mouth: 7" – $250.00; 9" – $300.00.

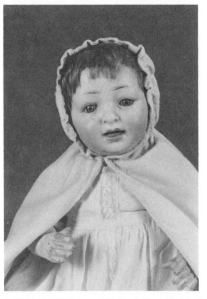

16'' Marked Kley and Hahn, in banner, and mold number 522. Five piece bent leg baby body, sleep blue eyes, original wig and clothes. Open/closed mouth. (Author).

Bisque head marked: 536/5/Kley & Hahn. Intaglio blue eyes, open/closed mouth and on fully jointed composition body. Courtesy Beres Lindus, South Australia.

KLEY AND HAHN

Kley and Hahn operated in Ohrdruf, Germany from 1895 to 1929. They made many different baby dolls, as well as extremely fine character children. Some of their mold numbers are: 50, 52, 66, 75, 76, 129, 130, 132, 133, 138, 140, 141, 142, 143, 149, 150, 154, 156, 158, 160, 162, 167, 176, 178, 179, 199, 210, 220, 250, 266, 277, 282, 331, 520, 525, 526, 531, 536, 546, 552, 568, 585, 680. Company marks are:

Walküre   K & H   ≥K & H≤

Character Children, boys and girls. Can have molded, painted hair or wigs. Closed or open/closed mouth. Intaglio eyes. ADD MORE FOR GLASS EYES. On jointed, or toddler body: All 500 (except #585) series mold numbers: 12" – $1,400.00; 16" – $2,400.00; 20" – $3,900.00; 24" – $4,300.00. Child doll. Jointed body and open mouth. Mold number 250-along with Walkure. The Walkure often will be found without the 250 mark, also: 16" – $275.00; 20" – $450.00; 24" – $525.00; 28" – $675.00; 32" – $995.00. Babies with five piece baby body. Add more for toddler body: Open/closed mouths. Mold numbers: 130, 142, 150, 199: 12" – $495.00; 16" – $595.00; 20" – $725.00; 24" – $900.00. Babies with open mouths: 132, 162, 167, 176, 585: 12" – $400.00; 16" – $500.00; 20" – $600.00; 24" – $700.00.

KLEY & HAHN
KRUSE, KATHE

19½" Key and Hahn 526 with brown painted eyes, full closed mouth and on fully jointed composition body. Courtesy Kimport Dolls.

15" Celluloid type face, cloth body, fully jointed, and blonde original wig. Clothes are original, but hat is replaced. Pre-World War II, or 1945 to 1949. Panther and donkey are Steiff and the Steiff donkey is still available. Courtesy Margaret Mandel.

Founded in 1910 by Kathe Kruse, the wife of a well known Berlin sculptor. Her first dolls were copies of a baby of the Renaissance period, and of her own children. The heads were hand painted in oils. In 1916 she obtained a patent for a wire coil doll. These dolls were Kathrinchen, a Dutch doll, Lutt Martin, Fritz, Christincen, and Michel. In 1923 she registered, as a trademark, a double K with the first one reversed, along with the name Kathe Kruse.

After World War II Kathe Kruse dolls were made of plastics by the Rheinische Gummi Celuloid Fabrik Company of Germany. These plastics were first shown at the Toy Fair in Nuremberg in 1955.

Marks: The early dolls had molded muslin heads that were hand painted, jointed cloth bodies, and have Kathe Kruse, in script, along with a number and sometimes Germany, on the sole of a foot. 17" – $675.00; 20" – $900.00. 1920's dolls with wigs, still have cloth bodies, and oil painted heads: 17" – $650.00; 20" – $900.00. Plastic dolls with glued on wigs, sleep eyes, and marked with Turtle in diamond and a number on head. On back: Modell/Kathe Kruse/, and a number, 16" – $400.00.

LADIES OF FASHION

The term "fashion dolls" should be restricted to those dolls used for transmitting fashion designs from shop to customer, or from country to country, but collectors refer to any "adult" type doll as a Fashion, even if the majority were only play dolls. Of all the ladies the most desirable are the Huret and Rohmer, and the articulated wood, bisque, or blown kid models. The most common seems to be the F.G. marked dolls. A great many fashions are unmarked. Dolls with articulated wood, or blown kid bodies and limbs. (Some have bisque lower arms): 16" – $2,900.00; 20" – $3,500.00. Those with articulated bisque arms and legs, with fine feet and hand detail: 16" – $3,400.00; 20" – $4,800.00. Marked Huret or Rohmer: 16" – $4,200.00; 20" – $5,400.00. Huret portrait lady: 18" – $9,800.00. Ladies with one piece shoulder and head (not jointed at neck): 12" – $900.00; 16" – $1,400.00; 20" – $1,800.00. Dolls with all kid bodies or bisque arms, swivel neck: 14" – $1,400.00; 18" – $1,800.00. F.G. marked head on a Gesland body with bisque hands and lower legs: 14" – $2,600.00; 17" – $3,200.00; 21" – $3,600.00. Gesland body, marked F.G. head, with hands and legs made of composition or Papier mache: 14" – $1,800.00; 17" – $2,400.00; 21" – $2,800.00. Marked Jumeau (body). Number on head: 14" – $1,900.00; 18" – $2,900.00; 24" – $3,600.00.

Smiling fashion called the "Mona Lisa" and made by Jumeau. All original clothes and wig. Glass eyes and pierced ears. Bisque swivel head on bisque shoulder plate. All kid body and limbs. Courtesy Barbara Earnshaw.

Rare incised Huret fashion that is fully articulated and has delicate metal hands. Nicely dressed in old materials. Very adult face with painted eyes. Courtesy Barbara Earnshaw.

LADIES OF FASHION

Unmarked swivel bisque head fashion on bisque shoulder plate, and with bisque lower arms. Glass eyes, pierced ears and kid over wood body with metal upper arms. Courtesy Barbara Earnshaw.

Side view of same fashion to see calf detail. Metal upper arms. Courtesy Barbara Earnshaw.

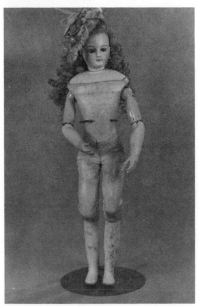

Front view of fashion with metal upper arms, bisque lower arms and blown kid lower legs. Courtesy Barbara Earnshaw.

Gesland stockinette covered body and limbs with bisque lower legs and gauntlet hands. Bisque swivel head on bisque shoulder plate. Head marked: F.G. Courtesy Barbara Earnshaw.

Close up of fashion face. Extremely fine quality bisque. Courtesy Barbara Earnshaw.

All original unmarked fashion with glass eyes and pierced ears. The body and limbs are all kid. Courtesy Barbara Earnshaw.

Close up of the unmarked fashion face and shows fine detail to brows and eyes. Courtesy "Tete" Cook.

All original fashion with her trunk and wardrobe. Bisque swivel head on bisque shoulder plate, pierced ears and glass eyes. All kid body and limbs. Unmarked. Courtesy "Tete" Cook.

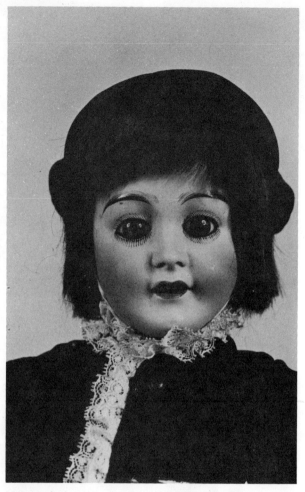

19" Marked Limoges - Favorite with the complete mark: FABRICATION/FRANCAISE, in square/"FAVORITE"/AL & Cie/LIMOGES. Open mouth and on fully jointed composition body. Courtesy Kimport Dolls.

A. Lanternier & Cie (Company) of Limoges, France made dolls from about the 1890's on into 1930's. Prior to making dolls heads they made porcelain pieces as early as 1855. The doll's heads will be fully marked, and will sometimes carry a name such as: Favorite, La Georgienne, Lorraine or Cherie. They will be marked with an anchor, or Fabrication/Francoise, in a square, along with an A.L., or AL & Cie. Generally found on papier mache bodies.

Child dolls with open mouths: 16" – $625.00; 20" – $725.00. Character doll marked: TOTO. Open/closed mouth. 16" – $895.00; 20" – $1,200.00.

21" Lenci character with large round painted eyes to the side, original clothes with tag sewn to hem of the skirt. Posed with two modern FECO (German) dogs. Courtesy Margaret Mandel.

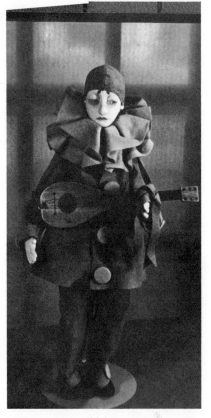

17" Down cast, all felt Lenci. Courtesy Barbara Earnshaw.

LENCI

Lenci dolls are all felt dolls, a few with cloth torso, and jointed at neck, shoulders and hips. The original clothes will be felt or organdy, or a combination of both. The features are oil painted, usually side glancing eyes. The *NEW* Lenci dolls have the eyes painted ahead. Sizes can be from 5" to 45". Marks: Lenci Torino-Made in Italy is often on paper tags or cloth tags. Lenci may be written on the bottom of the foot, or on the inside underneath one arm. Tiny dolls: 5" – $125.00; 9"-10" – $225.00. Children: 16" – $600.00 up; 20" – $850.00 up. Ladies with adult faces: 24" – $750.00 up. "Flapper" or "Boudoir" style with long limbs: 28" – $725.00 up. Clowns: 18" – $750.00; 26½" – $1,500.00. Golfer: 16" – $800.00. Indian: 16" – $900.00. Indian Chief: 22" – $1,200.00. Shirley Temple: Type: 30" – $1,200.00. Oriental: 16" – $900.00; 22" – $1,200.00. Bali Dancer: 22" – $1,200.00. Smoking Doll: 25" – $900.00. With glass eyes: 16" – $1,200.00 up; 20" – $1,800 up.

LENCI

23" "Primavera" by Anili, Turin, Italy. This is the style of dolls that Anili, who is the daughter of Lenci, is making her new and current dolls. The eye detail is especially well done and the eyes look to the side. The *new* Lenci dolls have the eyes straight ahead. Courtesy June Schultz.

16" Lenci - 1925. Mohair wig, brown eyes to side and the body is hollow felt with strung arms and legs. Original shocking pink felt coat and hat with gold embroidery and black felt trim. Felt shoes and silk socks. Original white lawn dress with lace trim and wears Teddies edged in lace. Courtesy Glorya Woods.

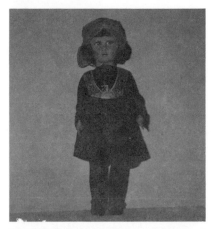

17" Lenci 598-397. All felt and all original in black with gold trim and headpiece. Original cross at neck. Courtesy Sally Bethscheider.

11" All felt Lenci-type. Oil painted features, glued on mohair wig, leather belt and metal horn. (Author).

LIMBACH

When Limbach started producing dolls is not known, but it was called Limbach Porzellanfabrik, Limbach, Thur., Germany. It is known that they made dolls in the late 1890's and early 1900's. They often carry names, such as "Norma", "Wally", "Willy". Marks:

Limbach

Limbach Children: Bisque head, composition jointed body. Open mouth: 16" – $325.00; 20" – $450.00; 24" – $550.00. Character Child or toddler: Molded hair, open/closed mouth. Includes mold number 8682: 12" – $700.00; 16" – $1,000.00; 20" – $1,800.00.

Bisque head with jointed composition child. Open mouth with four teeth. Large eyes with painted lashes over and beneath. Marks: Norma   Limbach 1. Courtesy Jane Walker.

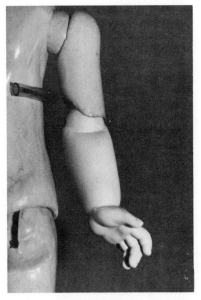

Lovely French "Belton" with paperweight eyes and an open/closed mouth with space between is only marked 9 J. Body is wood and composition with bisque lower arms. See following photo for detail of arms. Courtesy Millie Chappelle. 20" - $1,900.00.

Beautifully detail straight wristed bisque lower arms on doll marked only with a 9 J. Courtesy Millie Chappelle.

MAKER UNKNOWN

Close up of the unmarked dolls that collectors do not know if they are French or German. Most are marked only with a number. Paperweight eyes, open/closed mouth with modeled tongue and teeth. Decal brows. Courtesy Millie Chappelle. 19" - $1,800.00.

19" Round cheek, bisque head doll with open/closed mouth modeled teeth and tongue. Kid body with bisque lower arms. Paperweight eyes and decal brows. Could be French or German, maker is unknown. Courtesy Jane Walker. 19" - $1,800.00.

20" Unmarked bisque head on mache and composition German body. Beautiful set blue eyes, open mouth with teeth and pierced ears, dark feather brows. Most likely made by Kestner or Simon and Halbig. Dimple in chin. Looks very much like a S&H 939 or 949. Photos by Sally Freeman.

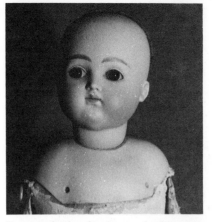

5" Tall with bisque head, sleep eyes and closed mouth. She has a composition five piece body with painted on shoes and socks. Dressed by owner. Courtesy Sylvia Bryant. $300.00.

Bisque socket head on bisque shoulder plate with closed mouth, set paperweight brown eyes and feathered brows. The socket is setted in a kid lining and she has sew holes, but is glued onto an all kid body with bisque lower arms. She could be a Kestner, or a Simon and Halbig although Kestner dolls often have the squared off corners to the mouth (which she has), and S & H has greater depth of detail (indentations) and the sew holes. Marked only with a 6. Courtesy Millie Chappelle. 18" - $1,200.00.

28" German bisque head doll with jointed composition body, blue sleep eyes, open mouth and only marked with: 1916/8. Eyebrows are modeled and lightly feathered, and are located close to the eyes. Courtesy Marcia Picewicz. 28" - $750.00.

Bisque head on fully jointed composition body. Sleep eyes and open mouth. Only marks: 101/6. Looks like the 101 My Sweetheart. Costumed by owner. Courtesy Sylvia Bryant. 22" - $425.00.

MAKER UNKNOWN

12" On five piece bent leg baby body and head is marked: 2B. Wide open with teeth and glass eyes. Bisque and coloring appear to be Nippon. Courtesy Sally Freeman. 12" - $155.00.

19" Shoulderhead with turned and tilted down slightly bisque head. Brown sleep eyes, open mouth with six teeth and deep modeling around nose, chin dimple. Auburn mohair wig, gusseted kid body with lower legs of cloth. The lower arms are bisque, and the arms have wire running through them. Original commercial bonnet and homemade dress of the late 1880's. High on the rim of the crown is marked: 𝒥 Price on body in pencil is $1.15 and inside shoulder is $1.60. Courtesy Sally Freeman. 19" - $475.00.

11½" Bisque head on five piece composition walker body with thin legs and painted on shoes and socks. Blue sleep eyes, open mouth, pierced ears and only mark is DEP, on head. Courtesy Verna Humphrey. 11½" - $1,100.00.

21" Bisque head that is incised: 150./Germany/2. Composition jointed body, blue sleep eyes with hair lashes and painted lashes below the eyes. Hand tied mohair wig, open mouth with upper teeth. Courtesy Sally Freeman. 21" - $725.00.

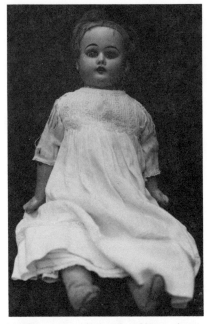

16" Bisque shoulderhead and bisque lower arms on kidalene and muslin body. Remains of original wig and may be original dress. Open mouth with three upper teeth, blue glass set eyes. Marks on shoulder: N (script) 184/9/0. Courtesy Carol Friend. 16" - $450.00.

24" Bisque head that is incised: 261. Dep. Germany. Sleep eyes with lashes, and painted lashes over and under the eyes. Open mouth with upper teeth. Delicate bisque color with heavy feathered eyebrows, mohair wig. Composition body. Courtesy Beres Lindus, South Australia. 24" - $600.00.

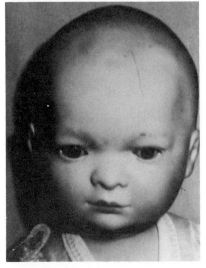

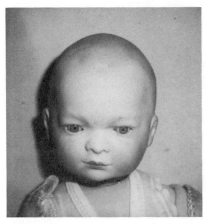

17" Character baby with bisque head that is incised: Germany/800/5. Grey sleep eyes, very pale colored brows and hair, full closed pouty-style mouth. 12½" head circumference. Courtesy Jimmy & Fay Rodolfos. 17" - $700.00.

MAKER UNKNOWN

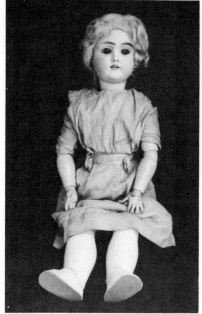

24" German doll that is unmarked. Bisque head with glued on mohair wig, blue set eyes, open mouth with four upper teeth. Composition and wood jointed body. The dress may be original. Courtesy Ruth Anderson. 24" - $385.00.

15" Bisque head on old Kestner, or Kestner style body that has five pieces and bent legs. Oriental with glass eyes and open mouth. Painted hair. This mold is exactly like the regular Kestner Oriental baby, but the head is totally unmarked. Courtesy Sally Freeman. 15" - $1,200.00.

26" Composition head on composition or heavy papier mache jointed body. Large painted brown eyes to the side, closed mouth and "pouty" look. The body is French of the S.F.B.J. period. No marks. (Author). 26" - $285.00.

Shows the jointed legs of the French composition doll. She is also jointed at the elbows.

14" Composition head boy of the "Can't Break 'em type". Side glance blue painted eyes, light brown hair and on excelsior stuffed, disc jointed cloth body and limbs with gauntlet composition hands. Courtesy Sally Freeman. 14" - $65.00.

8" Blue mohair covered body with covered, jointed legs in one piece and leatherette sewn on the bottom of feet. Matching leatherette belt, and hands to form mittens. Yellow mohair covered head, cloth in back and front half is painted bisque. Painted features with large eyes to side. These "fur" covered dolls became very popular after the discovery of the North Pole, with many made in the U.S.A., but most made in Germany. Courtesy Jayn Allen. 8" - $85.00.

19" "Mascotte" with large paperweight eyes, closed mouth, on French jointed body and marked with: M-8. Original clothes. Courtesy Barbara Earnshaw.

MASCOTTE

Mascotte dolls were made by May Freres Cie from 1890 to 1897, then this firm became part of Jules Steiner from 1898 into the 1900's. Some are marked with the full name: Bebe Mascotte/Paris. 16" – $2,200.00; 18" – $2,600.00; 20" – $3,200.00; 22" – $3,400.00.

MECHANICALS

Group of French mechanicals. All have closed mouths, and are all original clothes. Three are marked Jumeau, and the tallest with adult face is an early unmarked doll that has wheels, is key wound and waltzes. All are courtesy Barbara Earnshaw.

MECHANICALS

Mechanicals are also called Automatons, and were made as early as the 1840's. Many are mounted on a music box, and as the music plays the "dolls" move. They were mainly made in France and Germany by various firms. Some are on wheels and as they are pulled along the "doll" moves. There is such a great variety of the Automatons that an entire collection could be made of them alone. A. Theroude mechanical walker patented in France in 1840 with mache head and bamboo teeth in open mouth. Stands on three wheel (two large, and one small wheel) tin cart with mechanism attached to leg. 16" – $1,400.00. Autoperipatetikos of 1861. Base as clock like works and tin feet and when wound the doll walks. Heads can be china, untinted bisque or mache: 11", early china head – $995.00; 11", later china hairdo – $625.00. Untinted bisque head: 11" – $625.00. Mache head: 11" – $500.00.

George Hawkins walker with pewter hands and feet, wood torso. Hands modeled to push a carriage, which should be a Goodwin, patented in 1867-1868. Carriage has two large back wheels and one small front wheel. Molded hair doll's head will be marked: X.L.C.R./Doll head/Pat. Sept. 8,1868. 11" – $1,200.00. Jumeau. Raises and lowers both arms, and head moves. Hold items such as Hankie and bottle, book and fan, etc., in each hand. Key wound with music box in base. Closed mouth and marked: Jumeau. 15" – $2,800.00; 20" – $3,600.00. Same as above, but with open mouth: 15" – $1,600.00; 20" – $2,600.00. Marked Jumeau standing or sitting on music box that is key wound, and doll plays an instrument. 14" – $3,000.00; 17" – $3,600.00. Marked Jumeau walker standing on three wheel cart, and when cart is pulled doll's head turns and arms go up and down. Marked. 15" – $3,200.00; 18" – $3,800.00. Marked Jumeau walker with one piece legs, arms jointed at elbow, and she raises her arm to blow kisses, and the head turns. Cryer box. Open mouth. 16" – $1,200.00; 22" – $1,800.00. Mechanical Jules Steiner. Composition upper and lower torso, also lower legs and all of arms. Twill covered sections of hips and upper legs. Key wound. Cries, kicks and turns head. Open mouth with two rows teeth. 18" – $1,600.00. Same as above but with bisque torso section: 18" – $3,600.00. ALL PRICES ABOVE ARE FOR ORIGINALLY DRESSED MECHANICALS. THEY ARE LESS IF THE DOLL/FIGURE HAS BEEN RE-DRESSED.

21" Marked: Mon Tresor and made in 1914 by Henri Rostal. Open mouth with upper teeth, sleep eyes, feathered brows and on fully jointed composition body. Courtesy Yesterday's Child.

Henri Rostal of Paris used the initials H.R., and the name trademarks of Mon Tresor and Bebe Mon Tresor in 1914. The heads are bisque with bodies of composition and fully jointed. Open mouth dolls: 16" - $625.00; 18" - $750.00; 21" - $825.00; 24" - $950.00.

14" Munich Art Dolls. Boy and girl. Painted composition heads with painted features in oils. Both have closed mouths and are on fully jointed composition bodies. Courtesy Jane Walker.

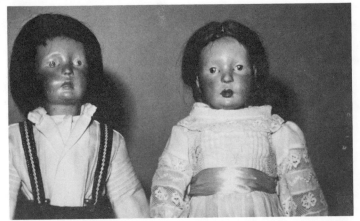

Closeup view of the detail in the faces of the Munich Art Dolls. Courtesy Jane Walker.

Munich Art Dolls are very rare. They were designed to look like real children, and were the forerunners of the "character" dolls that began to appear in the 1910's. Marion Kaulitz conceived the designs and had them modeled by Paul Vogelsanger. The dolls can have composition or fabric heads, and they are on fully jointed composition bodies. A few will be marked on back of the head. 14" – $525.00; 19" – $995.00.

PAINTED BISQUE

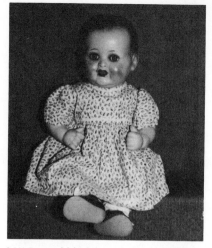

16" Marked Germany, on head. Painted bisque head with flirty sleep eyes and real lashes, open mouth with two upper teeth, dimples in cheeks and chin. Papier mache arms and bent baby legs, and excelsior filled cloth body. Free stancing thumbs with other fingers curled under. Molded, painted reddish brown hair and very rosy color to head. Made for Madame Hendron (Georgene Avrill). Ca. 1920's. Courtesy Shirley Merrill. 16" - $275.00.

16" Painted black bisque with mohair wig over molded hair. Brown sleep eyes, five piece body, and open, very red mouth. Unmarked. Courtesy Shirley Merrill. 16" - $185.00.

10" Painted bisque with one piece body and head. Painted hair and features. Not original. Stamped: Germany, on back. Courtesy Shirley Merrill. $40.00.

3¾" Painted bisque twins. Incised: Germany. Scotch outfits with green felt jackets, plaid kilt and gaiters, felt tie, organdy dickey, plaid tam on girl, hat on boy. Painted blonde hair and features. Courtesy Shirley Pascuzzi. 4" - $40.00 each.

2½″ Quints, painted bisque with one piece body and legs and head. Wire jointed shoulders. Red/white glued on pleated dresses with sailor collars. Curl molded on top of head, painted black eyes. Stamped in black on bottom of feet: Japan. In original card in original red paste board box: Has picture of toddler and on top: Made in Japan. Courtesy Shirley Pascuzzi. Set - $75.00.

3¾″ Twins in Greek style clothes. Skirt of fabric, tops of organdy. Cumberbund of girl and head dress of boy and pants are black felt. Ribbon trim at hem, on hat and waist. Painted black hair. Incised: Germany, on heads. Painted shoes over molded shoes. One piece body and head. 4″ - $40.00 each.

5″ Painted bisque incised: Germany, on head. Molded blonde hair, painted features. Black felt jumper with red pleated apron, white cotton sleeves. Free standing thumbs, painted on black shoes, but mold marks show sandles with straps. Elastic strung. Courtesy Shirley Pascuzzi. 5″ - $45.00.

PAPIER MACHE

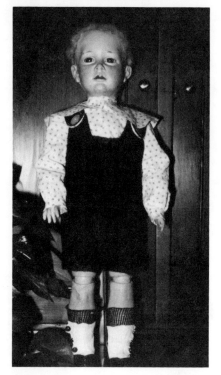

20" Beautifully modeled papier mache boys head with glass eyes, closed mouth, protruding ears and with top of crown cut. Wigged and on nice German fully jointed composition body. Marked: C.O.D., for Cuno and Otto Dressel. Courtesy Jane Walker.

PA'PI'ER MACHE'

Most so called "pa'pi'er mache'" parts on dolls were actually laminated paper and not pa'pi'er mache' at all. Laminated paper doll heads/parts are several thicknesses of molded paper that have been bonded (glued) together, or pressed after being glued.

Pa'pi'er mache' is a type of composition in that it was a plastic (meaning movable) material from paper pulp, wood and rag fibers, containing paste, oil or glue. Flour and/or clay, sand is added for stiffness. The hardness of pa'pi'er mache' depends on the amount of glue that is added.

As early as 1810 dolls of pa'pi'er mache' were being mass produced by molds. In 1858 Ludwig Greiner patented heads containing paper, whiting rye flour, glue and reinforced with muslin and linen. About 1870 pa'pi'er mache' was used on jointed dolls. In French the words Pa'pi'er mache' mean "chewed paper". Dolls marked: M&S Superior-2015. (Muller & Strassburger). 14" – $200.00; 18" – $400.00; 24" – $695.00. French and French type: Painted black hair with brush marks, on solid dome, some have nailed-on wigs. Open mouth with bamboo teeth, inset glass eyes or full closed mouth. All leather/kid body. 15" – $450.00; 20" – $725.00; 26" – $950.00; 30" – $1,300.00. Early mache with cloth body and wooden limbs. Early hairdo with top knots, buns, puff curls, or braiding. Ca. 1840's: 10" – $350.00; 14" – $500.00; 17" – $600.00; 20" – $850.00. Marked Greiner dolls of 1858 on: 23" – $650.00; 29" – $1,000.00. Motschmann types with wood and twill bodies. Separate torso section and separate hip section, glass eyes, closed mouth and brush stroke hair on solid dome: 16" – $325.00; 20" – $495.00. 1870's-1900's German mache with molded various curly hairdo, painted eyes and closed mouth. May be blonde or black hair. Cloth body with cloth or leather arms: 16" – $185.00; 20" – $225.00; 26"-32" – $725.00. Turned shoulder doll, solid dome, glass eyes and closed mouth: 18" – $695.00; 22" – $895.00. German character heads of mache and of the 1920's. Glass eyes, closed mouths on fully jointed composition bodies: 16" – $695.00; 20" – $850.00. 1920's on with pa'pi'er mache' heads, usually with brighter colors than the older ones. Wigged, and usually dressed as child, or in Provincial costumes. Stuffed cloth bodies and limbs, or have mache arms/hands: 12" – $85.00; 16" – $100.00.

Greiner doll of 1858 with glass eyes, papier mache shoulder head. Cloth body with leather arms and feet. Paper label: Greiner's/Improved/Patent Heads/ Pat. March 30th '58. Full exposed ears and hair-do puffed at sides. Courtesy Betty Shelley.

18" Ca. 1930 early French papier mache with black glass eyes without pupils, painted black hair that is parted in the middle and painted flat around the head. Cloth body with wooden arms and "spoon" hands. Clothes, including hat, are all original. Courtesy Pat Timmons.

PAPIER MACHE

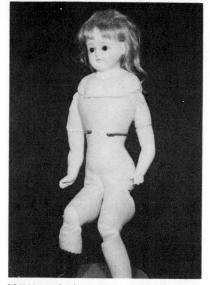

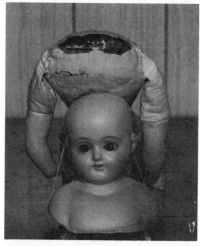

Shows the head of the 18" papier mache doll removed to see the blue Wagner & Zetzsche sticker across the shoulder of the body. Courtesy Penny Pendlebury.

18" Unmarked turned shoulder head that is made of papier mache. Set brown glass eyes, closed mouth, solid dome with hole in top to plug in the wig. Body has a blue Wagner & Zetzsche sticker with a 5 in the center of the sticker. Body is made of twill fabric with pink kid inserts at knees and hips. Composition lower arms. Courtesy Penny Pendlebury.

24" Wax over papier Mache with original wig and clothes. Cloth body with leather sewn on boots, and wax over papier mache lower arms. Closed mouth and glass eyes. (Author).

German wax over papier mache child's head of the 1880's. Paperweight blue glass eyes, original wig and closed mouth. On replaced body. Originally had cloth body with papier mache limbs. Courtesy Theo Lindley.

Papier Mache shoulder head (3½" tall-head only) that is very thin and almost like cardboard. Stamped: Germany. Light brown painted hair, blue painted eyes with red lines over the eyes. New body and limbs. Courtesy Sally Freeman.

11" Papier mache Oriental child with wig and black glass eyes without pupils. Open mouth with upper teeth. Body, lower arms and feet are also papier mache. Lightly sexed. Wood jointed legs. Courtesy Virginia Jones.

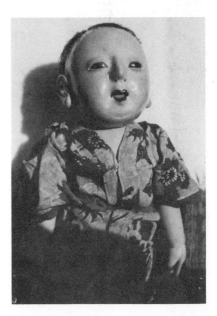

16" Papier mache type jointed at neck, shoulders, wrists, hips and ankles. Papier mache body. Original clothes. Black glass eyes and extremely large ears. Courtesy Marcia Piecewicz.

PAPIER MACHE

This group of dolls are 16" to 17" tall and reported to have been displayed at the Columbia Exposition in Chicago in 1893. This cannot be true as dates on four are after 1893. They are made of papier mache and some are wax. Some of the arms and hands are bisque, others papier mache and still others are wax. From the waists down the dolls are on a wire frame covered with cloth. They have human hair wigs. Each doll has a name tag fastened to her dress and some have a name tag fastened on the wire frame. Courtesy Vivian Lewis.

This single shot shows one of the dolls and the fine detail of face and clothes. This one is Marie-Amelia de Bourbon. Front row-left: Queen Elizabeth 1837-1898; Fru Ava 12th Century; Dame Ellen Terry 1848-1928; Eleanor Duse 1859-1924, Mrs. Hannah Duston 1657; Makrena Mieczyslawska 1797-1864. Second row - left: Marie-Amelia de Bourbon 1782-1866; Marie Therese Artner 172-1829, Maria Bibiana Benitez 1783; Adrienne Lecourreur 1692-1730; Katherina Frohlick 1800-1879. Back row - left: Eleanore d' Aquitaine (tall hat) 1122-1204; Minna Johnson Canth 1848-1897; Madame de Stael 1766-1817; Gertrude Gomez de Avellanedo 1814-1873; Hannah Moore 1745-1833. Courtesy Vivian Lewis.

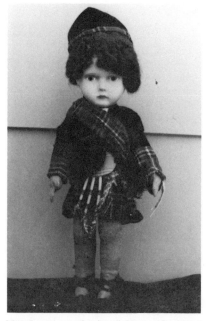

13" Papier mache head boy with closed mouth and painted eyes. Cloth body with stitched fingers and individual thumbs. Mohair wig, original Scottish outfit. Marked only with an E, on back. Courtesy Nancy Lucas.

PARIAN-TYPE (UNTINTED BISQUE)

PARIAN-TYPE (Untinted Bisque)

The use of the name "Parian" is incorrect for dolls, but the collectors have been using this term for so long that it would be difficult to change. The dolls are actually made of unglazed porcelain.

Parian-type dolls were made from the 1850's to the 1880's, most of which were made during the 1870's and 1880's. Almost all this style of dolls were made in Germany, and if marked, the marking will be found inside the shoulder plate. As to variety, there were hundreds of different heads modeled and an entire collection could be made up of them. It must be noted that the really rare and unique unglazed-white bisque "Parian" dolls are difficult to find, and their prices will be high.

The Parian-type dolls can be found with every imaginable thing applied to heads and shirt tops, from flowers, snoods, ruffles, feathers, plumes, ribbons, etc. Many have inset glass eyes, and most are blondes, although a few may have light brown or black hair which may be glazed.

Some of the Parian-type unglazed porcelain dolls and china dolls shared the same molds, and the men and boys as well as ones with swivel necks, can be considered rare.

Adelaine (Adelaide) Patti: Center part, roll curl from forehead to back on each side and "spit" curls at temples and above ears. 1860. 14" – $365.00; 18" – $625.00.

Alice in Wonderland: Hairdo is flat, pulled straight back with ribbon/hairband from middle to far back on head. Some have swivel necks. 1850-1860's. 12" – $365.00; 16" – $695.00; 20" – $1,100.00. Swivel necks: 12" – $450.00; 16" – $825.00.

Bald head: Solid domes that take wigs, full ear detail, 1850's: 14" – $750.00; 16" – $825.00; 20" – $1,200.00.

Countess Dagmar: Came with or without modeled on shirtwaist, and with both blonde and brown hair. This doll can also be found with glass eyes, or painted eyes. She has a ribbon bow at top of hairdo and many tiny ringlet curls in front of the bow that fall on the forehead: 1870's. The hair may also be glazed. 14" – $625.00; 16" – $775.00. Allow more for brown hair and glass eyes.

Lucy, also called *Empress Eugenia and Princess Alexandria:* Hair is in snood with gold and purple luster braided "material" across top of head and large white lustered feather that drapes from the top side of the head to the neck: 1863. 14" – $825.00; 17" – $1,100.00; 21" – $1,500.00.

Mary Lincoln Todd, also known as *Nancy Hanks:* Full snood in back and side with bows where the ears would be. 1870: 14" – $500.00; 16" – $725.00; 19" – $1,050.00. Various hairstyles with modeled combs, ribbons, flowers and/or head bands: 17", Glass eyes, pierced ears – $1,250.00 up; 17", Painted eyes, unpierced ears – $700.00. Modeled necklaces, jewels, or standing ruffled collars: 17", Glass eyes, pierced ears: – $1,250.00 up; 21" – $1,500.00 up; 17", Painted eyes, unpierced ears – $700.00; 21" – $1,000.00.

16" White bisque with modeled curls and deep comb marks with hair tinted brown. Blue painted eyes and rosy cheeks. On cloth body with white bisque lower arms and leather sewn on boots. Courtesy Kimport Dolls.

2 White bisque ("Parian") dolls. "Alice in Wonderland" hairstyles and clothes. Larger doll is 20" with original cloth body and leather arms to the elbows. Smaller matching is a white bisque "Frozen Charlotte", unjointed, flat sole feet with tan glazed boots with gold lustre on top edges of boots. Dresses are blue check gingham with white organdy aprons. Replaced shoes on a large doll. Courtesy Wanda Smith.

PARIAN-TYPE

Small white bisque with center part and puffed out curls. Courtesy Zoura Martinez.

Very nice white bisque with molded head band and deep comb marks through hairdo. Cloth and leather body. Pierced ears. Courtesy Zoura Martinez.

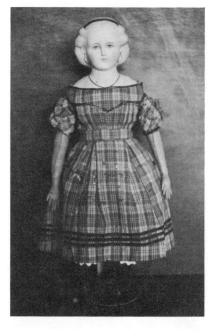

White bisque with pressed head that has a molded on head band and ribbons. Cloth body, "Parian" limbs. Courtesy Zoura Martinez.

PHENIX
PIANO BABIES

The Phenix marked dolls were designed by Henri Alexandre, and were registered and patented by him in 1889 in Paris. In 1890 Alexandre advertised thirty different models of the doll. In 1892 Alexandre sold out to Tourrel, who used the same advertisements. It was in 1895 that the Phenix trademark was registered by Mme. Marie Lafosse who was associated with the Jules Steiner firm. In 1900 the Jules Steiner firm went into the Jules Mettais company. Marked Phenix dolls: Closed mouth, good quality bisque: 16″ – $2,400.00; 20″ – $2,800.00; 25″ – $3,100.00. Open mouth, good quality bisque: 16″ – $1,400.00; 20″ – $1,800.00.

21″ "Star of Phenix". Marked: ⋆ . Full jointed composition body, closed mouth. (Author).

10″ Tall beautiful detailed Piano Baby. This one measures 11″ long. It is marked with a turtle/Germany. Courtesy Marjorie Uhl. This particular style has been reproduced in a large size and the painting detail is not as well done.

Many of the German firms made piano babies, such as Kestner and Gebruder Heubach. They were made from the 1880's on into the 1920's. They can run from 6″ on up to as large as 20″. Most piano babies are unsigned, but the most outstanding in detail, and usually marked are from the Gebruder Heubach firm. These are really figurines and not dolls as they are immobile, (unjointed) and will come in many different positions. They generally were in pairs. Piano babies, lying or sitting, excellent quality: 4″ – $85.00; 8″ – $195.00; 12″ – $400.00; 16″ – $525.00; 20″ – $700.00. Prices will vary on the uniqueness of the position they are in, and on quality. It must also be noted that a great many copies, reproductions and new piano babies have been on the market for a long time. The buyer should make certain that they are buying an OLD piano baby before paying the above prices.

PUTNAM, GRACE

PUTNAM, GRACE

The Bye-lo baby was designed by Grace Storey Putnam, distributed by George Borgfeldt, in 1922. Several German manufacturers produced the bisque heads for these babies. The celluloid heads were made by Karl Standfuss of Germany with the all bisque Bye-los made by J.D. Kestner. The composition heads were produced by the Cameo Doll Co. of New York. Bodies for the Bye-lo are called a "frog" body due to the shape of the legs, and all the bodies were made by the K & K Toy Co. of New York. Schoenhut made an unauthorized Bye-lo in wood. Bye-lo babies had cloth bodies with celluloid hands. Later ones and the composition headed dolls, have composition hands. All will be marked with the name of the doll and designer, some having a date added. The cloth bodies are often stamped with this information also. Bisque head Bye-lo: Measured by head circumference: 10" – $385.00; 12" – $485.00; 15" – $685.00; 18" – $1,300.00. Bye-lo with smiling closed mouth: 14" – $4,400.00 up. Bisque socket head on five piece bent leg composition baby body: 14" – $585.00; 17" – $800.00. All bisque Bye-lo: Jointed only at hips and shoulders, painted eyes: 6" – $365.00. Jointed at neck, shoulders and hips, glass eyes: 6" – $600.00. Cut pate with wig, glass eyes, jointed shoulders and hips: 6" – $625.00. Painted eyes, immobile, in different positions: 3½" – $350.00. Composition head Bye-lo with cloth body, composition hands: Head circumference: 10" – $175.00; 12" – $300.00; 15" – $400.00. Painted bisque head Bye-lo with cloth body, composition hands: Head Circumference: 10" – $250.00; 13" – $365.00; 15" – $550.00. Schoenhut wood head Bye-lo: Cloth body, wood hands: Head Circumference: 13" – $1,200.00. Celluloid head Bye-lo: All celluloid: 6" – $145.00.

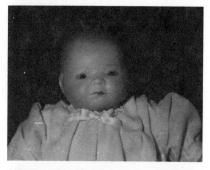

10½" Bye-lo with sleep brown eyes, all cloth "frog" shape body and celluloid hands. Marks: Copr J/ Grace S. Putman/Made in Germany. Courtesy Lorraine Weston.

3½" Bye-lo that is immobile and modeled all in one piece. Painted hair and features. This type was also used as salt and pepper shakers. Courtesy Jackie Barker.

Rabery and Delphieu began making dolls in 1856. The very first dolls had kid bodies, but are extremely rare. The majority of the R.D. marked dolls are on French composition/wood and mache bodies. They will be marked with: R.D., a few marked: Bebe Rabery, and a few with Bebe de Paris. Dolls with closed mouths. 14" – $1,700.00; 17" – $2,000.00; 20" – $2,600.00; 22" – $2,800.00; 25" – $3,100.00. Dolls with open mouths: 14" – $900.00; 17" – $1,600.00; 20" – $1,900.00; 22" – $2,000.00.

21½" Marked: R 2 D. On French ball jointed body, closed mouth, blue paperweight eyes and pierced ears. Courtesy Marcia Piecewicz.

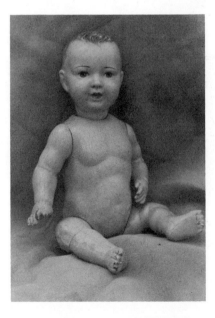

18" Raleigh doll that is all composition. Brown painted eyes, brown modeled hair and two painted teeth in open/closed mouth. Spring jointed and originally came dressed in diaper and cap. Courtesy Carole Friend.

Raleigh dolls were made from 1916 to 1920 by Jessie McCutcheon Raleigh of Chicago, Illinois. They are all composition, or can have cloth bodies with composition head and limbs. The dolls are considered very rare, and were excellent quality. They came as boys or girls, with molded hair or wigged, with closed mouth and open/closed with painted teeth. 13" – $250.00; 16" – $300.00; 18" – $325.00; 22" – $400.00.

RECNAGLE OF ALEXANDERINETHAL

19" Marks: 1909/Dep/R. 3 A./Germany. Made by Recnagle of Alexanderine. Bisque socket head with blue sleep eyes, open mouth with four teeth. Blonde mohair wig. Body is five piece papier mache. All original. Long waisted deep rose bottom with light pink top, hat to match. Courtesy Eloise Godfrey.

6" Bisque bonnet head child with marks: R.A. Made by Recnagle of Alexanderine. Painted features, molded on bonnet with bows over the ears and etched in detail. Shoulder heads on excelsior stuffed gauze type bodies. Bisque lower arms and legs. Courtesy Sally Swain.

Dolls marked with an R.A. were made by Recknagel of Alexandrinethal, Thur, Germany. They came also marked with a number and/or Germany. They came with bisque heads, composition bodies, as well as pa'pi'er mache' and wood jointed bodies. Children: Set or sleep eyes, open mouths, with small dolls having painted on shoes and socks: 9" – $100.00; 13" – $165.00; 16" – $200.00; 19" – $295.00; 22" – $345.00. Character child or baby. Ca. 1909-1910. Came on five piece bent leg baby body, toddler body or child body. Sleep or set eyes, open mouth: 12" – $185.00; 16" – $250.00; 19" – $325.00; 22" – $400.00.

Character baby with painted eyes, and modeled on various styles of bonnets. Open/closed mouth, generally with painted, modeled in teeth: 8" – $475.00; 12" – $545.00.

Dolls marked with a P.M. were made by Otto Reinecke of Hof-Moschendorf, Bavaria, Germany from 1909 into the 1930's. The most often found mold number from this company is the 914 baby or toddler. The marks include the P.M., as well as a number and Germany. Child with open mouth, set or sleep eyes: 15" – $285.00; 18" – $375.00; 22" – $450.00. Baby with open mouth, set or sleep eyes: 12" – $250.00; 16" – $375.00; 22" – $500.00; 25" – $600.00.

19" German baby marked: P.M. 914/-Germany/10. Five piece bent leg baby body, open mouth with tongue and teeth and set brown eyes. Made by Otto Reinecke. The P.M. stands for name of the factory: Porzellanfabrick Moschendorf. Courtesy Marcia Piecewicz.

14" Marks: Revalo. Made by Gebruder Ohlhaver, Germany. Jointed composition body, bisque head with deeply modeled hair and ribbon head band with two side bows. Painted eyes and laughing open/closed mouth with painted upper teeth. Old dress. Courtesy Elizabeth Burke.

The Revalo marked dolls were made by Gebruder Ohlhaver of Thur, Germany in 1921 into the 1930's. Bisque heads on composition bodies. Children: Sleep or set eyes, open mouth: 14" – $350.00; 17" – $450.00; 20" – $525.00; 24" – $600.00. Coquette style with molded hair and ribbon, intaglio eyes and open/closed mouth: 11" – $565.00; 14" – $695.00. Character toddler or baby: Sleep eyes, open mouth, bent leg baby body or toddler bodies: 15" – $450.00; 17" – $500.00.

SCHMIDT, BRUNO
SCHMITT & FILS

BRUNO SCHMIDT

Bruno Schmidt manufactured dolls from 1900 into the 1930's and operated from Walterhausen, Thur, Germany. He not only worked in porcelain, but also in pa'pi'er mache' and celluloid. His trademarks all include hearts, and he registered Mein Goldhertz (My Golden Heart) in 1904 and the BSW in the heart the same year. Other years he registered hearts were: 1908, 1910 and 1915. Some of the Bruno Schmidt mold numbers are: 204, 529, 2033, 2048, 2072, 2094, 2096, 2097. Some mold marks:

Wendy, mold number 2033. Closed mouth: 16" — $5,000.00 up; 20" — $6,500.00 up. Children, open mouths: 20" — $450.00; 24" — $550.00; 29" — $950.00. Character children with molded, painted hair and eyes, closed mouth: 16" — $2,600.00; 20" — $3,200.00. Mold number 2048, called "Tommy Tucker": 16" — $850.00; 20" — $1,200.00. Babies, wigs, sleep eyes: 14" — $375.00; 17" — $485.00; 21" — $650.00.

Rare Bruno Schmidt character girl. All original, and has intaglio eyes and closed mouth. Ball jointed composition body. Marks: B.S.W., in a heart. Courtesy Barbara Earnshaw.

17'' and 23'' Schmitt & Fils of France. Marks: on head and body. Both have closed mouths, pierced ears and set paperweight eyes. The 17'' is all original, except necklace has been added. Courtesy Barbara Earnshaw.

Schmitt and Fils produced dolls during the 1870's, 1880's and 1890's in Paris, France. They will be marked on head and body with a shield: 🛡 They have composition/wood jointed bodies, and came with fully closed and open/closed mouths. 15" — $3,000.00; 18" — $4,500.00; 20" — $5,000.00; 23" — $6,200.00; 25" — $6,600.00.

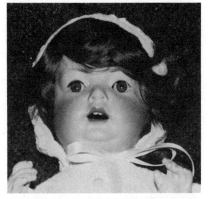

Marks: S H and PB in a five point star-Hanna/Germany. Made by Schoenau & Hoffmeister. Comes as a baby on a five piece bent leg baby body, or on a toddler body. Open mouth with two upper teeth and sleep eyes. Courtesy Beres Lindus, South Australia.

24" Marked Schmitt with crossed hammers in a shield on head and body. Ball jointed body with straight wrists. Closed mouth. Courtesy Kimport Dolls.

SCHOENAU & HOFFMEISTER

Schoenau & Hoffmeister began making dolls in 1901, and were located in Bavaria. The factory was called "Porzellanfabrik Burggrub" and this mark will be found on some doll's heads. Dolls are also marked with a five point star with the initials SH and PB inside the star: Some of their mold numbers are: 21, 169, 170, 769, 900, 914, 1800, 1906, 1909, 1923, 4000, 4500, 4900, 5000, 5300, 5500, 5700, 5800, Hanna.

Oriental: Mold number 4900: Open mouth: 10" — $365.00; 14" — $895.00; 18" — $1,100.00.

Hanna: Brown or black bisque. Open mouth. Grass skirt, or native print cloth gown: 8" — $165.00; 10" — $200.00.

Princess Elizabeth: Smiling open mouth, marked on head: 16" — $2,300.0; 20" — $2,700.00; 24" — $3,400.00.

Character Baby: Mold number and five piece bent leg baby body: 12" — $300.00; 17" — $475.00; 20" — $500.00; 24" — $575.00.

Character Toddlers: Same description and marks as the babies: 14" — $465.00; 17" — $595.00; 20" — $625.00.

Character Baby with closed mouth; and sleep eyes: 13" — $550.00; 16" — $725.00; 20" — $995.00.

Children: Mold numbers such as 1909, 5500, 5700, 5800. Open mouths: 10" — $100.00; 15" — $285.00; 18" — $325.00; 21" — $385.00; 26" — $550.00.

SCHOENHUT
SCHUETZMEISTER & QUENDT
SCHOENHUT

The Albert Schoenhut & Co. was located in Philadelphia, PA in 1872. His grandfather and father were both woodcarvers in Germany. It was in 1909 that Albert Schoenhut applied for the patent for a swivel, spring jointed dolls, but did not receive the patent until 1911. In 1911 he brought out his line of "All Wood Perfection Art Dolls" and in 1913 he started to produce the infant doll with curved limbs. The infant was designed by son Harry E. Schoenhut, and they came with wigs or molded hair, as well as toddler bodies and the infant bodies.

In 1924 the Schoenhut company brought out the "Bass Wood Elastic Dolls" that were jointed by elastic instead of springs, and were cheaper in price.

Schoenhut dolls will be incised: Schoenhut Doll/Pat. Jan, 17, '11, U.S.A./& Foreign Countries, and will have a paper label with the same mark in an oval. Boy or girl character with molded hair/ribbon/comb: 14" – $1,000.00; 16" – $1,150.00; 20" – $1,375.00.

Pouty, open/closed mouth/painted teeth or closed mouth: 16" – $500.00; 19" – $675.00.

"Baby" common face on baby or toddler body: 16" – $525.00; 17" – $595.00.

"Dolly" faced common doll: 17" – $385.00; 20" – $445.00.

Sleep eyes: 17" – $525.00; 20" – $685.00.

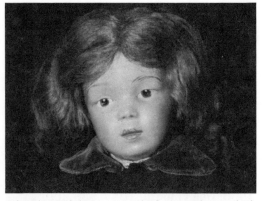

Schoenhut girl that is mint. She has a sticker marked: 00237, on back. All wood with spring jointed body. Painted brown eyes, closed mouth and original wig and clothes. Courtesy Lorraine Weston.

22" Marked: S & Q/101. Made by Schuelzneister and Quenot. Bisque head with open mouth, sleep brown eyes and on fully jointed composition body. Courtesy Glorya Woods.

Schuetzmeister & Quendt only operated for a few short years, 1893 to 1898. The factory was located in Boilstadt, Thur., Germany. Sample marks: SQ   Q   S
                                                                  Q

10", bald head with two stringing holes, closed mouth. Mold number 101, 201, 301: 16" – $265.00; 20" – $375.00; 24" – $450.00. Bent leg baby, open mouth: 17" – $425.00; 22" – $485.00.

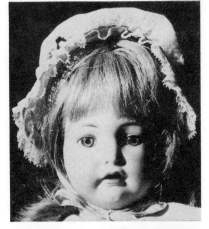

16" Marked: Simon Halbig/600/6½. Sleep blue eyes, open mouth, dimple in chin, and on fully jointed body. Courtesy Jane Walker.

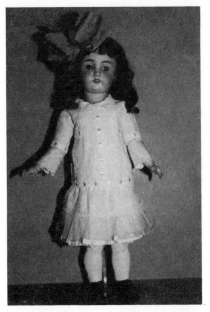

21" Marked: 53/Germany/Simon & Halbig/ S & H. Brown sleep eyes, open mouth with four teeth and on fully jointed composition body. The body marked on right hip: Heinrich Handwerck/Germany. Costumed by owner. Courtesy Glorya Woods.

SIMON & HALBIG

The following is for Simon & Halbig dolls with their mark only, and not in combination with other marks such as K star R/S & H. "Dolly" faced dolls with open mouths, kid or composition bodies. Mold numbers such as: 130, 550 (most common), 1009, 1010, 1040, etc.: Allow extra for flirty eyes: 15" – $385.00; 18" – $495.00; 22" – $525.00; 26" – $675.00; 30" – $950.00. Mold number 1079: 15" – $575.00; 18" – $675.00; 22" – $895.00. Closed mouth characters: Mold numbers: #120: 14" – $1,000.00. 150, 151: 18" – $5,200.00. 153: 18" – $4,400.00. 600: 14" – $765.00. 718, 719: 16" – $1,800.00; 20" – $2,200.00. 905, 908: 14" – $1,600.00; 17" – $2,600.00. 939, 949: 17" – $1,800.00; 20" – $1,950.00; 24" – $2,600.00. Same mold numbers with open mouths: 16" – $750.00; 20" – $950.00; 25" – $1,200.00; 28" – $1,600.00. Mold number 950, kid body: 10" – $385.00. Mold number 1279: 16" – $965.00. 1299: 18" – $895.00. 1388: 20" – $7,600.00. 1428: 20" – $1,400.00. 1488: 20" – $3,900.00. Mold number 1039, walker body. Key wound: 16" – $975.00. Mold number 1160, referred to as "Little Women": 6" – $300.00; 9" – $375.00. Mold number 1159, 1179, lady with adult body and open mouth: 18" – $1,200.00; 22" – $1,300.00; 25" – $1,600.00. Mold number 1303 lady with closed mouth: 18" – $5,200.00. 1469. Lady with closed mouth: 18" – $2,300.00. Babies, open/closed mouth characters: 1924: 15" – $525.00; 20" – $700.00. Incised Baby Blanche: 20" – $625.00; 24" – $895.00. Incised: Santa: (mold number 1249): 16" – $575.00; 20" – $695.00; 26" – $995.00.

SIMON & HALBIG

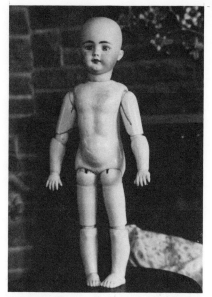

22" Marked: S 13 H 719 DEP. Three hole saucer dome. Line around dome looks like it was meant to be cut off. Set eyes, closed mouth with dimple in chin. On German jointed body with straight wrists. Courtesy Pat Landis.

Shows the body of the Simon and Halbig mold number 719. Lower knee detail, and straight wrists. Courtesy Pat Landis.

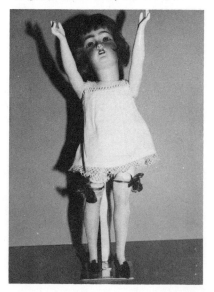

21" S & H 1030/10 DEP. Blue sleep eyes with lashes, open mouth. A pull string from the back of the neck positions the eyelids to open and cover. (The lids come down over the eyes). Another pull string in side of body for voice box. Courtesy Penny Pendlebury.

14" Marked Simon Halbig/S & H 1159. Limbs are slim, arms one piece and legs are jointed well above the knees to allow doll to wear very short styles. Feet are modeled to take heeled shoes. Original white cotton chemise, silk hose and shoes. Courtesy Glorya Woods.

Three sizes of the Simon and Halbig lady dolls with mold number 1159. The two larger dolls are all original. All have open mouths and real lashes. Thin waists and adult bodies. Courtesy Barbara Earnshaw.

13½'' Marked: S.H. 1249/DEP/Germany. Blue sleep eyes, open mouth with four teeth and on fully jointed body. Courtesy Lorraine Weston.

32'' Marks: 1249/Germany/Halbig/S & H/15. Brown sleep eyes, open mouth with four teeth, pierced ears and on fully jointed composition body. Costumed by owner. Courtesy Glorya Woods.

32'' Marks: Halbig-S&H-1249. Brown sleep eyes, open mouth with four teeth, pierced ears and on fully jointed body. Holds a 12'' Baby Gloria with molded hair, blue sleep eyes, cloth body and dimples in cheeks. Courtesy Glorya Woods. Wicker chair was gift to owner in 1927.

STEIFF
S.F.B.J.

STEIFF

Margarete Steiff of Wurtemberg, Germany made dolls and puppets, as well as stuffed animals. The dolls and puppets have a seam down the center of the face, button eyes, and a metal button in the ear. They will be made of velvet, plush or felt. Steiff dolls: Characters: 15″ – $675.00; 20″ – $895.00. Children: 10″ – $345.00; 15″ – $565.00. Puppets: 10″ – $65.00.

10″ Steiff hand puppet. Flannel and wool lower part with brushed felt head and shoulder plate, and hands. Seam down middle of face, button eyes and applied ears.

19″ Walker, turns head as legs move. Sleep eyes with lashes and open mouth. Marks: Depose/S.F.B.J./6. Courtesy Pauline Hoch.

S.F.B.J.

The Societe Francaise de Fabrication de Bebes et Jouets (S.F.B.J.) was formed in 1899, and known members were Jumeau, Bru, Fleischmann & Blodel, Rabery & Delphieu, Pintel & Godchaux, P.H. Schmitz, A. Bouchet, Jullien, and Danel & Cie.

The director was Fleischmann, and at the beginning of World War I, he was deported and his properties taken from him because he was an alien (German). By 1922 S.F.B.J. employed 2,800 people. The Society dissolved in the mid-1950's.

There are a vast amount of common "dolly" faced S.F.B.J. dolls, but also some extremely rare, and character molds. Most of the character dolls are in the 200 series of mold numbers. Sample marks:

S.F.B.J.
239
PARIS

Children: Open mouth, sleep or set eyes. Mold number 301: 8" – $195.00; 14" – $565.00; 18" – $785.00; 22" – $895.00; 28" – $1,100.00; 32" – $1,550.00. Mold number 60: Open mouth: 14" – $465.00; 20" – $625.00. S.F.B.J. Kiss throwing, walking doll: Head moves side to side, flirty eyes, open mouth: 21" – $1,500.00. Character molds, 1910, on. 211: 16" – $4,700.00. 226: 16" – $1,700.00; 21" – $1,900.00. 227: 16" – $1,800.00; 21" – $2,000.00. 230: 23" – $1,600.00. 233: 14" – $1,600.00; 17" – $3,000.00. 234: 16" – $2,550.00; 21" – $2,950.00. 235: 16" – $1,700.00; 21" – $1,900.00. 236: 16" – $1,300.00; 21" – $1,700.00. 237: 16" – $1,700.00; 21" – $1,900.00. 238: 16" – $2,500.00; 21" – $2,900.00. 239 (Poubout): 14" – $3,700.00; 17" – $4,300.00. 242: 17" – $3,200.00. 247: 16" – $1,700.00; 21" – $2,500.00. 251: Baby: 10" – $895.00; 16" – $1,300.00; 21" – $1,600.00. Toddler: 16" – $1,700.00; 21" – $2,000.00. 252: Baby: 10" – $2,000.00; 16" – $2,400.00. Toddler: 16" – $3,500.00; 20" – $5,000.00; 26" – $7,000.00. 257: 16" – $1,800.00. 266: 20" – $1,700.00. Googly 245: 14" – $5,000.00.

14" Marks: S.F.B.J./60/Paris/2/0. Brown set eyes, open mouth and fully jointed composition body. Original clothes. The stomach part of this doll is padded with excelsior, wrapped in cheese cloth, and has been done at the factory. Courtesy Penny Pendlebury.

12½" Bisque socket head with pierced ears, blue set eyes, blonde mohair wig, open mouth and all original clothes. Key wind walker with head marked: Depose/ S.F.B.J./9. Tag: Je Marche. Courtesy Verna Humphrey.

S.F.B.J.

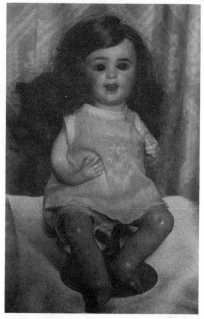

17" Marked: S.F.B.J. 238 character girl. Set brown eyes, open mouth with four teeth and on French jointed body. All original wig and clothes. Courtesy Susan Harrin.

8" "Laughing Jumeau" marked: S.F.B.J. 236/Paris. Has red and blue and white sticker on body: Fabrication Francaise Paris, along with S.F.B.J., in a circle. Five piece bent leg and arm baby body. Courtesy Penny Pendlebury.

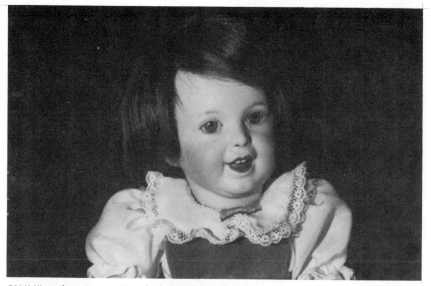

9½" "Laughing Jumeau" marked: SFBJ/236. Blue sleep eyes, open/closed mouth with two upper teeth modeled in, and on five piece bent large baby body. Courtesy Lorraine Weston.

Left to right: 11" Marked: Unis France/251, and called "The Twerp". Next is marked: S.F.B.J./301/Paris, and label says Paris Bebe. 11". Right: Marked: 21/60/S.F.B.J./Paris and is 10½" tall. Courtesy Lorraine Weston.

17½" Marked: Paris Fire A 11. Made by Jules Steiner. Pierced ears, closed mouth and blue set eyes. Jointed body with straight wrists. Courtesy Marcia Piecewicz.

15½" Googly marked: S.F.B.J. 245 with sleep eyes. Closed smile mouth and has original red wig. On jointed French body. Small doll is an 8" googly marked: A. 233 M. Courtesy Barbara Earnshaw.

STEINER, JULES

JULES NICHOLS STEINER

Jules Nichols Steiner operated from 1855 to 1892, when the firm was taken over by Amedee LaFosse. In 1895 this firm merged with Henri Alexander (maker of Bebe Phenix), and May Freres Cie (maker of Bebe Mascotte), then in 1899 Jules Mettais took over the firm. In 1906 the company changed again, to Edmond Daspres.

In 1889 the firm registered the girl with the banner and the words "Le Petite Parisien", and in 1892 Lafosse registered the trademark "Le Parisien". This should help to date a few marked Steiner bodies.

Sample marks: Steiner BTe SGDG. Bourgoin c-4. Paris A 13. "A" Series Steiner: Closed mouth: 12" – $1,500.00; 16" – $2,100.00; 20" – $3,300.00; 25" – $4,400.00; 28" – $4,800.00. "A" Series with open mouth: 16" – $1,200.00; 20" – $2,300.00; 26" – $3,400.00. "A" Series with head incised, along with "Le Parisien" red stamp (1892): Closed mouth: 16" – $2,200.00; 20" – $3,400.00. Open mouth: 16" – $1,200.00; 20" – $2,300.00. "A" Series with full head stamp; and paper label of doll carrying a flag on the body: (1889): Closed mouth: 16" – $2,800.00; 20" – $3,400.00; 25" – $4,400.00. Bourgoin Steiner with "Bourgoin" incised, or in red script on head, along with rest of the mark: Closed mouth: 16" – $3,600.00; 20" – $3,900.00; 25" – $4,800.00. Bourgoin Steiner with eyes that operate by a wire control: Closed mouth: 16" – $2,800.00; 20" – $4,200.00; 25" – $4,600.00. "C" Series Steiner: Closed mouth: 16" – $3,500.00; 20" – $3,900.00. Mechanical Steiner (kicking, crying). Key wound, open mouth with two rows teeth: 18" – $1,600.00. "Bisque hip" Steiner. Motschmann style body with bisque head, shoulders, lower arms and legs and bisque torso section. 18" – $3,600.00. Early white bisque Steiner with round face, open mouth with two rows pointed teeth. Unmarked. On jointed Steiner body: 14" – $1,200.00; 18" – $2,600.00.

21" Marked: TANAGRA/Perle-Depose/-9/Paris. Open mouth with four teeth, sleep blue eyes with long lashes with painted lashes over and under the eyes. On fully jointed French body. Courtesy Eloise Godfrey. 16" - $495.00; 20" - $645.00.

13" Marked: Trion Toy, on head. Straw stuffed body and upper arms. Cloth stuffed (circular print cloth) legs with attached composition boots. Composition lower arms. Pin jointed hips and shoulders. Composition head, painted blue eyes, closed pouty mouth and molded painted hair. Original cotton dress. (Author). 13" - $95.00-110.00.

14" "Twinkie". Composition swivel head with tin flirty eyes, jointed cloth body with celluloid hands. Molded hair and closed smiling mouth. All original. Marks: Genuine Twinkie Doll Copyr. 1920. Made by S. Kirsch & Co. (S.K. Novelty Co.), who operated from 1919 to 1924. The Kirsch Company was located in Brooklyn, NY. (Author). 14" - $245.00.

STROBEL & WILKEN WAX

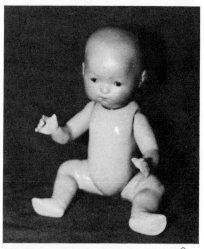

8" Bisque head marked: 221 15/0/Germany. Made by Strobel & Wilken. Closed mouth and painted hair. Not original body. Courtesy Florence Black Musich.

8" Painted bisque head with blue sleep eyes, open mouth, curly mohair wig and cardboard pate. Papier mache body, composition arms and legs which are strung. Five piece body. Clothes are sewn and glued on. All original. Marks: ⚜ , on head. Made by Strobel and Wilken, Germany. Courtesy Shirley Pascuzzi. 8" - $95.00.

21" Poured wax portrait lady with cloth body, upper arms and legs with poured wax lower arms and legs. Inset glass eyes. Original beautiful gown. Courtesy Barbara Earnshaw. 21" - $1,900.00.

14" Poured wax child with inset hair and glass eyes. This 1870's wax has cloth body with poured wax lower arms and legs. Courtesy Barbara Earnshaw. 14" - $1,000.00.

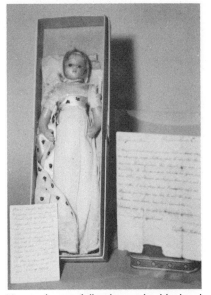

Very early wax doll with wax shoulder head, arms and legs. Cloth body. Glass eyes. Letter is dated 1821 that describes that doll as a gift. Courtesy Barbara Earnshaw. 16'' - $1,900.00.

20'' Turned shoulder head with no marks, brown set eyes, closed mouth and solid dome head with one hole for wig. All kid body with bisque lower arms and the Wagner & Zelzsche sticker #8. The body is cork filled with little bags of B.B.'s, also has B.B.'s mixed with the cork. Given as a Christmas gift to a child in 1886. Courtesy Penny Pendlebury.

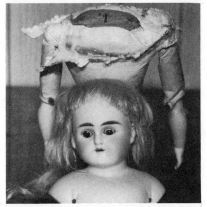

17'' Turned shoulder head with open dome, original blonde mohair wig, brown sleep eyes, open mouth and chin dimple. Pin jointed all kid body with bisque lower arms. Shoulder marked: 1123 ※ 5. Blue Wagner & Zelzche sticker on body. This doll has the heavy, flat undersided eyebrows made by Wagner & Zelzche. Courtesy Penny Pendlebury.

WAGNER & ZETZCHE

Richard Wagner and Richard Zetzsche made dolls, doll's bodies, doll's heads and doll's shoes. They operated in Ilmenau, Thur. Germany between the 1870's and the 1930's. They used a blue paper label on the shoulder (inside) with the initials W & Z, which were in heavy interwoven script, as well as block printed letters. They EXPORTED both kid and cloth bodies, and to export from Germany not only meant the United States, but to other countries as well. The majority of the turned head dolls where the head has been removed to examine the Wagner & Zetzsche label, are unmarked.

Marked heads that have been found on W & Z bodies are, Simon and Halbig, Kestner, and Heinrich Handwerck. Turned head dolls. Closed mouth. 16" – $700.00; 20" – $1,100.00; 24" – $1,500.00. Open mouth: 20" – $495.00; 24" – $750.00.

WAGNER & ZELZCHE

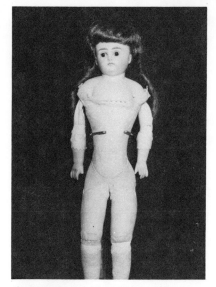

14½'' Turned head shoulder plate with closed mouth, set brown eyes, and on kid body. Open dome head with cork pate. Has a Wagner & Zelzche blue sticker on body. The head is marked with an E. This head looks like a Kestner, for sure, with the body made by the Wagner and Zelzche firm. All kid body with lower arms of bisque. Courtesy Penny Pendlebury.

Shows the turned head doll on her body which is all kid with bisque lower arms. Courtesy Penny Pendlebury.

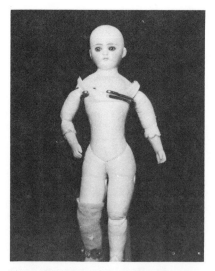

9½'' Turned shoulder head with decal eyebrows, solid dome, (Bald head), paperweight blue eyes and full closed mouth. Head marked: 2/0. Body is all kid with bisque lower arms and has the interwound W & Z mark of the Wagner & Zelzche firm. The head looks extremely Simon and Halbig, and was most likely made by them. Courtesy Penny Pendlebury.

Shows the body and head of the 9½'' turned shoulder head. Bisque lower arms. Courtesy Penny Pendlebury.

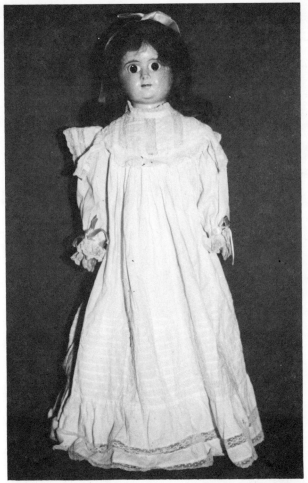

24" Webber Singing Doll. Wax over composition with large set in glass eyes, cloth torso with singing box and wax over composition and lower legs. May be original clothes and wig. The Webber dolls are marked with "The Webber Doll" in fancy script, on the cloth body. Courtesy Pat Timmons.

William Augustus Webber of Medford, Mass. only made his "Webber Singing Doll" for a period of two years, from 1882 to 1884. In 1882 he advertised two sizes, the 22" and 30", with one in each size having waxed head and set eyes, or having sleep eyes. The bodies of these dolls are cloth and they have a wooden box in the stomach, with a button on front, to make the doll sing. The songs included, "Home Sweet Home", "America", as well as several others. In 1883 and 1884 the Webber Singing Doll came in sizes 22", 24", and 26", and additional songs were offered, such as "God Bless the Prince of Wales", "Pop Goes the Weasel", etc. Also in 1883 Webber advertised that the bodies were made in America, and could sit easily. Webber Singing Dolls with wax over composition head and limbs, or with leather arms and cloth legs. All with cloth bodies and the Webber singing mechanism. 22" – $995.00; 24" – $1,195.00; 30" – $1,400.00.

mini-marTians

From up above the
sky so high came the
MINI-MARTIANS
"pinky" high

Professor Pook   Marti   Mini

Bonnie   Meri   Teenie

Mini-Martians $1.49 each

Futuristic sprites a mere 4½ inches tall. They'll take you to their world above where make-believe is so much fun. Made of soft vinyl, their arms and head move. Comb and wash their rooted hair. Remove boots for barefoot space walks. Dressed in supersonic styles. From Japan. Collect all 6 and have your own Mini-Martian community.

49N3246—Prof. Pook. Painted glasses. Wt. 3 oz.$1.49
49N3247—Marti. Space lad. Shpg. wt. 3 oz. . . . 1.49
49N3248—Mini. In silver-color cape. Wt. 3 oz. . . 1.49
49N3249—Bonnie. In lunar sarong. Wt. 3 oz. . . . 1.49
49N3250—Meri. In solar shift. Shpg. wt. 3 oz. . . 1.49
49N3251—Teenie. In cosmic tent dress. Wt. 3 oz. 1.49

Martian Star House $3.99

Far beyond earth's bustling pace
Mini-Martians dwell at ease

Zooming around in "outer space", Mini-Martians live and play. Nestled among the stars and comets . . a home so streamlined, all their own. Brightly colored outside and in. Space car parks on terrace platform.

Two elevated bunks for sleeping. Video scanner to check on pals. All furnishings vacuum formed. Vinyl house closes for visits to "other planets" . . . 15½x5x9 in.
49 N 9203—Shpg. wt. 2 lbs. 14 oz. $3.99
Mini-Martians not included with Star House

Offered nowhere in the universe but at Sears

"Carnaby Comet" Clothes for Mini-Martians

Two outfits in each space-age set.

1. **Star Time Togs.** For all the Mini-Martian girls. Bright colored stripes . . one tent dress and hostess pajamas.
49 N 3296—Shpg. wt. 3 oz. . . . Set 98c

2. **Zoom Suits.** Just the thing when the girls take the scooter for a spin. Each dress has matching helmet.
49 N 3297—Shpg. wt. 3 oz. . . . Set 98c

3. **Stellar Shifts.** Just meant for special parties. Gold-color dress has gold-color headband. Blue dress has star trimmed headpiece.
49 N 3298—Shpg. wt. 3 oz. . . . Set 98c

4. **Lunar Leisure Wear.** For lounging, games of star tag. Yellow, red jumper, beadband. Blue, white jumper.
49 N 3299—Shpg. wt. 3 oz. . . . Set 98c

5. **Galaxy Garb.** For Marti or Professor Pook. Full cape for cold weather, short jacket and helmet for scooter rides.
49 N 3292—Shpg. wt. 3 oz. . . . Set 98c

6. **Jet Jumpers.** Professor Pook wears them, Marti can too. Silver-color is ever so dashing for Martian parties.
49 N 3293—Shpg. wt. 3 oz. . . . Set 98c
Dolls not included with above outfit sets

$2.99
Jet Car for jaunts from star to star

Two Mini-Martians can take a trip in this round car. Clear plastic dome top lets them see everything along the way. Made of molded plastic . . . 7½ in. long. Travels on three wheels. Mini-Martians not included.
49 N 9208—Shipping weight 1 pound. $2.99

1967

Sporty Space Scooter for errands on the run $1.99

One Mini-Martian drives this scooter for trips to a "meteor grocery" or "lunar laundromat". It's great for just buzzing around in, too. Made of molded plastic, about 8 inches long. Runs on 3 wheels. Has clear plastic windshield. Mini-Martian not included with space scooter. So easy to buy when you just use the phone.
49 N 9247—Wt. 12 oz. . . $1.99

596 Sears

ADVANCE DOLL CO.

Advance Doll Company: 18" "Wanda The Walking Wonder" – $65.00. 18", "Walking Wabbit" (Wanda) dressed in fleece bunny outfit with bonnet that has ears – $65.00. 24", "Winnie The Wonder Doll" – $100.00.

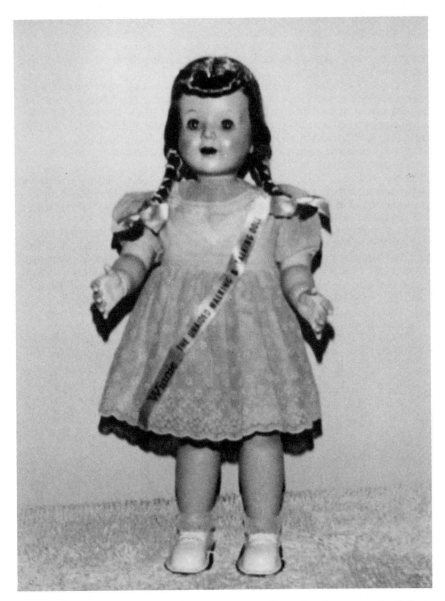

24" "Winnie the Wonder Doll". 1957 by Advance Doll Co. Blue dress trimmed with flocked flowers and collar trimmed with lace. Sleep eyes, open mouth with two teeth. Key wind doll that walks and sings nursery songs, head turns and she swings her arms. Tag: "Winnie the Unaided Walking and Talking Doll". Courtesy Ann Wencel.

ADVERTISING DOLLS

ADVERTISING DOLLS

Alka Seltzer "Speedy". 7½" all vinyl boy with name on Alka Seltzer "hat" – $8.00.

American Beauty "Roni Mac". 11" printed on fabric to be cut and sewn. Printed on features, collar and bow tie, also shoulder strap with books and ruler. Head is shaped like a cylinder – $30.00.

Betty Crocker doll. 13" All cloth with brown suede hair and yarn ponytails, very large eyes and wears a red/white checked dress, white apron with a red applique – $14.00.

Borden Company "Elsie cow" 15". Plush toy with vinyl head, horns. 1950's cow has an aqua plush body, and 1970's has yellow felt hooves and a brown plush body. 1950's – $16.00; 1970's – $12.00.

Campbell Kids. 10" vinyl Bicentennial dolls. Dressed in colonial style. He has brown molded hair, she, blonde. $38.00 pair.

Chiquita Banana Doll. All printed cloth. (see photo) – $8.00.

Diaparene baby. 6" (see photo) – $4.00.

Fab Doll. 8" All hard plastic. (see photo) – $20.00. 9" All hard plastic dressed in pink cotton dress trimmed in white – $25.00.

Faultless Starch. Printed on cloth to be cut and sewn. "Miss Phoebe Primm (see photo), and Miss Lilly White – $45.00 each.

Gerber Baby, 12" 1954. All rubber – $14.00. 14" soft vinyl 1966. Marked Gerber Baby – $14.00. 18" Made by Sun Rubber Co. – $22.00. 11" 1972 made by Uneeda Doll Co. White: – $10.00. Black – $25.00.

Green Giant all cloth doll: 16" – $9.00. "Country Girl". 18" vinyl 1957 (see photo) – $50.00. 1956 – $50.00. 6", "Sprout" – $2.00. 9", "Jolly Green Giant" – $8.00. 12", "Sprout" – $5.00.

"Itylyti", 16" All cloth made for Brunswick – $12.00.

Jack Frost all cloth dolls: 14" – $4.00; 16" – $6.00.

Keebler Elf made for Keebler Cookie Co. 6½" – $6.00; 16" – $9.00; All fleece/felt – $12.00.

McDonald, Ronald: 13½" – $5.00; 17" – $7.00.

Luvs Diaper dolls. 12" – $6.00.

Libby cloth doll. 14" – $12.00.

Nestle Chocolate doll, "Hans". 13" – $22.00.

Shoney Restaurant doll: 14" Cloth boy – $6.00; 10", Dog – $5.00; 14", "Dolly" – $6.00; 16", Shoney Boy. 8" – $4.00; 9" – $7.00; 10" – $8.00; 11" – $10.00.

Sunbeam Bread all cloth doll: 17" – $15.00.

7" Campbell Kids. All vinyl and jointed only at the neck. She has yellow molded hair and he has brown molded hair. Dolls are not marked. Molded on clothes and painted features. Courtesy Jeannie Mauldin.

16" 1974 "Chiquita Banana" doll. Stuffed cloth with printed on features and clothes. Tag: Made in U.S.A. by Chaseline Div. Chase Bag Co. Doll came with record and banana cook book. Courtesy Jeannie Mauldin.

6" Diaparene advertising baby. Plastic with full joints, painted hair and features. Marks: Sterling Drug, Inc. 1980. Product of Korea. Courtesy Jeannie Mauldin.

ADVERTISING DOLLS

11" "Miss Phoebe Primm" by the Faultless Starch Co. Printed cloth that was stamped on a flat sheet of fabric to be cut out and sewn. The dolls offered by this Kansas City firm were printed by the Saalfield Publishing Co. Courtesy Jeannie Mauldin.

8" Hard plastic walker that was offered by the Fab soap in 1957. The dress is pink with blue trim and a pink straw-type hat. This same doll was also offered by Luster Creme Shampoo Co.

16" First "Jolly Green Giant" doll of all one piece green stuffed cloth. 1966. Courtesy Jeannie Mauldin.

146

This picture shows the array of Gerber Baby Food dolls that have been offered over the years. Courtesy Jeannie Mauldin.

Left to right: 6" "Sprout", all green vinyl and molded on leaves for hair and clothes. No marks. 9" "Jolly Green Giant". All vinyl and all one piece. No marks. Box: Jolly Green Giant. Trademark of the Green Giant Co. Product People, Inc. 12" "Sprout" all felt made in one piece with green leaves for hat and clothes. Eyes are plastic. Tag: Exclusively for Green Giant Mf'd by Animal Toys, Inc. obtained with product labels in 1980. Courtesy Jeannie Mauldin.

16" "Itylyti" all stuffed cloth with pink shoes on all three yellow legs, yellow head with pink hair. One printed eye open and other winking. Marks: Itylyti Brunswick, Itylyti the acronym for: "I Told You Last Year, Try It". Courtesy Jeannie Mauldin.

ADVERTISING DOLLS

18" "Country Girl" made for the Green Giant Company. Vinyl head with rooted hair and latex one piece body and limbs: "coo" cryer when pressed. Sleep eyes and closed mouth. Green and white check blouse with yellow buttons, yellow pinafore dress with green trim, white shoes and socks. Yellow bonnet and carries shoulder bag that is yellow with green/white check shoulder strap, and has ears of corn inprinted. This doll was made in 1957. Courtesy Carroll & Bob Skell.

The Green Giant Company had the same doll the year before (1956) that was dressed in a white dress with green dots and removable white apron with "Jolly Green Giant" holding peas, and with green trim. The hat is starched cotton lace with green trim and ribbon. Green Giant magazine ad.

18" and 14" "Jack Frost" advertising dolls. All stuffed cloth with printed on clothes and features. Courtesy Jeannie Mauldin.

The Keebler Cookie Company doll, "Keebler Elf" made of stuffed flannel and felt with "fur" hair. Courtesy Jeannie Mauldin.

12" Advertising dolls for Luvs disposable diapers. All one piece cloth in pink or in blue. Diaper is sewn on, and the dolls have no face features. Tag: 1978 Sheram Puppets, Inc. Courtesy Jeannie Mauldin.

13½" Variation of Ronald McDonald clown. Not only is the face different from the 17" size, but also this smaller size has pointed collars and larger patches showing the "twin arches" and they are in different locations. The hands are more defined, also. Courtesy Arlene Mitgel.

14" "Libby Premium" doll that is marked: Made in Mexico/7930 Libby. 1974 Mattel. Pull string talkers and says: "Libby, Libby on the table, table". All cloth with yarn hair and painted features. Courtesy Shirley Pascuzzi.

ADVERTISING DOLLS

14" "Shoney Boy" and "Dolly", shown with the Shoney dog, "Nugget". All are stuffed, printed cloth. "Shoney's Big Boy" is stamped: Wen. Adv. Corp. Los Angeles, Cal., on back of foot. The dog is 10" and has his name on both sides of collar. "Dolly" holds a printed on "Big Boy" behind her. Courtesy Jeannie Mauldin.

13" "Hans, the Nestle Chocolate" man. All vinyl with painted features, inset beard and hair and molded glasses and hat. Original clothes, with the shoes being molded vinyl. Marks: 1969 The Nestle Co, on head. Courtesy Sally Freeman.

Left: Is the older Shoney's "Dolly" dressed in green and is 16" tall, the right doll is newer and dressed in pink with white dots. Each holds a tiny "Big Boy" behind her. Both are stuffed, printed cloth. Courtesy Jeannie Mauldin.

Left to right: 9" All vinyl "Big Boy" with jointed neck. Molded hair and painted features. Name on shirt. Clothes molded on. 2nd doll: 8" Plastic body and legs. Vinyl head and arms, jointed at neck and shoulders. Removable clothes and molded hamburger in hand. Painted features and molded hair. 3rd: 10" All vinyl with jointed neck. Molded clothes, painted features. Mark: Product of Big Boy Restaurants of America. 11" All vinyl bank, molded on clothes and painted features. Courtesy Jeannie Mauldin.

17" Cloth doll advertising Sunbeam Bread. All stuffed cloth with clothes printed on. Yellow printed on hair, large blue eyes and blue dress with white apron. Blue ribbon in hair. Courtesy Jeannie Mauldin.

ALEXANDER DOLLS (ALEXANDER-KINS)

ALEXANDER

7½" & 8" Madame Alexander dolls are referred to as "Alexanderkins", "Wendy Ann", "Wendy-kins", and all these names are correct.

7½", 1953-1954. Straight legs, non walkers, and were of heavy hard plastic. This group also included the "Quiz-kins" with a push button in the middle of the back that made the head move. 8" 1955 (and part of 1954) had straight legs, but were walkers. 8" 1956 to 1966 had bend knees and were walkers. 1966 to 1973 had bend knees only. 1973 to late 1977 these dolls had straight legs, non-bend knees and marked with "Alex." From 1978 to date the dolls are still straight leg, non-bend knees, but are marked with the full name, "Alexander", on the backs.

Alexander-kins/Wendy-kins, prices based on: short dress and ballgown. Mint, including shoes & socks, short dress – $125.-145.00; ballgown – $145.-175.00. Clean, played with, but all original, short dress – $100.-110.00; ballgown – $120.-150.00. Hair mussed, original clothes washed – $85.00-95.00; ballgown – $100.-110.00. No original clothes, but dressed and clean, short dress – $70.-80.00; ballgown – $90.-100.00. Nude doll, hair in fair condition, short dress – $50.00-60.00. Allow $50.00 more for early straight leg, non walker. Add $35.00 for straight leg, walker.

The following is a list of discontinued Alexander-kin/Wendy-kin dolls. The first price is for a mint, unplayed-with doll. The second for a doll that is dirty, played-with, or part of original clothes gone. African – $350.00 up; Amish boy or girl – $350.00 up; Argentine boy – $400.00; Bible Characters – $1,200.00 up; Bolivia – $350.00; Bride (Walker) – $200.00; Ecuador – $350.00 up; Eskimo – $475.00; First Communion – $275.00; Hawaiian – $350.00 up; Greek Boy – $350.00 up; Groom – $175.00; Guardian Angel – $1,000.00 up; Indian Boy – $425.00; Indian Girl – $425.00; Korea – $350.00; Little Minister – $950.00 up; Morocco – $350.00; Miss U.S.A. – $275.00; Peruvian Boy – $425.00; Quiz-kins – $300.00; Spanish Boy – $350.00 up; Story Princess – $500.00; Vietnam – $400.00. Add $75.00 more for "Maggie" face on mint doll, $20.00 more for dirty doll.

Guardian Angel, 1954 straight leg walker. Gold halo, harp and shoes. Blue taffeta gown with silver stars. Wendy-kins wrist tag. Courtesy Bernice Heister.

8" 1955 Groom/Best Man and 1956 Bride. Courtesy "Tete" Cook.

8" "Alexander-kins in school dress. Dress came in blue and white and red and white. Courtesy Linda Crowsey.

8" 1956 "Story Princess" in rose color net and satin gown. Tiara missing. There is also a matching 15" "Story Princess". Courtesy Pat Spirek.

Alexander-kin/Wendy Ann shown as "Ruth" from the Bible Character series of 1955. The gown is blue and she holds a sheath of wheat. All original. An extremely rare doll. Courtesy Billie McCabe.

ALEXANDER DOLLS
BABIES

20" "Kathy". All vinyl, sleep eyes, one with rooted hair and other with molded hair. Both are marked: Alexander, on the head. Courtesy Jeannie Mauldin.

Two desirable Madame Alexander babies, Rusty is on left and is a red head, and "Happy" is on the right and has dark brown hair. Not original clothes. Both have sleep eyes. Courtesy Jeannie Mauldin.

ALEXANDER BABIES

First price is Mint & Original, the second is Played-With, Dirty, Not Original. Baby McGuffey, compo., 20" – $200.00---$50.00; Bonnie, vinyl, 19" – $100.00---$30.00; Cookie, compo., 19" – $$125.00---$40.00; Genius, vinyl, flirty eyes – $$50.-90.00---25.00; Happy, vinyl, 20" – $200.00---$50.00; Honeybun, vinyl, 23" – $65.-95.00---25.00; Kathy, 20" – $75.00---$20.00; Little Genius, compo., 20" – $85.00---$20.00; Littlest Kitten, vinyl, 8" – $125.00---$30.00; Pinky, compo., 23" – $85.00---$25.00; Precious, compo., 12" – $85.00---$25.00; Princess Alexandria, 24" – $125.00---$35.00; Rusty, vinyl, 20" – $200.00---$50.00; Slumbermate, compo., 12" – $150.00---$40.00; Sunbeam, vinyl, 16" – $95.-145.00---$35.00.

Brenda Starr. 12. Hard plastic. 1964. In box, mint and unplayed with: In street dress – $165.00; In ball gown – $185.00; Bride – $185.00. Played-with, but mint in box: Street dress – $130.00; Ball gown – $155.00; Bride – $155.00. No box, but mint: Street dress – $150.00; Ball gown – $170.00; Bride – $. As "Yolanda", mint & in box – $185.00; Mint, but no box – $165.00.

A 12" mint in box Brenda Starr. Hard plastic, glued on red wig and has jointed knees and high heels. Some blondes have been found tagged: Brenda Starr, and in the box. This doll was used as "Yolanda", who had blonde hair, but tagged, mint in the box ones have been found with red hair, also. Courtesy Pat Timmons.

Cissette as Scarlett. Made from 1968 through 1973. Courtesy Mary Williams.

10"-11" "Cissette". Hard plastic. In street dress – $145.00; Ball gowns – $300.00; Set with three wigs – $450.00 up; Queen – $400.00; Gibson Girl – $950.00 up; Gold Rush – $950.00 up; Iceland – $950.00; Klondike Kate – $950.00 up; Used as Margot – $300.00. Used as Portrettes: Agatha – $425.00; Godey – $425.00; Jenny Lind – $500.00; Melinda – $450.00; Renoir – $425.00; Scarlett – $375.00; Southern Belle – $400.00. Used as Jacqueline. Street dress – $475.00; Ball gown – $575.00. Used as Sleeping Beauty – $375.00.

ALEXANDER DOLLS
CISSY

Cissy in street dress of navy with white dots, white trim at sleeves, navy and white shoes, purse with red flower, corsage and white hat. Courtesy Charmaine Shields.

Cissy in ballgown. The gown is red taffeta with wide attached sash off the hips and has three rhinestone pins. Courtesy Charmaine Shields.

Cissy as a Bride with two long sashes of satin. (Author).

Cissy: In ballgown, mint – $250.-500.00; fair condition – $85.00. Bridesmaid, mint – $250.00; fair condition – $65.00. Street dress, mint – $175.00; fair condition – $45.00. Miss Flora McFlimsey, mint – $375.00; fair condition – $100.00. Portrait (Godey, etc.) – $525.00; fair condition – $150.00. Scarlett, mint – $500.00; fair condition – $150.00. Queen, mint – $525.00; fair condition – $150.00.

Plush blue cat with flower felt nose and original clothes, except the hat is copy of the original one. Tag. Madame Alexander/New York, N.Y. Courtesy Mimi Hiscox.

13" "Little Shaver" of 1939-1940, also called "So-Lite" babies. All cloth with oil painted features and fine yarn hair.

17" "So-Lite Baby". Soft stuffed stockenette body and legs, cotton filled arms with free formed thumbs. Same material on back of head and around base of neck. (Neck jointed). Felt style velour molded face mask, hand painted in oils. Brown eyes with inset lashes. One small sewn in piece of hair in front. Cotton sleeveless slip, yellow organdy baby dress and bonnet, white lace trim and yellow ties. Tag: So-Lite Baby/Madame Alexander/New York.

Cloth Dolls: Animals – $300.00 up. Characters: Alice in Wonderland – $350.00. Clarabelle Clown 19" – $165.00. Dionne Quint, 24" – $650.00. David Copperfield – $400.00. Eva Lovelace – $300.00. Little Shaver, 7" – $175.00; 10" – $225.00; 20" – $375.00. Little Shaver Baby – $325.00. Little Women – $300.00. Funny – $65.00. Muffin – $65.00. So-Lite baby or toddler – $300.00 up.

ALEXANDER DOLLS
COMPOSITION

11" "Three Pigs" all composition with painted features. Original clothes with felt gloves that tie over hands. Left has black top and pink suspender short pants. Middle has blue top, pink pants and the one on the right has blue overalls. Gloves are tied with black ribbon. Marks: Madame Alexander, on backs. Courtesy Martha Silva.

Composition Dolls. Alice in Wonderland, 9" – $200.00; 14" – $250.00; 20" – $350.00. Babies, Baby Genius, McGuffey, etc., 11" – $125.00; 22" – $200.00. Baby Jane, 16" – $500.00. Brides-Bridesmaids, 7" – $125.00; 9" – $165.00; 15" – $200.00; 21" – $275.00. Dionne Quints:

	Mint/ original	Played-with, not original	Set of five
8"	$135.00	$ 50.00	$ 900.00
11"	$225.00	$ 85.00	$1,600.00
14"	$300.00	$100.00	$1,800.00
16"	$375.00	$135.00	$2,200.00
19"	$400.00	$175.00	$2,400.00

Flora McFlimsey (marked Princess Elizabeth). Freckles. 15", mint – $300.00; 15", fair condition – $125.00. 16"-17", mint – $375.00; 16"-17", fair condition – $135.00. 22", mint – $450.00; 22", fair condition – $150.00.

Internationals/Storybook, 7" – $125.00; 11" – $165.00. Jane Withers: 13", mint, closed mouth – $675.00. 14", fair – $150.00. 17", mint – $675.00. 17", fair – $150.00. 21", mint – $850.00. 21", fair – $175.00. Jeannie Walker. 13", mint – $275.00. 13", fair – $100.00.

18", mint – $400.00. 18", fair – $150.00. Karen (and other compositions) Ballerina: 15", mint – $250.00. 15", fair – $85.00. 21", mint – $400.00. 21", fair – $100.00. Kate Greenaway: (Marked Princess Elizabeth): 14", mint – $300.00. 14", fair – $125.00. 18", mint – $400.00. 18", fair – $135.00. Little Colonel: 9", mint – $175.00. 9", fair – $75.00. 11"-13", mint – $350.00. 11"-13", fair – $135.00. 23", mint – $575.00. 23", fair – $175.00. Margaret O'Brien: 14½", mint – $300.00. 14½", fair – $125.00. 18", mint – $400.00. 18", fair – $145.00. 21", mint – $650.00. 21", fair – $150.00. Marionettes: Tony Sarg – $165.00.

McGuffey Ana. (Marked Princess Elizabeth): 13", mint – $265.00. 13", fair – $100.00. 20", mint – $345.00. 20", fair – $135.00. Portrait Dolls, 21", mint – $500.00. 21", fair – $200.00. Princess Elizabeth: 13", (closed mouth), mint – $275.00. Fair – $100.00. 18", mint – $350.00. 18", fair – $145.00. 24", mint – $400.00. 24", fair – $165.00. Scarlett: 9", mint – $225.00. 9", fair – $100.00. 14", mint – $350.00. 14", fair – $150.00. 18", mint – $550.00. 18", fair – $175.00. Sonja Henie: 17", mint – $395.00. 17", fair – $150.00. 20", mint – $450.00. 20", fair – $165.00. 14", Jointed waist, mint – $275.00. Three Pigs. 11", set of three mint – $900.00; Fair – $300.00. Each: Mint – $250.00; Fair – $100.00.

18" "Karen Ballerina". All composition and all original with pale blue with gold trim. Marks: MMe. Alexander, on head and Alexander, on back. Courtesy Glorya Woods.

9" "China". All composition with painted features, glued on wig and all original clothes and tag. Marks: MMe. Alexander, on back. (Author).

ALEXANDER DOLLS
COMPOSITION
ELISE

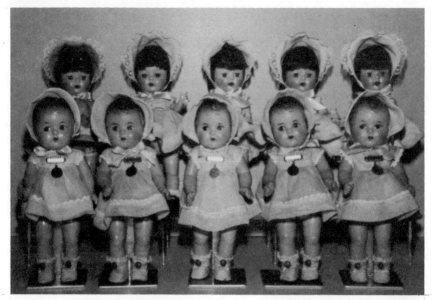

Set of Madame Alexander Dionne Quints (front). All composition, original pins and clothes, are shown with a set of "Muffie" by Nancy Ann Storybook. Courtesy Glorya Woods.

16½" Elise in ballgown. Net over cotton and satin with scattered flowers on skirt. Courtesy Charmaine Shields.

Elise: 16½" (only made 1957-1960. Hard plastic, vinyl arms. Street dress, mint/original – $185.00 up; not original – $85.00. Ball gown, mint/original – $200.00 up; not original – $85.00. Mary-bel head, mint/original – $185.00 up; not original – $95.00. Ballerina, mint/original – $225.00; not original – $85.00. Bride, mint/original – $225.00; not original – $85.00. Elise, 17", vinyl head, rooted hair, plastic & vinyl body and limbs. 1966 to date. Portrait Elise, mint – $250.00; Played with – $170.00; Nude – $50.00. Ballerina Elise (except current one in silver): mint – $135.00; Played with – $90.00; nude – $50.00.

14" Hard plastic of 1949, and called "Godey Lady". (Author).

HARD PLASTIC

Alice in Wonderland: 14" – $250.00; 17" – $225.00; 23" – $350.00. Annabelle: 15" – $250.00; 18" – $300.00; 23" – $400.00. Babs: 20" – $250.00. Babs Skater: 18" – $300.00; 21" – $375.00. Binnie Walker: 15" – $165.00; 25" – $225.00. Ballerina: 14" – $165.00. Cinderella: 14" – $385.00; 18" – $450.00. Cynthia (Black doll): 15" – $495.00; 18" – $550.00; 23" – $650.00. Fairy Queen: 14½" – $265.00; 18" – $350.00. Glamour Girls: 18" – $525.00. Godey Lady: 14" – $400.00; 18" – $465.00. Bride: 14" – $400.00; 18" – $465.00. Godey Man-Groom: 14" – $475.00; 18" – $525.00. Kathy: 15" – $285.00; 18" – $365.00. Lady Churchill: 18" – $525.00. Lissy: 12", Street dress – $275.00; Ballgown – $350.00; Ballerina – $295.00; Bride – $200.00; Bridesmaid – $225.00; Classics, such as McGuffey Ana, Cinderella, etc. – $1,000.00 up. Little Women: 14" – $250.00 each; 14" – $1,325.00 set of five; 8", straight leg, walker – $125.00 each; 12" (Lissy) – $275.00 each; 12", Laurie – $450.00. Maggie: 15" – $225.00; 17" – $250.00; 23" – $275.00. Maggie Mixup: 8" – $275.00; 16½", 1960 – $300.00. Margaret O'Brien: 14½" – $450.00; 18" – $500.00; 22" – $550.00. Margaret Rose, Princess: 14" – $250.00; 18" – $300.00. Mary Martin, 14", Sailor suit – $600.00. Nina Ballerina: 14" – $225.00; 17" – $300.00; 23" – $375.00. Prince Charming: 14" – $495.00; 18" – $550.00; 21" – $600.00. Prince Phillip: 17" – $450.00; 21" – $550.00. Queen: 18" – $425.00. Shari Lewis: 14" – $225.00; 21" – $350.00. Sleeping Beauty: 16½" – $400.00; 21" – $475.00. Story Princess: 15" – $325.00; 18" – $400.00. Violet, Sweet: 18" – $325.00. Wendy Ann: 14½" – $225.00; 17" – $250.00; 22" – $400.00; 25" – $400.00. Winnie Walker: 15" – $165.00; 18" – $200.00; 23" – $250.00.

ALEXANDER DOLLS
JANIE & TODDLERS

14" "Godey Man/ or Groom" of 1949. He could be used with the Bride or the Godey Lady. All hard plastic. (Author).

12" Lissy. All hard plastic, sleep eyes and glued on wig. Courtesy Barbara Schilde. The earlier "Lissy" dolls had jointed elbows and knees.

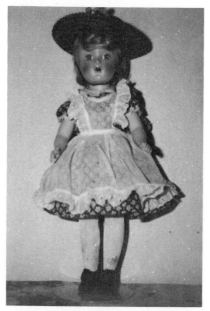

16" "McGuffey Ana". All hard plastic using the "Margaret" face doll. Red flowered print dress, red straw hat and white pinafore. Courtesy Sally Bethscheider.

12" "Janie Ballerina" that is blonde and shown with a brunette "Janie" that is also all original, but the dark haired one has freckles. Courtesy Renie Culp.

12", Janie Toddler – $200.00. 12", Rozy Toddler – $200.00. 12", Smarty Toddler – $200.00.

Little Genius: 12″-14″, composition/cloth – $65.00. 18″-20″, composition/cloth – $85.00. 8″, hard plastic, vinyl – $150.00.

Little Genius-1960. Tagged Little Genius. Blue cotton overalls, matching bonnet. Other in pink check romper. Courtesy Bernice Heister.

8″ Maggie Mix-up in pale blue tagged Alexander-kin nightie. Straight red hair with full bangs and freckles. Courtesy Beth Donor.

Maggie Mixup: 8″ – $275.00. 8″ with Wendy face – $275.00. 8″, Angel – $900.00 up. 8″, Angel – $900.00 up. 8″, Riding Habit – $275.00. 8″, Skater – $275.00.

ALEXANDER DOLLS
MIMI & OTHER LARGE DOLLS

Large dolls: Mimi, 30" – $375.00; Penny, 34" – $275.00; Barbara Jane, 29" – $275.00; Mary Ellen, 31" – $300.00; Timmie Toddler, 30" – $165.00; Joanie, 36" – $225.00.

30" "Mimi". Plastic body and limbs, vinyl head with sleep, flirty eyes with long lashes. Eye shadow and dimple in chin. Delicate designed hands. Extra joints at wrist, waist and ankles. All original in tagged Madame Alexander gown and matching bonnet. Has panty hose, pantaloons, black shoes with pink ribbon. Earrings and necklace match. Courtesy Jeannie Mauldin.

ALEXANDER DOLLS
MISCELLANEOUS & PORTRAITS

MISCELLANEOUS MADAME ALEXANDER DOLLS

Caroline. 15" – $300.00; In riding habit – $375.00. First Ladies: First set of six dolls 1976-1978 – $1,400.00; Second set of six dolls 1979-1981 – $750.00.

"Fisher" Quints. Hard plastic head, vinyl body, limbs – $325.00 set of five.

Gidget. 14" – $250.00.

Jacqueline in ball gown. 21" – $700.00 up; 10" – $575.00; Riding habit, 21" – $700.00 up; In street dress, 21" – $700.00; 10" – $475.00.

Jenny Lind & Cat, 14" – $425.00.

Leslie, 17" (Black doll). Ball gown – $225.00; Ballerina – $185.00; Bride – $225.00; Street dress – $225.00.

Madame Doll: 14" – $250.00

Madelaine: 18", 1952 with extra joints (elbows, knees, etc.) – $300.00; 16½", Rigid vinyl – $250.00.

Mary-bel, 16" – $150.00; In case – $275.00.

Peter Pan set. (Peter and Wendy-all hard plastic), 15" – $350.00 each; 14" Peter Pan, 14" Wendy, 10" Tinkerbell, 11" Michael with bear – $1,400.00 set; 8" Peter Pan – $350.00.

Sound of Music sets: Large set of seven dolls. 11"-14" & 17" – $1,400.00 set. Small set of seven dolls. 8"-10"-12" – $1,200.00 set.

21" 1978 Portrait Gainsbough. Courtesy Renie Culp.

Portraits: 1965 to present date. All have the "Jacqueline" face, are 21" and ALL will still be marked 1965, on the neck as the same molds have been used for 18 years. 21" – $350.00. up, depending upon the individual doll. The 1966 "COCO" Portraits, or in street dress, and ball gowns are: 21" – $1,500.00 up.

165

AMERICAN DOLL CO.
AMERICAN CHARACTER

23" Baby style toddler that has cloth body, composition shoulder head and limbs. Deeply molded hair, painted blue eyes. Marks: AM. Doll. Co. Courtesy Jeannie Mauldin. This company made dolls from 1912 through 1930 and were located in New York City. Dolls in excellent condition: Babies: 20" - $65.00; 23" - $85.00; 28" - $100.00. Girls: 20" - $85.00; 24" - $95.00; 28" - $115.00. Boys: 23" - $110.00; 28" - $150.00.

24" Marked: AM. Doll Co. Made in 1918. Composition shoulder head with papier mache body and limbs. String jointed. Molded brown painted hair, painted blue shoes. Decal blue eyes. Crier set in back. Courtesy Edith Evans.

AMERICAN CHARACTER DOLL CO.

All American Character Dolls are highly collectible. This company produced excellent quality dolls and is no longer in business. The dolls marked American Doll and Toy Co. are also their products, as the name was used from late 1959 to 1968 when they went out of business. Early dolls were marked: Petite. Annie Oakley, 17" – $125.00. Betsy McCall, 8" – $57.50; 14" – $65.00; 36" – $175.00. Butterball, 19" – $85.00. Cartwright, Ben, Joe or Hoss, 8" – $45.00. Chuckles, 23" – $125.00. Baby, 18" – $65.00. Composition babies/cloth bodies, 14" – $45.00; 22" – $65.00; 25" – $75.00. Cricket, 9" – $12.00. Hedda-Get-Betta, 21" – $60.00. Marie Ann, 13" – $50.00. Marie Lee, 13" – $50.00. Miss Echo, Little, 30" – $110.00. Popi, 12" – $16.00. Ricky, Jr., 13" – $45.00; 20" – $75.00. Sally, composition, 14" – $120.00; 18" – $155.00; Other girls: 20" – $150.00. Sally Says, 19" – $75.00. Sweet Sue & Toni, hard plastic, 15" – $75.00; 18" – $100.00; 22" – $125.00; 30" – $295.00. Groom, 20" – $150.00. Vinyl, 10½" – $50.00; 17" – $75.00; 21" – $125.00; 30" – $295.00. Tiny Tears, 8½" – $22.50; 13" – $45.00; 15" – $60.00; 17" – $75.00. Tiny Tears, vinyl, 8" – $22.50; 12" – $40.00. Toodles, Baby, 14" – $45.00. Tiny, 10½" – $75.00. Toddler, or child with "follow me eyes": 22" – $85.00; 28" – $125.00; Black Toodles, 22" – $175.00. Toodle-loo, 18" – $95.00. Tressy, 12" – $18.00 up. Whimette, 7½" – $12.00. Whimsey, 19" – $75.00 up.

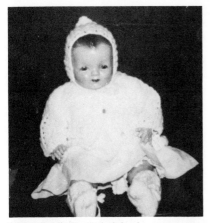

22" "Toddle-Tot" cloth body, composition head and limbs. Molded hair, sleep blue eyes, open mouth with two upper teeth, and has smile. Ca. 1932. Marks: A Petite Doll, on head. Courtesy Jeannie Mauldin.

7½" "Tiny Betsy McCall Marine". Excellent detail to the uniform, which is made of felt. Replaced wig, and has original glue lines for a boy's wig. Uniform is not removable. (Author).

14" Betsy McCall by the American Character Doll Co. Blue sleep eyes, auburn hair. All original dressed in pink and has pale pink nail polish. Unmarked. Courtesy Shirley Merrill.

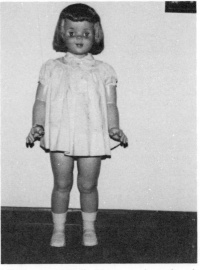

36" Betsy McCall. Plastic and vinyl with rooted hair, sleep eyes and closed mouth. Marked: Amer. Char. Hair has been cut AND SHE IS NOT ORIGINALLY DRESSED. Courtesy Jeannie Mauldin.

AMERICAN CHARACTER

18" Sweet Sue. All hard plastic walker, very blue sleep eyes, original clothes. Unmarked. Made by the American Character Doll Co. Courtesy June Schultz.

23" Sweet Sue by American Character. Walker and all hard plastic. All original with wrist tag, and hair in original set. Courtesy Evelyn Samec.

Left: 17" Annie Oakley (Sweet Sue) by American Character Doll Co. All original and hard plastic. 1952. Right: 19" Sweet Sue Sophisticate that is all hard plastic with a vinyl head. All original, except addition of white fur stole. This same doll used also as the Toni by American Character. Courtesy June Schultz.

30" Sweet Sue by American Character. All original with wrist tag. Has jointed knees and elbows. Made of hard plastic and vinyl. Courtesy Evelyn Samec.

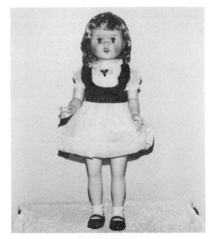

30" "Little Miss Echo" Battery operated tape recorder, records, plays back and erases tape. Marked 26, on head. All plastic with vinyl head and rooted hair. Open mouth with teeth. Nylon dress with black velvet vest. Made by American Doll & Toy Corp. Takes one 9 volt and two "D" cell batteries. Courtesy Ann Wencel.

30" and 24" Toodles by American Character Doll. Plastic body with vinyl head and limbs. Sleep eyes that follow you, but are not flirty. Open mouths with four upper and two lower teeth. Marks: American Doll & Toy Corp. 1960 on both dolls. Smaller one has on original pajamas, robe and shoes. Courtesy Jeannie Mauldin.

23" Chuckles. All vinyl with elastic strung legs. Painted brown eyes with molded lashes and lids. Also came with painted blue eyes. Rooted hair and chunky body and limbs. Marks: Amer. Doll & Toy Co. 1961. Shown with 27" all vinyl Kewpie made by Amsco, under contract with Cameo Doll Co. (Joseph Kallus). Courtesy Jeannie Mauldin.

AMERICAN CHARACTER

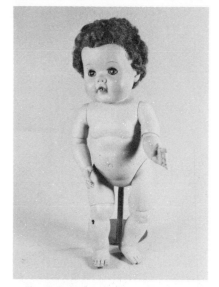

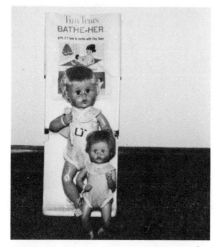

12" Teeny Tiny Tears and 8" Teen Weeny Tiny Tears. All vinyl, open mouth/nursers. Sleep eyes and rooted hair. Both are original. Courtesy Jeannie Mauldin.

20" Toodles marked: Amer. Char. Doll, on head. Has extra joints at the knees and elbows. Open mouth/nurser. Sleep eyes with lashes and made of very heavy vinyl. Courtesy Virginia Jones.

Whimsies by the American Doll & Toy Co. 1960. Left to right: Unidentified and 19", 19" Miss Take, 21" Blushing Bride, 19" Lollipop. All have original clothes. Courtesy Florence Black Musich.

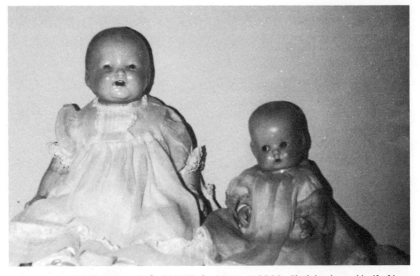

Left: 16" "Baby Nancy" 1928. Cloth body and half of legs. Composition head, lower legs and arms. Both arms and legs are disc jointed to body. Sleep eyes, open mouth with felt tongue and two upper teeth. Smiling and also has dimples. Some had wigs. Marks: Arranbee, on head. Right: 10" All composition baby with molded hair, painted eyes, closed mouth. Marks: Arranbee Doll Co, on back. Courtesy Jeannie Mauldin.

15" Baby Nancy Lee. 1950. Marked Arranbee, on head. Early vinyl with puckered features, painted eyes, deeply molded hair and wide open/closed mouth. Courtesy Sally Freeman.

ARRANBEE DOLL CO.

The Arranbee Doll Co. was founded in 1922, and purchased by the Vogue Doll Co. in 1959. The molds were still used, as well as the name (R&B), until 1961.

Bottle Tot. Composition with celluloid hand and molded bottle: 13" – $95.00; 18" – $145.00. Debu-Teen. Composition girl with cloth body: 14" – $100.00; 18" – $125.00. All composition: 14" – $95.00; 18" – $110.00. Dream Baby. Vinyl/cloth, 16" – $65.00; 26" – $100.00. Kewty: All composition with molded hair: 14" – $30.00. Littlest Angel: All hard plastic: 10" – $22.00. Miss Coty: Vinyl: 10" – $20.00. My Angel: Plastic/vinyl: 17" – $20.00; 22" – $45.00; 36" – $95.00. Nancy: All composition: 12" – $90.00; 17" – $140.00; 19" – $165.00; 23" – $195.00. Nancy Lee: All composition: 14" – $100.00; Hard plastic, 14" – $95.00. Unusual eyebrows/vinyl, 15" – $85.00. Baby: Painted eyes, and looks as if crying: 15" – $50.00. Nanette: All hard plastic: 14" – $55.00; 17" – $100.00; 21" – $145.00; 23" – $175.00. Sonja Henie: All composition: 18" – $140.00; 21" – $175.00. Taffy: Looks like Alexander's "Cissy": 23" – $.

ARRANBEE

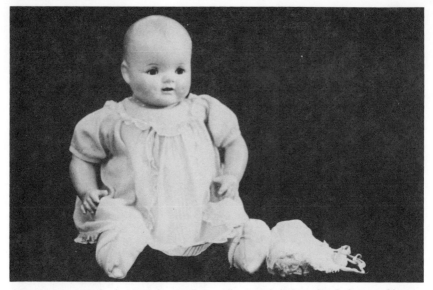

21" My Dream Baby by Arranbee Doll Co. All original clothes of pink dress and bonnet trimmed in lace. Dress has tag: Dream Baby. An Arranbee Doll. The doll is unmarked. Composition head and limbs with cloth body. Molded blonde hair, blue tin sleep eyes, dimples and open mouth with two teeth. 1936-7. Courtesy Martha Sweeney.

20", 17" and 19" "Nancy" dolls that are all composition. Left two are original and right is redressed. All have human hair wigs. Courtesy Martha Sweeney.

19" "Nancy" by Arranbee. All composition, blue sleep eyes, open mouth with four teeth and human hair wig. Marked: Nancy, on head. Redressed, but in original shoes and socks. Courtesy Martha Sweeney.

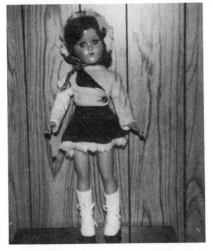

17" Closed mouth Sonja Henie. All composition and original. Sleep brown eyes. Marked: R & B, on head. Courtesy Jeannie Mauldin.

14" "Nancy Lee". Early hard plastic in all original taffeta gown with lace gloves. Gold canvas shoes. Marks: "Nancy Lee". An all durable doll", on tag and R & B, on head. Courtesy June Schultz.

10½" "Littlest Angel" by Arranbee with original wardrobe. All hard plastic, walker and made in 1958. Doll is unmarked. Sleep eyes and open/closed mouth. Courtesy Helena Street.

ASTER
AVERILL, GEORGENE (MADAME HENDRON)

20" Aster Walker. All hard plastic with glued on wig, sleep eyes, and upper teeth. One piece walker legs, both arms slightly curved and second and third fingers slightly curled. All original. Looks very much as the Ideal "Saucy Walker" dolls. Doll is unmarked. Box: Aster Corp. Courtesy Marjorie Uhl. 20" - $85.00.

28" Oil cloth stuffed body with oil cloth legs and arms. Vinyl hands and head. Very fat looking, has brown sleep eyes, wide open/closed smiling mouth with molded upper and lower teeth and has dimples. Original clothes except shoes and socks. Marks: Georgene Averill, on head. Molded hair. Courtesy Jeannie Mauldin.

GEORGENE HENDREN AVERILL

Madame Hendron-Averill first started making dolls in 1913, and the names used by her are: Madame Georgene Dolls, Paul Averill Mfg. Co., Averill Mfg. Co., Georgene Novelties, Madame Hendron, Brophey Doll Co. (Canada). She also designed a great many dolls for George Borgfeldt. For animals, Bonnie Babe, or cloth dolls see bisque section. Baby Georgene. Composition/cloth, 21" – $110.00; 23" – $135.00. Baby Hendron: Composition/cloth, 22" – $120.00. Baby Yawn: Composition-closed eyes-yawn mouth: 17" – $250.00. Dolly Record. Composition/cloth with record player in back: 26" – $425.00. Indians: Googly: Composition/cloth: 14" – $195.00; 16" – $225.00; 19" – $300.00. Snookums: 14" – $225.00. Whistling Boy: Composition/cloth. 14" – $125.00.

BABY BERRY

Alfred E. Newman: Vinyl head: 20″ – $95.00. Christopher Robin: Vinyl head: 18″ – $65.00. Daisy Mae: Vinyl head: 14″ – $85.00; 21″ – $100.00. Emmett Kelly (Willie the Clown): Vinyl head: 24″ – $95.00. Lil' Abner: Vinyl head: 14″ – $95.00; 21″ – $125.00. Mammy Yokum: Molded vinyl hair: 14″ – $125.00; 21″ – $150.00; Yarn Hair: 14″ – $100.00; 21″ – $125.00. Pappy Yokum: Vinyl head: 14″ – $125.00; 21″ – $150.00.

21″ "Pappy and Mammy Yokum" by the Baby Barry Doll Co. Cloth bodies, arms and legs with vinyl head, hands and vinyl boots molded on the Pappy doll with the Mammy having black felt boots. Pappy has rooted hair and molded beard, and painted brown eyes. Original clothes. Mammy has molded on black hat, molded hair and painted brown eyes. All original. Courtesy Jeannie Mauldin.

CAMEO

Baby Bo Kaye: Composition head: 18″ – $450.00. Baby Mine: Vinyl head: Sleep eyes, 15″-16″ – $100.00; Painted eyes, 15″-16″ – $150.00. Betty Boop: Composition head: 12″ – $375.00. Champ: Composition head, freckles: 16″ – $525.00. Giggles: Composition, molded loop for ribbon: 11″ – $225.00; 14″ – $385.00. Ho-Ho: Plaster: 4″ – $45.00; Vinyl: 4″ – $15.00. Joy: Composition head: 10″ – $225.00. Kewpie: Composition, jointed body: 9″ – $100.00; 14″ – $165.00; Unjointed body: 9″ – $65.00; 14″ – $100.00. Celluloid: 3″ – $35.00; 10″ – $75.00. Bean bag body: 10″ – $20.00; Cloth body, vinyl head & limbs: 16″ – $165.00. Gal with molded hair/ribbon: 8″ – $25.00. Hard plastic: 16″ – $275.00. Ragsy, vinyl one piece molded clothes: With heart on chest. 1964: 8″ – $60.00; Without heart, 1971, 8″ – $45.00. Thinker, one piece, sitting down: Vinyl, 4″ – $8.00. Vinyl, jointed shoulders and hips: 9″ – $45.00; 14″ – $95.00. Not jointed: 14″ – $40.00; Black: 14″ – $65.00; 27″ – $150.00; 27″ – $225.00. Wards Anniversary: 8″ – $35.00. Little Annie Rooney: Composition head: 16″ – $625.00. Margie: Composition head: 6″ – $165.00; 10″ – $185.00. Miss Peep: 1960's: 18″ – $45.00; Black: 18″ – $65.00. Miss Peep, Newborn: 18″ – $65.00. Peanut, Affectionately: Vinyl: 18½″ – $90.00. Pete the Pup: Composition head: 8″ – $145.00. Pinkie: Composition head. 1930's – $125.00. Vinyl & plastic 1950's – $65.00. Scootles: Composition: 12″ – $325.00; 15″ – $425.00; Black: 15″ – $600.00; Vinyl: 14″ – $85.00; 27″ – $200.00.

CAMEO

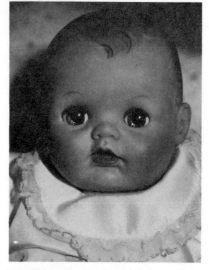

15" "Baby Mine" with molded hair and very large sleep eyes, open/closed mouth and on the "Miss Peep" style body. Courtesy Phyllis Teague.

18" "Baby Mine" by Cameo. Lambs wool wig, molded tongue in closed mouth and sleep blue eyes. Has the pin jointed "Miss Peep" style body. All vinyl. Redressed. Courtesy Phyllis Teague.

Shows the "Miss Peep" style body on the 15" "Baby Mine". All vinyl with pin joints at shoulders and hips. Courtesy Phyllis Teague.

14" Composition Kewpie by Cameo with joints at the shoulders, hips and neck. Painted eyes to side and has molded blue wings at base of neck. Courtesy Diane Hoffman.

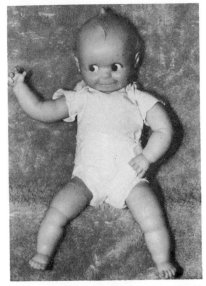

18" Kewpie marked: Cameo. All vinyl with pin joints like the "Miss Peep" doll. Is marked on head and body. Molded hair and painted eyes to the side. Courtesy Shirley Merrill.

27" Kewpie. Vinyl with painted eyes, modeled top knot and tufts of hair, all original. Courtesy Pat Timmons.

Shows 17½" "New Born Miss Peep" along with a "Miss Peep" doll to compare the styling of the design of the heads. Courtesy Phyllis Teague.

5½" Rare size "Margie" by Joseph Kallus of the Cameo Doll Co. Wood multi-jointed body with composition head with molded ribbon. Googly eyes and smile mouth. Sticker on chest. (Author).

CAMEO
CENTURY

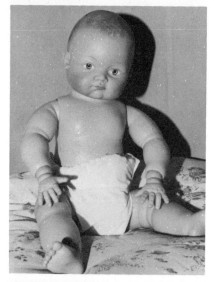

17½" "New Born Miss Peep" marked Cameo on head and body. Excellent body detail and has jointed wrists. Inset glassene eyes, closed mouth and molded hair. Courtesy Phyllis Teague.

12" "Black Scootles". All composition and jointed at neck, shoulders and hips. Molded hair and painted features. Ca. 1940's. Courtesy Karen Miller.

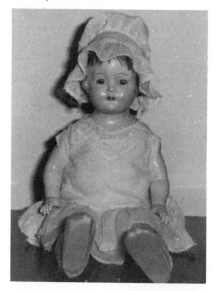

24" "Marleena" of 1926 by the Century Doll Co., and so marked on the shoulder plate. Head, shoulders, arms and legs are composition. Cloth body, sleep eyes, brown wig, and open mouth with four painted teeth. Cryer box. All original. Courtesy Arlene Wacker.

CENTURY DOLL COMPANY

Babies with cloth bodies, composition head and limbs: 18" – $100.00; 24" – $125.00. Toddlers and girls: Cloth bodies, composition head and limbs: 18" – $125.00; 24" – $175.00. Boy Dolls: Cloth bodies, composition heads and limbs: 18" – $150.00; 24" – $200.00.

10½'' Cloth doll with note, "This doll given by Helen Louise to Lenore when she was born, 10-23-31." Cloth covered body of same material as dress. Printed on material, black, full bang hair, and has large painted black eyes to the side. Courtesy Jayn Allen. 10½'' - $45.00.

15½'' All cloth, original with hat and dress. Wig that is glued on, painted features with eyes to the side. Cloth body with cloth legs, having side seams and oil cloth sewn on feet. Fat hands with chubby free formed thumbs. Made by Primrose Doll Co. of Chicago in 1932 to 1937. Courtesy Jayne Allen. 15½'' - $75.00.

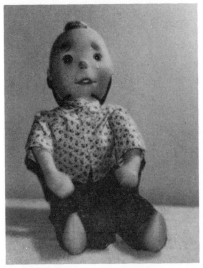

20'' Cloth dolls, approximately sixty years old. Both have yarn hair, embroidered features, and may be originally dressed. They were made by different companies. The girl has no formed fingers and the boy has stitched fingers with separate thumb. Courtesy Marjorie Uhl. 20'' - $85.00.

All cloth crying child (came as boy, or girl). Has painted features with painted tear under left eye, single top knot hair. Called "Tear Drop Baby", he was made by the Madame Hendron (Averill) company, under the name of Georgene Novelties. Courtesy Jeannie Mauldin. 14'' - $50.00.

CLOTH

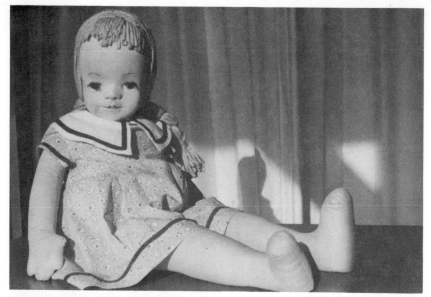

24" Cloth that is unmarked. Hand painted cotton cloth mask face that is nailed to composition molded head. Blue painted eyes, inset long brown lashes and jointed at neck only. Stitch jointed at shoulders and hips. Contour shaped legs with seam in front and back. Limbs are flesh color cotton, torso is off white cotton. Yellow yarn wig in pigtails stitched to wig cap. Courtesy Margaret Mandel. 24" - $100.00.

23" "Wednesday" made by the Aboriginals Inc. for cartoonist Charles Addams. The cartoon series was called "Addam's Evils" 1962. Also sold at this same time was Wednesday's mother, "Morticia", who was 45" tall, and brother, 20" "Irving". All cloth with yarn hair. Courtesy Elaine Kaminsky. 23" - $125.00.

15" Grandpa made by Mattel and is a pull string talker. The 14" Grandma is tagged Amsco Toys-Raggi Grandma. They have face features painted alike, both are original, made of one piece and stuffed, and both have black cloth shoes. Grandma's dress is removable, Grandpa's clothes are sewn on. His tag reads: Mattel-Grandpa-1968. He has grey painted hair and she has grey yarn hair. Courtesy Jeannie Mauldin. $12.00 each.

8" Dark skin "It's a Small World" exhibit-ride doll from Disneyland and Disneyworld. All vinyl with string hair and painted eyes. Marked W. Disney Prod. These dolls were also sold from stores across the U.S. (Author).

11½" "It's a Small World Doll". All vinyl with large painted eyes, rooted hair and thin, closed smile mouth. Marked: W. Disney Prod. (Author).

DISNEY, WALT

Christopher Robin: All polyfoam & wire by Bendy: 10" – $25.00. Cloth/vinyl, molded hair by Swedlin: 12" – $35.00; 19" – $95.00.

Donald Duck: All one piece vinyl. By Dell: 6" – $6.00. One piece squeeker toy by Sun Rubber Co.: 10" – $12.00. With binoculars. All vinyl. By Dell: 10½" – $10.00. Roly-Poly. All plastic and musical: 11" – $15.00.

Fairy Princess from "Babes in Toyland": Plastic and vinyl with deep "V"'ed forehead hairline of black rooted hair. By Uneeda: 32" – $75.00.

Ferdinand: All composition. By Ideal: 9" – $150.00.

Mary Poppins: Plastic and vinyl. 1964 by Horsman: 12" – $22.00. Plastic and vinyl, sleep eyes, walker. By Horsman: 26" – $50.00. Plastic and vinyl. By Horsman: 36" – $75.00.

Michael: Plastic and vinyl. By Horsman: 8" – $20.00.

Mickey Mouse: Composition head. By Knickerbocker: 9" – Roly-Poly. Vinyl face mask. By Gund: 10" – $20.00. All rubber. 1945. By Sun Rubber Co.: 11" – $16.00. Vinyl face mask & large ears, plush body: 12" – $22.00. All cloth Cowboy. By Knickerbocker: 13" – $25.00. Suede face mask, rest cloth: 17" – $35.00. Porous vinyl. By Bend-a-Twist: 18" – $85.00. Hard plastic, walker, mask face, felt ears. 1954: 26" – $95.00.

Minnie Mouse: All rubber. By Sun Rubber Co.: 11" – $16.00. Wood filled velvet, felt hands. 1940's by Wood Bey Products: 8½" – $20.00.

Mousketeer: "Ginger" in felt clothes & hat: 8" – $22.00. "Ginger", blue pleated skirt, white sweater & Mickey Mouse plastic mask: 8" – $25.00. Boy & girl. Vinyl, one piece body and legs, sleep eyes and

DISNEY, WALT
DOLL ARTIST

separate hats. By Horsman. 1971: 8" – $18.00. All vinyl with molded on clothes: 12" – $18.00.

Peter Pan: One piece vinyl, molded on clothes. By Sun Rubber: 10" – $25.00. Vinyl head & arms, rest cloth, by Ideal: 17" – $60.00.

Pinocchio: Composition head. By Ideal: 11" – $175.00. Composition head. By Knickerbocher: 12" – $150.00. Composition head and shoes: 16" – $295.00.

Pollyanna: All vinyl. By Uneeda: 10½" teen type – $35.00. All vinyl, white rooted hair. By Uneeda: 17" – $50.00. Plastic and vinyl. White hair. By Uneeda: 31" – $75.00.

Seven Dwarfs: All composition. By Knickerbocher: 9" – $85.00. Composition & cloth. By Ideal: 11" – $135.00.

Small World Dolls: Internationals: 8" – $20.00; 11½" – $30.00. Snow White: All early vinyl. By Sayco: 21" – $65.00.

Tinkerbell: One piece polyfoam & wire, vinyl head. By Bendy: 6" – $18.00. All soft vinyl. By Sayco: 12" – $35.00.

20" "Lady Guenevere". Parian-type shoulderhead with applied bonnet and beading. Cloth body with detailed porcelain hands and feet. Marks: Clear (Emma). (Author).

18" N.I.A.D.A. Artist Sharon Johnson portrait of her youngest child with baby doll. Named "Dainie & Doll". Bisque heads, hands and feet. Doll has bisque head and all cloth body and limbs. Painted features. Tag: Mother & Daughter Doll House/Originals by Sharon. Courtesy Kimport Dolls.

DOLL ARTIST

Clear, Emma: Blue Scarf Doll: 20" – $225.00. Chinas: 20" – $200.00; 26" – $275.00. Chinas, early hairdo: 20" – $250.00. Danny Boy: 20" – $365.00. George & Martha Washington: 20" – $700.-1,200.00 set. Lady Guenevere: 20" – $365.00. "Parian": 16" – $225.00; 20" – $400.00. Johnson, Sharon: 18" – $325.00 set.

Kane, Maggie Head: Caldonia: 14" – $300.00. Marigold: 14" – $150.00. Nicodemus: 13" – $225.00. Peach Blossom: 14" – $300.00. Uncle Ned: 15" – $225.00.

LaMott, Gerald: Snow Boy: 18" – $300.00.

Mann, Polly: Empress Charlotta: 15½" – $275.00. Patti-Jean: "Parian": 15" – $150.00; 17" – $175.00.

Wallace, Sheila: Charles 1.: 13" – $995.00. Elizabeth 1.: 13" – $995.00. Sir Walter Raleigh: 13" – $995.00. Family of Louis XVI – $1,800.00.

Wilson, Lita: Cinderella: 16" – $225.00. Elizabeth Taylor: 16" – $265.00. Prince Rainier: 16" – $200.00.

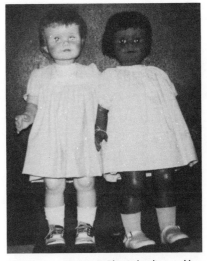

14" Baby Luv. 1970. Cloth body with vinyl head and limbs. Large painted eyes with stars in the middle. Open/closed smile mouth and wide spread fingers, as well as separate formed toes. Rooted hair. Marks: Eegee, on head. Courtesy Jeannie Mauldin.

28" "Annette" 1961. Plastic bodies and legs with vinyl arms and heads. Rooted hair and sleep eyes. Both are marked: Eegee 1961, on heads. Courtesy Jeannie Mauldin.

EEGEE

The name of this company is made up from the name of the founder, E.G. Goldberger. Founded in 1917, the early dolls were marked: E.G., then later, E. Goldberger, and now Eegee.

Andy: Plastic & vinyl boy. Marked: EG-1961. 12" – $ . .

Annette: 11½" Teen type: $22.00. Plastic and vinyl walker legs: 25" – $32.00; 28" – $40.00; 36" – $60.00.

Baby Luv: Cloth and vinyl, large painted eyes. Marks: B.T. Eegee: 14" – $40.00.

Baby Tandy Talks: Foam body, rest vinyl. Sleep eyes, pull string talker: 1963 – $40.00.

Flowerkins: Plastic and vinyl. Marks: F-2, on head. 16" – $22.00 each.

Gemmette: Plastic and vinyl. Teen type. 14" – $16.00.

EEGEE

Georgette and Georgie: Cloth & vinyl. 22"23" – $20.-25.00 each.

Gigi Perreaux (child star). Hard plastic & early vinyl head. 17" – $125.00.

Granny from Beverly Hillbillies. Plastic & vinyl. "Old lady" modeling. Grey rooted hair. Painted, or sleep eyes. 14" – $55.00.

Miss Charming. All composition. Shirley Temple look-a-like. Marks: E.G., on head. 19" – $165.00.

My Fair Lady: All vinyl, jointed waist. 19" – $45.00.

Posey Playmate: Foam and vinyl. 18" – $16.00.

Susan Stroller: Hard plastic and vinyl. 20" – $45.00; 23" – $50.00.; 26" – $65.00.

Tandy Talks: Plastic and vinyl. Freckles. Pull string talker: 20"-21" – $60.00.

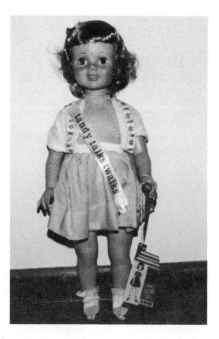

14" "Gemette". Plastic body and legs, vinyl head and arms. Rooted hair and sleep eyes. Dressed as Bride, but also came in various style outfits. Made by Eegee. Courtesy Phyllis Teague.

21" Tandy Talks-Walks. 1961. Plastic body and legs, vinyl arms and head. Sleep eyes, open/closed mouth with upper teeth, freckles and all original. Pull string talker that says 10 different things. Marks: Eegee, on head. Courtesy Jeannie Mauldin.

5" Unknown personality. Marked: EEgee. Jointed at neck only with rooted hair and eyes painted to the side. One piece vinyl body and limbs with clothes molded on. Courtesy Sally Freeman.

EFFANBEE

American Children: All composition, designed by Dewees Cochran. Painted or sleep eyes. Closed mouth: Girl: 15" – $550.00; 18" – $800.00; 21" – $1,000.00; Boy: 15" – $800.00; 17" – $1,000.00.
Open mouth: 15" – $585.00; 18" – $650.00; 21" – $695.00.
Anne Shirley: All composition: 15" – $150.00; 21" – $225.00; 27" – $325.00.
Babyette: Cloth & composition: 12½" – $150.00.
Babykin: All composition. Boy or girl: 9"-12" – $135.-150.00. All vinyl, sleep eyes. 1964: 10" – $45.00.
Baby Cuddleup: Vinyl coated cloth body, rest vinyl. Open mouth, two lower teeth. 1953: 20" – $60.00.
Baby Dainty: Cloth & composition: 15" "135.00.
Baby Evelyn: Cloth & composition. 17" – $165.00.
Baby Tinyette: Composition: 8" – $135.00. Composition toddler: 8" – $135.00.
Bi-Centennial boy and girl (Pum'kin), 1976. 11" – $125.00 each.
Bridal Sets. 1970's (4 dolls): Plastic and vinyl: White – $165.00; Black – $285.00.
Bubbles: Cloth & composition: 14" – $165.00; 16" – $175.00; 20" – $185.00; 26" – $235.00.
Button-nose: All composition: 8"-9" – $125.00. Cloth & vinyl. 1968: 18" – $50.00.
Candy Kid: All composition: White: 12" – $150.00; Black, 12" – $225.00.
Carolina, made for Smithsonian. 1980: 12" – $65.00.
Cinderella: All hard plastic: 16" – $165.00.
Colonial Lady: 1877-1978 only. Plastic & vinyl: 15" – $65.00.
Currier & Ives. Plastic & vinyl: 12" – $65.00.
Disney Dolls: Cinderella, Snow White, Alice in Wonderland, Sleeping Beauty: 1977-1978, 14" – $125.00 each.
Dy Dee Baby: Hard plastic head, vinyl body: 15" – $65.00; 20" – $85.00.
Fluffy: All vinyl. 10" – $35.00. As Girl Scout, Brownie, etc.: 10" – $45.00; Black – $45.00.
Grumpy: Cloth & composition: 12" – $150.00; 18" – $225.00.
Historical Dolls: All composition: 21" – $1,100.00; 14" – $450.00.
Honey: All composition: 14" – $75.00; 18" – $125.00; 27" – $250.00. All hard plastic: 14" – $75.00; 18" – $125.00; 21" – $250.00.
Ice Queen: In skating outfit. All composition. Open mouth. 17" – $450.00.
Lamkin: Cloth & composition: 16" – $275.00.
Limited Edition Club dolls: 1975, Precious Baby – $450.00; 1976, Patsy – $285.00; 1977, Dewees Cochran – $175.00; 1978, Crowning Glory – $250.00; 1979 Skippy – $185.00; 1980, Susan B. Anthony – $150.00; 1981, Girl With Watering Can – $150.00; 1982, Princess Diane – $175.00; 1983, Sherlock Holmes – S.A.
Little Lady: All composition: 15" – $125.00; 21" – $175.00; 27" – $325.00. Cloth body/yarn hair: 21" – $175.00.
Lovums: Cloth & composition: 15" – $150.00; 22" – $185.00.
Mae Starr: Cloth & composition with record player in torso: 30" – $425.00.

EFFANBEE

Marionettes: Composition and wood: 14″ – $110.00.

Martha Washington: 1976, plastic & vinyl: 11″ – $75.00.

Mary Jane: Plastic & vinyl, walker & freckles: 31″ – $165.00.

Mary Ann & Lee: Cloth & composition, and all composition: 16″ – $150.00; 18″ – $175.00; 24″ – $225.00.

Mickey: All vinyl. Some with molded on caps: 11″ – $95.00.

Patricia: All composition: 14″ – $185.00.

Patsy: Cloth & composition: 14″ – $185.00; All composition: 14″ ″185.00.

Patsyette: 9″ – $150.00.

Patsy Ann: 19″ – $225.00. Vinyl, 15″ – $95.00.

Patsy Joan: 16″ – $200.00.

Patsy Jr: 11″ – $155.00.

Patsy Lou: 22″ – $275.00.

Patsy Mae: 30″ – $450.00.

Patsy Ruth: 26″-27″ – $425.00.

Patsy, Wee: 5″-6″ – $200.00.

Polka-dottie: 21″ – $150.00.

Portrait dolls: All composition: 12″ – $150.00 each.

Prince Charming: All hard plastic: 16″ – $175.00.

Rootie Kazootie: 21″ – $165.00.

Rosemary: Cloth & composition: 14″ – $150.00; 22″ – $200.00; 28″ – $300.00.

Skippy: All composition: 14″ – $225.00.

Sunny Toddler: Plastic & vinyl: 18″ – $65.00.

Suzette: All composition: 12″ – $125.00.

Sweetie Pie: Cloth & composition: 14″ – $115.00; 19″ – $150.00; 24″ – $175.00.

W.C. Fields: Cloth & composition: 22″ – $600.00. Plastic & vinyl. 1980: 15″ – $175.00.

15″ "American Child" designed for Effanbee by Dewees Cochron. All composition with latex painted arms. Green sleep eyes. Marked Effanbee, on head and Effanbee/Anne Shirley, on body. Not original. Courtesy Shirley Merrill.

9" "Button-nose". All composition with painted brown eyes, all original clothes and marked: Effanbee, on the back. Courtesy Pat Timmons.

1979 Bridal Party using the "Nicole" face for the large bride, the "Caroline" face for the Bridesmaid and "pumpkin" for the Flowergirl and Ringbearer. They are in white and blue. Courtesy Hazel Adams.

13" "Candy Kid". All composition toddlers that are all original (missing shoes). Marked Effanbee on head and back. Left is 1946 in pink sold through Wards in suitcase with extra clothes. (In yellow for Easter), and was also sold in white dress same year. Childhood dolls of owner, Shirley Merrill.

12" "Caroline" face doll made exclusively for the Smithsonian and limited to 1980. Russet gown, ecru taffeta slip and pantaloons with lace trim. Courtesy June Schultz.

EFFANBEE

12" "Charleston Harbor" of the Currier & Ives collection made in 1980 only. Uses the "Nicole" face. Head is marked: Effanbee/1979/1279. Courtesy Renie Culp.

15" "Colonial Lady" 1977 and 1978 only. White cotton pantaloons, heavy net half slip with cotton ruffle and lace trim. Blue flowered cotton gown with white eyelet trim on waist wrap, white bonnet with navy ribbon trim. Blonde hair. (Author).

8½" Black Fluffy used as Girl Scout (old uniform). Box says: Junior Girl Scout #11-966. Marked: Effanbee, on head. All vinyl with sleep eyes/molded lashes. 1965. Courtesy Treasure Trove.

14" Historical Doll: 1607 Indian. All composition with painted eyes, and is marked: Effanbee/Anne Shirley, on the back. Courtesy Eloise Godfry.

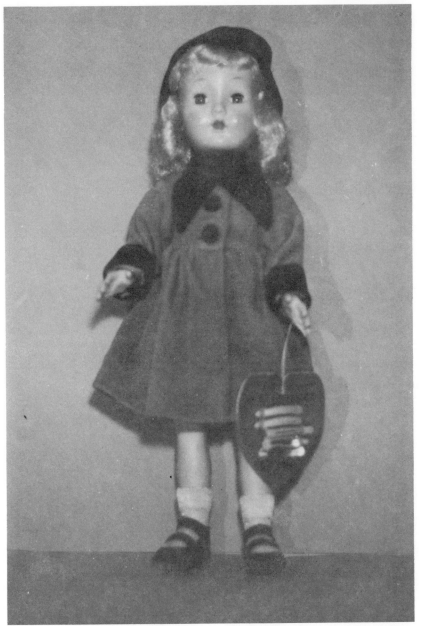

14" "Honey-Tintair Girl". Original with dress under coat, brown suede shoes and comes with curlers. All hard plastic with sleep blue eyes and saran glued on wig. Courtesy Kay Bransky.

EFFANBEE

21" "Little Lady". All composition with sleep brown eyes. Marks: Effanbee/Anne Shirley. 1943. Came with booklet for Little Lady doll. Replaced wig-originally had yellow yarn hair in braids. Replaced clothes. Courtesy Mrs. Frank Miller.

27" "Little Lady". All composition with original black glued on wig, blue sleep eyes and unmarked. Heart shape bracelet says: Effanbee Durable Doll. Not original dress. Courtesy Pat Timmons.

Shows both sides of the booklet that came with the "Little Lady" doll of 1943. Courtesy Mrs. Frank Miller.

One of the many Marionette made by the Effanbee Doll Co. Made of composition and wood. This one is a Walt Disney character, "Captain Hook". All original. Shown in 1953 Sears Catalog, along with Peter Pan, Clarabell Clown & Howdy Doody. Courtesy Marjorie Uhl.

11" "Martha Washington" 1976, 1977 only. Cotton pantaloons, half slip, soft satin navy gown with white trim, white lace. Shawl and poke bonnet. Blue ribbon trim. White slippers, black cameo on black ribbon. Marks: Effanbee/1976/1276. Courtesy Beverly Harrington.

All composition "Patsy" with molded hair, sleep blue eyes and has second and third fingers molded together. Right arm is more bent at the elbow, left, fairly straight. Marked Effanbee. Courtesy Joleen Flack.

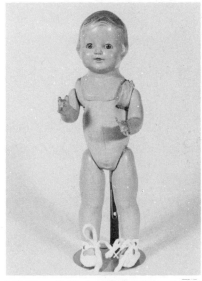

14" "Patsy". Marks: Effanbee/Patsy, in oval on composition shoulderplate. Molded light brown hair that is parted on the side. Blue tin sleep eyes, excelsior stuffed cloth body and composition limbs. Cry box in back, and slight dimple in each cheek. Courtesy Shirley Pascuzzi.

Snow White made by Effanbee exclusively for Disneyland and Disneyworld. 1977-1978. There were four storybook dolls made by Effanbee for Disney during 1977-1978. Courtesy Hazel Adams.

Effanbee's Rootie Kazootie and Polka Dottie. Cloth bodies and legs with vinyl arms and head. Rootie has brown deeply molded hair, blue painted eyes, freckles, open/closed mouth with molded tongue. Original. Marked on head: Rootie Kazootie Effanbee. Polka Dottie has blue painted eyes, open/closed mouth with tongue and dimples, molded brown hair. Clothes may be original. Marked: Rootie Kazootie-Polka Dottie Effanbee. Courtesy Jeannie Mauldin.

18" "Sweetie Pie". All composition with brown sleep eyes, molded brown hair and marked Effanbee on head and body. Not original. Courtesy Shirley Merrill.

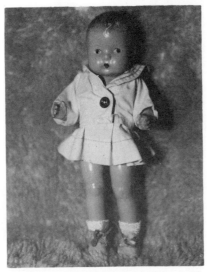

Left: 18" "Sunny" Toddler. Plastic and vinyl and all original. Blue sleep eyes and rosebud mouth. Rooted white hair. Marks: 15 Effanbee 1968 9305, on head. By 1970 was called "Luv". Right: 17" "Binny" that is plastic and vinyl with rooted hair and sleep eyes. Redressed. Marks: Alexander 1964. Courtesy June Schultz.

8" "Tinyette Toddler". Composition with molded painted hair, painted eyes and all original clothes. Marks: Effanbee, on head and Effanbee Baby Tinyette, on body. Courtesy Shirley Merrill.

EUGENIA

17" "Roberta", also sold as "Sandra Sue", and used as a blank doll to dress by Mollye Goldman. All composition with brown sleep eyes, closed mouth and dimples in cheeks. Box reads: A Personality Pla-mate styled for Montgomery Ward by Eugenia Doll Co. A touch of Paris. Copyright 1945. She is marked 17 on the back and her dress is tagged: Made in U.S.A. Eugenia Doll Co. America's finest dolls. Courtesy Jeannie Shipi. 17" - $125.00; 21" - $150.00.

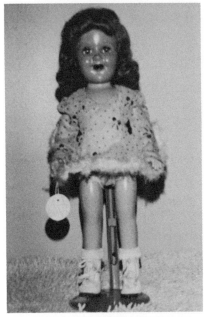

16" All composition with molded brown hair, brown sleep eyes and tiny bow mouth. Marks: Harriet Flanders, on head. Courtesy Jeannie Mauldin. 16" - $100.00.

14" Barbara Ann Scott. All composition, sleep eyes and open mouth. All original outfit has pink nylon lined body, sheer sleeves and overall pattern in glitter design. Marabou trim. White ice skates, and socks. Marks: Reliable. Made in Canada. Courtesy Ann Wencel. 14" - $225.00; 20" - $350.00.

14" Collection DeLuxe-Historique series made by Atelier D'Art of Saint-Brieuc, France. The wigs are glued on and the eyes are painted. 1978. $65.00 each.

FOREIGN DOLLS

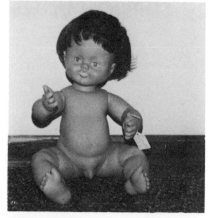

22" Marked Clodrey/Made in France, on head. All vinyl boy, rooted hair, sleep eyes and open/closed mouth with smile and painted lower teeth. Courtesy Jeannie Mauldin. 22" - $85.00.

16" Marks: By Laflex 1965/Made in France. Shirt is marked: Pitchdum, or Pitchoun Laflex 1965. All vinyl, has bowed legs, thin waist, bright orange hair and bright green eyes. Courtesy Marcia Piecewicz. 16" - 32.50.

12" Girl from Germany. Blue sleep eyes, movable head, arms and legs. Blonde wig. Original clothes. All plastic. Marks: AD, on head. Courtesy Mrs. Frank Miller. 12" - $18.00.

16" All vinyl sexed dolls with blonde hair, blue sleep eyes and wearing original tops. Marks: Turtle, in diamond, on head and back. By Rheinische, Germany. Courtesy Shirley Merrill. 16" - $65.00 each.

196

36" Made by Princess Christina and marked with M.G. in box/Zapf/1976, on paper sticker. Rooted hair, painted eyes and made of plastic and vinyl. Vinyl hands, and jointed between wrist and elbow. Very good quality. Not original clothes. Courtesy Nancy Lucas. 36" - $195.00.

14" Hard plastic doll with brown mohair wig, sleep eyes and original. 1950's. Cryer in back. Marks: Furga Italy. Courtesy Nancy Lucas. 14" - $45.00.

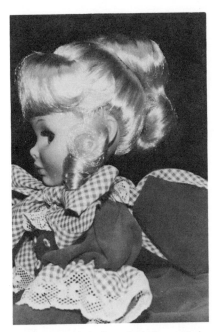

21" "Eugenia" #45 plastic and vinyl doll that is all original. Doll marked: Furga, Italy, on head. Furga/Made in Italy, on back. Courtesy Renie Culp. 21" - $85.00.

FOREIGN DOLLS

All original Furga with beautiful hairdo, and excellent quality clothes. Missing umbrella that matched her gown. Courtesy Marjorie Uhl. 21'' - $85.00.

13'' "Viviana". Plastic and vinyl. Original. Marks: No marks on head. 27/Italy/zz, on lower back. Tag: Zanini & Zambelli/Made in Italy/Canneto 5/0 Italy. Courtesy Renie Culp. 13'' - $45.00.

Japanese Traditional-souvenir style doll. Painted papier mache body with crushed oyster shell white face. Painted on shoes without pupils. Courtesy Diane Hoffman. 6'' - $8.00; 10'' - $15.00. Bisque head: 6'' - $40.00; 10'' - $95.00. Painted flesh color bisque heads: 6'' - $20.00; 10'' - $65.00.

22'' Jumeau made of plastic and vinyl. Head marked: Collections/Doll/C D-30. Tag: Collector's Collection Doll. Made in Japan. Open mouth and original clothes. Courtesy Virginia Jones. 22'' - $175.00.

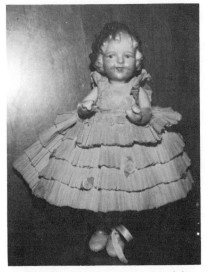

8" Shirley Temple made in Japan and dressed in original pink crepe paper dress. Doll is made of painted bisque. Courtesy Mildred Busch. $150.00.

15" Doll made in Korea, very elaborate. Marks: Korean Souvenir Co. Manufacturers and exporters. Authorized Concessionaire. Seoul, Korea, on bottom of stand. Courtesy Renie Culp. 15" - $70.00.

13" Man and woman dancers from Spain. Made by Jose Marin in Verdugo-Cadiz. They have excellent detail in features and clothes. Courtesy Mrs. Frank Miller. 13" - $95.00 set.

15½" "Jackie Kennedy Visiting Spain". Rigid plastic shoulder head, painted eyes, open/closed mouth with painted teeth and glued on black hair. Cloth body and rigid plastic arms and legs. Molded bracelets, shoes and has metal cross. Carries prayer book, Rosary and white gloves. Tag: Marvin-Chiclane-Made in Spain. Jose Marin of Verdugo-Cadiz used same head as he used for his Spanish dancers. Courtesy Ann Wencel. 15½" - $85.00.

HASBRO

4" Monkees. Body and legs are wire armature, vinyl covered, vinyl heads with painted brown spot on top with rooted hair. Painted features. Heads not marked. Marks on body: 1967/Hasbro/Hong Kong. Removable clothes. Left to right: Dimples, one shoe missing is Peter Tork. Next, not smiling, and both shoes missing is Mike Nesmith, who records on his own. Next with full bangs is Davey Jones who records on his own. Far right: Mickey Dolenz. Courtesy Virginia Jones.

HASBRO

Adam. 1971. (World of Love boy), 9" – $12.00.
Aimee. 1972. Plastic & vinyl: 18" – $40.00.
Defender. 1974. One piece arms and legs: 11½" – $10.00.
Dolly Darling. 1965: 4½" – $6.00.
Flying Nun. 1967. Plastic & vinyl: 5" – $15.00.
G.I. Joe: Flocked or molded hair, no beard. 1964: 12" – $30.00.
Flocked hair and beard – $22.50. Eagle eyes. 1975. 11½" – $12.00.
Foreign, includes: Australian, Japanese, German & Russian. 1964: 12"
– $75.00. Nurse, 1967: 12" – $125.00. Talking: 11½" – $22.50.
Leggy: 10" – $8.00.
Little Miss No Name. 1965: 15" – $60.00.
Monkees. (Set of four): 4" – $30.00.
Storybooks. 1967: 3" – $9.00 each.
Sweet Cookie. 1972: 18" – $15.00.
That Kid. 1967: 21" – $.   .
World of Love girls. 1968: 9" – $.   .

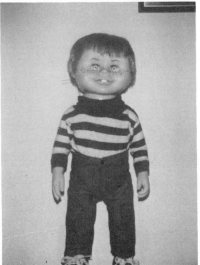

12" G.I. Joe, Talking. Has pull string at neck. Brown flocked hair and beard. Blue painted eyes. Marks: 1975 Hasbro/Pat. Pend. Pawt. R.I. Multi-jointed. Courtesy Dorothy Judge.

21" That Kid. Marks: Hasbro/1967. Patent Pending. Plastic and vinyl. Freckles. Battery operated. Reposition head and he says different things. Built in sling shot in hip pocket and if pulled, he talks. Courtesy Jeannie Mauldin.

HORSMAN

Answer Doll. Button in back to make head move. 1966: 10" – $10.00.

Billiken. Composition head, slant eyes, plush or velvet body. 1909: 12" – $250.00.

Baby Bumps. Composition & cloth. 1910: 11" – $135.00; 16" – $165.00; Black: 11" – $185.00; 16" – $225.00.

Baby First Tooth: Cloth & vinyl, cry mouth, one tooth, tears on cheeks: 16" – $40.00.

Baby Tweaks: Cloth & vinyl. Inset eyes. 1967: 20" – $28.50.

Betty: All composition: 16" – $90.00. Plastic & vinyl: 16" – $18.00.

Betty Jo: All composition: 16" – $90.00. Plastic & vinyl: 16" – $18.00.

Betty Ann: All composition: 19" – $90.00. Plastic & vinyl: 19" – $18.00.

Betty Jane: All composition: 25" – $125.00. Plastic & vinyl: 25" – $40.00.

Betty Bedtime: All composition: 16" – $90.00; 20" – $125.00.

Bright Star: All hard plastic. Open mouth. 1952: 15" – $90.00.

Brother: Composition & cloth: 22" – $95.00. Vinyl: 13" – $25.00.

Christopher Robin: 11" – $32.00.

Child Dolls: All composition: 15" – $85.00. 19" – $110.00.

Cindy: All hard plastic. 1950's: 15" – $50.00; 17" – $65.00. All early vinyl: 15" – $20.00; 18" – $40.00. Lady type, swivel waist: 19" – $45.00.

HORSMAN

Country Girl: 9" – $12.00.

Crawling Baby: Vinyl. 1967: 14" – $28.00.

Dimples, Baby: Composition & cloth: 20" – $165.00; 24" – $195.00. Toddler: Composition & cloth: 20" – $175.00; 24" – $210.00. Laughing: Composition & cloth, painted teeth: 22" – $250.00.

Gold Medal Doll: Composition & cloth, upper & lower teeth: 21" – $95.00. Vinyl, molded hair, one piece body & limbs: 26" – $150.00.

Early babies: Composition & cloth: 15" – $90.00; 22" – $125.00.

Ella Cinders: Comic character. Composition & cloth: 14" – $275.00; 18" – $495.00.

Hebee-Shebee: All composition: 10½" – $90.00 each.

Jackie Coogan: Composition & cloth: 14" – $425.00.

Jackie Kennedy: Plastic & vinyl. 1961: 25" – $90.00.

Jeanie Horsman: All composition: 14" – $100.00. Composition & cloth: 16" – $100.00.

Life Size Baby: Plastic & vinyl: 26" – $100.00.

Lullabye Baby: Cloth & vinyl. Music box: 12" – $18.00.

Mary Poppins: 12" – $25.00; 16" – $45.00; 26" – $100.00.

Mama Style Babies: Composition & cloth: 16" – $80.00; 22" – $95.00. Hard plastic & cloth: 16" – $65.00; 22" – $90.00. Vinyl & cloth: 16" – $20.00; 22" – $30.00.

Patty Duke: 1965: 12" – $45.00.

Pippi Longstockings: Cloth & vinyl. 1972: 18" – $22.50.

Pipsqueaks: four in set. 1967: 12" – $14.00 each.

Polly & Pete: Black dolls molded hair: 13" – $95.00 each.

Poor Pitiful Pearl: 12" – $20.00; 17" – $30.00.

Roberta: All composition: 1937: 14" – $100.00.; 20" – $150.00.

Ruthie: All vinyl, or plastic & vinyl: 14" – $10.00; 20" – $20.00.

Ruthie's Sister: Plastic & vinyl. 1960: 26" – $65.00.

Sleepy Baby: vinyl & cloth, eyes modeled closed: 24" – $35.00.

Tessie Talks: Plastic & vinyl: 18" – $20.00.

Tuffie: All vinyl. Upper lip molded over lower: 16" – $40.00.

Made by Horsman this all composition doll's name is "Betty Bedtime". The chubby doll is shown in original box and with original tag. White organdy with large red flower print. Yellow mohair wig, blue sleep eyes, open mouth. Marks: Horsman, on head. Courtesy Jeannie Mauldin.

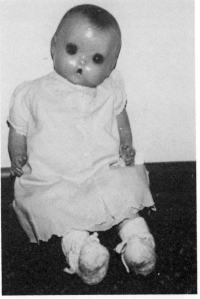

13" "Brother" 1955. Blue sleep eyes, open/closed mouth, brown molded hair. Vinyl head with one piece stuffed vinyl body. Marks: Horsman, on head. Courtesy Carol Friend.

22" Horsman's "Brother" of 1937 and marked: Horsman, on head. Cloth and composition with lightly molded brown hair, brown sleep eyes with eyeshadow. Small closed mouth. Also this year was "Sister" who has a top knot molded hairdo and painted tufts of hair. Courtesy Jeannie Mauldin.

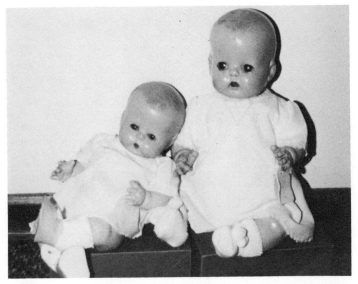

18" "Chubby" babies of the 1930's. Cloth bodies with composition head and limbs. Lightly molded and painted blonde hair, brown sleep eyes. Courtesy Jeannie Mauldin.

HORSMAN

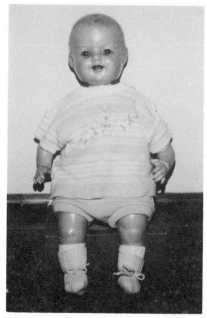

9" Country Girl by Horsman. Comes with tea set. Plastic body and legs, vinyl arms and head. Jointed knees with flat feet. Rooted hair and painted eyes. Marks: 1973 Universal Associated Co. Ltd./Made in Hong Kong, runs up and down on back. Sold in 1976-77. Courtesy Marie Ernst.

Horsman made these "Gold Medal Baby" dolls in the 1930's and they are marked: E.I.H. Co., on head. Cloth and composition with lightly molded hair. Has sleep eyes, open mouth with two upper and two lower teeth. Redressed. Courtesy Jeannie Mauldin.

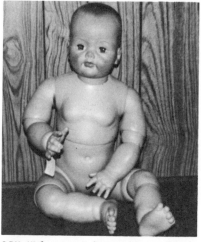

25" "Jackie Kennedy" marked: Horsman 1961/JK 25-4. Vinyl with rooted hair, blue sleep eyes, high heel feet and shown in original box. Schiffli embroidered dress, felt pill box hat and pearl necklace and earrings. Courtesy Ann Wencel.

25" "Life-size Baby" similar to Ideal's "Bye-Bye Baby". Plastic body, arms and legs, vinyl head with molded hair, sleep blue eyes and open/closed mouth. Jointed at neck, shoulders, elbows, hips and knees. Marks: Horsman, on head. Courtesy Jeannie Mauldin.

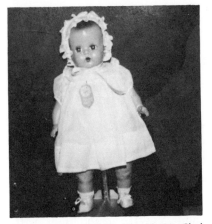

"Ma-ma; Pa-pa Baby" of the 1940's. Cloth and composition with large brown glassene eyes, molded brown hair and all original. Marks: Horsman, on head. Courtesy Jeannie Mauldin.

16" "Mary Poppins". Plastic and vinyl. Marks: Horsman Dolls, Inc./1964/210, on head. Sleep blue eyes. Courtesy Kathy Walters.

19½" "Ruthie". 1955. One piece body, arms and legs. Red-blonde rooted hair. Not original clothes. Marks: Horsman, on head. Courtesy Mrs. Frank Miller.

18" Tessie Talk Ventriloquist Gal. Plastic with vinyl arms. Mouth is hinged with pull strings in the back of head. Rooted orange hair, painted blue eyes. Heavily modeled nipples and navel and knees. Very large feet and hands. Marks: Horsman Dolls Inc. 3000, high on head. Horsman Dolls Inc. 1974, on back. (Author).

IDEAL

Baby Belly Button: Plastic & vinyl. 9", White – $7.00; Black – $14.00.

Baby Big Eyes: Vinyl coated cloth & vinyl: 21" – $45.00.

Baby Crissy: Plastic & vinyl. 24", White – $32.50; Black – $42.50.

Baby Ruth: Cloth & early vinyl: 12" – $20.00; 23" – $32.00.

Bam Bam: Plastic & vinyl, and all vinyl: 8" – $10.00; 12" – $12.00; 16" – $15.00.

Batgirl/other Super Women. Vinyl: 12" – $65.00 each.

Betsy McCall: Hard plastic & vinyl: 14" – $125.00.

Betsy Wetsy: Hard plastic & vinyl: 12" – $30.00; 14" – $40.00; 18" – $85.00; All vinyl: 12" – $20.00; 18" – $60.00.

Betty Big Girl: Plastic & vinyl: 30" – $95.00.

Bizzy Lizzy: Plastic & vinyl, 17" – $28.00.

Blessed Event: Called "Kiss Me" (1950-1951). Cloth body with plungee in back that makes doll cry or pout. Vinyl head and limbs, with eyes almost squinted closed: 21" – $50.00.

Bonnie Braids: Hard plastic & vinyl: 13" – $42.50.

Brandi: Plastic & vinyl: 18" – $45.00.

Brother/Baby Coos: Composition & latex: 24" – $23.00. Hard plastic & vinyl: 24" – $45.00.

Bye Bye Baby: Plastic & vinyl: 12" – $90.00; 25" – $175.00.

Cinnamon: Plastic & vinyl: 12" – $45.00; Black – $85.00.

Cricket: Plastic & vinyl: 16" – $50.00.

Crissy: 18" – $20.00; Black – $50.00; Look-a-Round – $20.00.

Daddy's Girl: Plastic & vinyl: 42" – $750.00 up.

Deanna Durbin: All composition: 17" – $300.00; 21" – $400.00.

Dianna Ross: Plastic & vinyl: 18" – $125.00.

Dina: Plastic & vinyl: 15" – $45.00.

Fanny Brice and other "Flexie" wire and composition (Baby Snooks, Mortimer Snerd, etc.): 12" – $200.00.

Flossie Flirt: Composition & cloth, flirty eyes: 22" – $95.00.

Giggles: Plastic & vinyl: 16" – $35.00; 18" – $45.00.

Goody Two Shoes: 18" – $50.00.   Walking & talking: 27" – $75.00,

Harriet Hubbard Ayers: Hard plastic & vinyl: 14½" – $95.00; 18" – $125.00.

Judy Garland: All composition: 14" – $750.00; 18" – $950.00. Marked with backward 21: 18" – $250.00.

Kerry: Plastic & vinyl: 18" – $35.00.

Kissy: 12" – $30.00; Black – $75.00; Tiny: 16" – $42.00; 22" – $50.00. Black: 22" – $100.00.

Little Lost Baby: Three faced dolls: 22" – $35.00.

Magic Lips: Vinyl coated cloth & vinyl: 24" – $55.00.

Mama Dolls: Composition & cloth: 18" – $45.00; 23" – $65.00. Hard plastic & cloth: 18" – $35.00; 23" – $50.00.

Mary Hartline: All hard plastic: 15" – $100.00; 21" – $150.00.

Mia: Plastic & vinyl: 15½" – $28.50.

Miss Curity: Hard plastic: 14" – $95.00.

Miss Ideal: Multi-jointed: 25" – $75.00; 28" – $95.00.

Miss Revlon: 10½" – $45.00; 17" – $60.00; 20" – $80.00.

Mitzi: Teen type: 12" – $40.00.

Patti Playpal: 30" – $105.00; 36" – 135.00.

Pebbles: Plastic & vinyl and ail vinyl: 8″ – $10.00; 12″ – $12.00; 15″ – $15.00.

Penny Playpal: 32″ – $95.00.

Peter Playpal: 38″ – $185.00.

Pinocchio: Composition/wood: 11″ – $175.00; 21″ – $450.00.

Sandy McCall: 36″ – $185.00.

Saralee: Cloth & vinyl: Black, 18″ – $95.00.

Saucy Walker: 16″ – $50.00; 19″ – $75.00; 22″ – $85.00. Black: 22″ – $145.00.

Shirley Temple (See next section)

Snow White: All composition: 12″ – $385.00; 18″ – $450.00.

Sparkle Plenty: 15″ – $45.00.

Tara: Plastic & vinyl: Black, 16″ – $20.00.

Tammy: 9″ – $20.00. Black – $35.00. Grown-up: 12″ – $20.00.

Thumblina: Kissing: 10½″ – $12.00. Tearful: 15″ – $20.00. Wake-up: 17″ – $18.00. Black: 17″ – $30.00.

Tickletoes: Composition & cloth: 15″ – $60.00; 21″ – $85.00.

Tippy & Timmy Tumbles: Plastic & vinyl: 16″ – $35.00. Black – $50.00.

Toni: 14″ – $75.00; 21″ – $95.00.

Tressy: Plastic & vinyl: 18″ – $28.50. Black $50.00.

Velvet: Plastic & vinyl: 16″ – $18.00. Black $50.00. Look Around – $18.00.

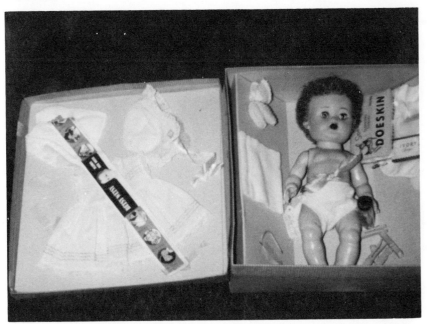

14″ Betsy Wetsy. All vinyl and original in original case. Courtesy Jeannie Mauldin.

IDEAL

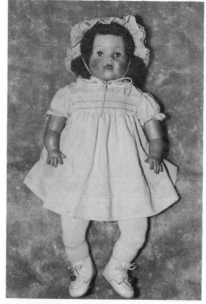

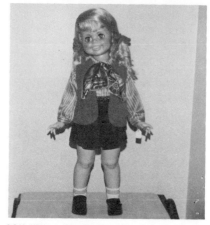

30" "Betty Big Girl". All original. Plastic and vinyl with sleep eyes, rooted hair and open/closed smiling mouth. Marks: 1968 Ideal Toy Corp/HD-31-H-127. Walker and talks by using batteries. Courtesy Ann Wencel.

23" Baby Ruth. Cloth and early vinyl head and limbs, glued on dark brown wig, blue sleep eyes, open/closed mouth with molded tongue. Marks: Ideal Doll/B-23, on head. Not original. 1952. Courtesy Shirley Merrill.

17" Bizzy Lizzy. All original with battery operated case to plug into doll's back. Has ironing board, irons, rug cleaner, duster and carry box. Plastic body and legs, vinyl head and arms. Marks: 1970 Ideal Toy Corp./ H-K-18-H 171, on head. 1971 Ideal Toy Corp. H,K, 18, on back. Courtesy Jeannie Mauldin.

14" Bonnie Braid from the comic strip, "Dick Tracy". Vinyl head with latex one piece body. All original. Marks: Chicago Tribune/Ideal Doll. 1951. Courtesy Marjorie Uhl.

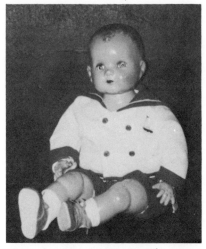

24" Brother Coos. Late 1940's with composition head, and limbs and cloth body. Also called "Baby Coos", and "Baby Squeezums" with latex body in 1950. Sleep eyes, eye shadow. Jointed neck on shoulder plate. Marks: Ideal Doll Inc., on head. Courtesy Jeannie Mauldin.

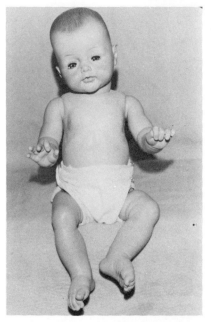

25" Bye-Bye Baby-Life Size Baby. Plastic and vinyl with excellent modeling, sleep eyes and molded hair. Courtesy Phyllis Teague.

18" Crissy wearing extra boxed outfit by Ideal Fashion Boutique, called "The Turned on Mini". Dress is gold with hot pink trim on sleeves, gold mesh stockings and gold shoes. Courtesy Ann Wencel.

24" Baby Crissy, both White and Black. All vinyl. Marks: 1972 Ideal Toy Corp./G.H.B.-H-225, on head. 1972 Ideal Toy Corp./G.H.B. 2-M-2-611, on back. The White version is marked the same on the head and 6-2M-5611-7, on the back. Courtesy Jeannie Mauldin.

22" Flossie Flirt. Cloth and composition with hard rubber arms. Mohair wig, grey tin, celluloid covered flirty sleep eyes. Marks: Ideal, in a diamond. Courtesy Shirley Merrill.

14" Harriet Hubbard Ayers. Hard plastic with early vinyl head, glued on wig, sleep eyes and vinyl arms with finely detail fingernails. (Author).

22", 16" and 12" Kissey. Plastic and vinyl. Jointed wrists. Put arms forward, and push together, mouth puckers and makes a kissing sound. Courtesy Jeannie Mauldin.

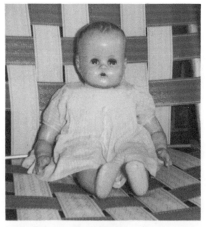

Poppa Mama Doll Ideal Toy Corporation. 18" composition head, arms and straight legs, with cloth body. Crier in stomach says "mama" when turned one way, and "papa" when turned the other way. Brown sleep eyes, molded hair and closed mouth. Mark on back of head: Ideal Doll, Made in USA. Original dress. Received Christmas 1942, collector's last childhood doll. Courtesy Pat Potts Collection.

23" "Mary Hartline". All hard plastic with sleep eyes and glued on saran wig. Redressed in correct styling. Marks: Ideal Doll, on head. Ideal Doll P-94, on back. Courtesy June Schultz.

20" Miss Revlon. All vinyl with jointed waist, rooted hair and sleep eyes. All original. (Author).

10½" Little Miss Revlon. Blue sleep eyes/molded lashes. Jointed waist. All vinyl. All original. Marks: Ideal Doll/VT 10½", on head. Courtesy Shirley Pascuzzi.

25" and 28" Miss Ideal. Plastic body and legs with vinyl arms and head, sleep eyes. Strung arms. Jointed at neck, shoulders, wrists, waist, hips and ankles. Marks: Ideal Toy Corp/ SP-30-S, on head of 28". G-30-S, on back. The 25" head is marked: S.P. 25-S, and Ideal Toy Corp/P-25, on back. Courtesy Jeannie Mauldin.

IDEAL

36'' Patti Playpal. Both have blue sleep eyes, left has dark brown hair and other is blonde. Both are marked: G-35 Ideal Doll, on head. Ideal, in oval on backs. Brunette is original and blonde is not. Courtesy Shirley Merrill.

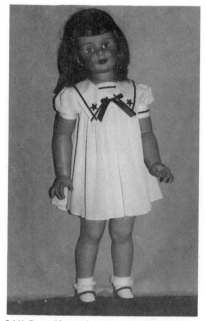

36'' Patti Playpal with tosca blonde hair, blue sleep eyes. Courtesy Phyllis Teague.

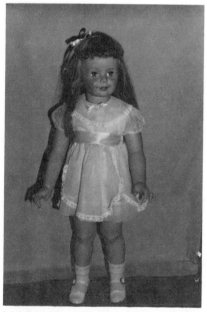

36'' Patti Playpal with red hair and blue sleep eyes. Courtesy Phyllis Teague.

32″ "Penny Playpal". Vinyl head and arms with plastic body and legs. Blue sleep eyes/lashes, open/closed mouth and posable head. Marks: Ideal Doll/B-32-B, on head. Ideal Toy Corp./B-32/Pat. Pend., on back. 1959. Courtesy Phyllis Teague.

32" and 28" Super Walkers. Both have sleep eyes, rooted hair, are all vinyl and toddlers. 32" marked: Ideal Toy Corp/Bye-32-35, on head. 28" marked: Ideal Toy Corp./T 28 X 30, on head. Not original. Courtesy Shirley Merrill.

28" Suzy Playpal. All vinyl with green sleep eyes, brown rooted hair and one of the "Playpal" series. Marks: OB-28-5/Ideal Doll Corp., on head. Courtesy Shirley Merrill.

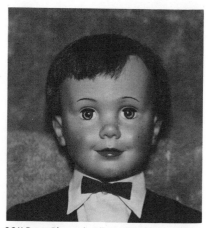

38" Peter Playpal. All vinyl with green sleep eyes, red rooted hair. Not original. Marks: BE-35-38, on head. Ideal, in an oval on back. Courtesy Shirley Merrill.

22" Saucy Walker. All hard plastic and all original. Flirty eyes. Marked: Ideal Doll, on head and body. Courtesy Pat Timmons.

Large 21" size Pinocchio made of composition and wood. Multi joints, molded on clothes, except tie and hat. Molded hair and painted features. Marks: CP WDP/Ideal Doll/Made in USA, on head. Sticker: Pinocchio/Dis. & Co. Walt Disney/Made by Ideal Novelty & Toy Co. Courtesy Marge Meisinger.

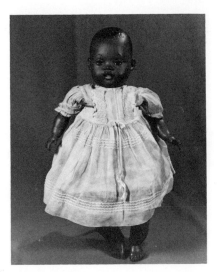

18" Saralee. Cloth body with vinyl head and limbs. All original. Dress tag: The genuine Saralee Doll made by Ideal Toy Corp. Marks on head: C-17/Ideal Doll. Courtesy Virginia Jones.

IDEAL

12" Tammy dressed in her original tennis outfit. Her arms do not bend and the fingers are not molded to hold anything. Marks: Ideal Toy Corp./BS-12, on back & head. Painted eyes to side with four painted lashes. (Author).

14½" Tickletoes. Composition head, flirty eyes, rubber arms and legs. Cloth body and completely original. The original price of $2.50 shows on the box. Courtesy Valna Brown.

12" Thumbelina with cloth body, vinyl head and limbs. Painted blue eyes, blonde rooted hair. Original. Marks: Ideal Toy Corp. OTT14, on head. Courtesy Shirley Merrill.

10" Kissing Thumbelina. Cloth with vinyl head and limbs. Blue painted eyes, dark rooted hair. Orignal. Tag: Kissing Thumbelina Doll/1970 Ideal Toy Corp/KT-9P-H-174/Hong Kong, on head. Courtesy Shirley Merrill.

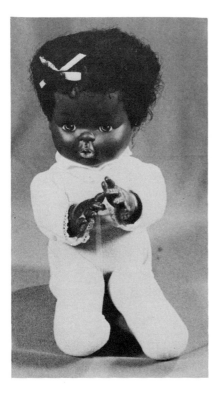

17" Wake Up Thumbelina. Marks: 1976/Ideal Toy Corp./WB-18-H-251, on head. 1976/Ideal, in oval,/Hollis NY 11423, on back. Battery operated. Raises body and rolls over on back, holds arms out to be picked up. Cloth stuffed legs are part of clothes. Plastic body in one piece. Rigid vinyl arms, vinyl head. Rooted hair and painted features. Courtesy Treasure Trove.

11" "Toddler Thumbelina". Cloth body with vinyl head and limbs, rooted hair, closed mouth with smile, and painted blue eyes. Operated by pull string, and she rocks on her horse. Her shoes are molded on, and her suit is orange and blue fringed at pant legs, arms, waist and neck. Marks: 1968 Ideal Toy Corp. 9770-M-124, on head. Body has tag: Toddler Thumbelina/Ideal. Courtesy Jeannie Mauldin.

IDEAL

16'' Tippy Tumbles. 1977. Marks: 1976/Ideal Toy Corp./T-18G-H-276, on head. U.S. Pat. No. 3500577/Ideal Toy Corp./Hollis NY 11423, on back. Also on back is a sidewards: 1977. Plastic with rigid vinyl arms. Vinyl head, painted features, rooted hair. Two plugs on side of leg to attach battery box. Courtesy Treasure Trove.

16'' Timmy Tumbles. Sits and stands on head, does a front flip, pulls himself up and does a back flip. Marks: 1976/Ideal Toy Corp./T-18G-H-276, on head. U.S. Pat. No. 3500577/ Ideal Toy Corp./Hollis NY 11423/1977, sidewards on back. Plastic with rigid vinyl arms, vinyl head with painted features. Two plugs in side of leg for battery box. Courtesy Treasure Trove.

14'' Toni. Original clothes and has dark hair. All hard-plastic, sleep eyes. Courtesy Mary Williams.

A tree of composition Shirley Temples of various sizes and in many original costumes. Courtesy Glorya Woods.

IDEAL'S SHIRLEY TEMPLE

Shirley Temple: All composition, marked both head and body. *First,* prices are for mint and original dolls, *second* price for dolls with light craze, clouded eyes, and with original clothes. *Third* price is for small cracks, badly crazed dolls, and not originally dressed. 11″ – $595.00; $400.00; $85.00. 11″ Cowgirl – $650.00; $125.00; $85.00. 13″ – $475.00; $300.00; $85.00. 16″ – $500.00; $300.00; $95.00. 18″ – $550.00; $325.00; $95.00. 20″ – $595.00; $345.00; $100.00. 22″ – $625.00; $400.00; $120.00. 25″ – $725.00; $500.00; $130.00. 25″ Cowgirl: $800.00; $595.00; $150.00. 27″ – $800.00; $595.00; $175.00. 27″ Cowgirl – $875.00; $500.00; $175.00. Allow extra for outfits such as Little Colonel, Wee Willie Winkie, Bluebird, etc.

Shirley Temple Baby: Price scale same as for dolls. 16″ – $550.00; $325.00; $95.00. 18″ – $625.00; $400.00; $120.00. 22″ – $700.00; $425.00; $130.00. 25″ – $785.00; $450.00; $140.00. 27″ – $825.00; $500.00; $140.00.

Shirley Temple: 1950's. Marked: Ideal Doll, and size number. (12, 15, 17, or 19) Made of vinyl, has set-in teeth. 12″ Mint in box – $125.00; Mint – $100.00. 15″ Mint in box – $175.00; Mint – $150.00. 17″ Mint in box – $195.00; Mint – $150.00. 19″ Mint in box – $250.00; Mint – $200.00. 35″-36″ Mint in box – $1,400.00; Mint – $1,300.00; Redressed – $1,200.00. Re-issue for Montgomery Ward. 1972 – $150.00.

1973 with box that has many pictures of Shirley on it, and the red polka dot dress. 16″ Mint in box – $65.00; Mint – $50.00. Shirley Temple *old* pin – $45.00.

IDEAL
SHIRLEY TEMPLE

27" Shirley Temple Ranger - Cowgirl doll. All composition and original except for the cowboy hat. Courtesy Evelyn Samec.

13" Shirley Temple in trunk with three outfits. The shoes are replaced. Courtesy Evelyn Samec.

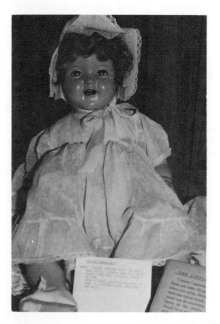

24" Shirley Temple baby. Original, has flirty eyes, cloth body and composition head and limbs. Courtesy Beres Lindus (South Australia).

16'' Shirley Temple. Plastic and vinyl in dotted swiss dress. Shoes marked: 1972 Ideal Toy Corp. Head is marked: ST-14-H-213/Hong Kong. Ideal, in oval, 1972/2M-5634, on back. On market in 1973. Courtesy Mary Wheatley.

IDEAL
SHIRLEY TEMPLE

10" Teen-Shirley Temple. Uses the Little Miss Revlon body, jointed waist, sleep eyes/molded lashes, has unpierced ears and dimples. Stand is marked. Courtesy Joan Amundsen.

Re-issued Shirley Temple for the Montgomery Ward anniversary in 1972. The doll is 12" tall. Courtesy Phyllis Houston.

This shows the prototype of both the Sara Stimson doll from the movie Little Miss Marker, along with the Shirley Temple that was not marketed at the same time. The Sara Stimson was not as successful at the box office as expected, and that was a shame, as she is a delightful little girl, just as Shirley was, but in a different way. Photo: Courtesy Ideal Toy Corp.

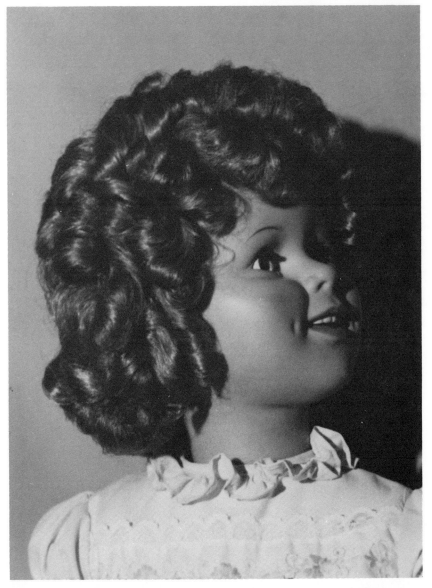

Large 36″ Shirley Temple which, to a great many collectors, looks more like Shirley than any other size. Courtesy Phyllis Teague.

INDIAN & ESKIMO DOLLS

INDIAN & ESKIMO SOUVENIR DOLLS

7″-8″, Indian: American – $12.00; Alaska – $18.00. 10″, Indian: American – $15.00; Alaska – $20.00. 12″, Indian: American – $18.00; Alaska – $25.00. Eskimo dolls with real fur: Baby, 4″ – $20.00. Toddler, 5″ – $20.00; 8″ – $27.50; 12″ – $32.50; 15″ – $45.00; 18″ – $57.50; 20″ – $62.50.

Left to right: Northwest Coast Indian, Navajo, Eskimo, Eskimo, Apache. Made by Heritage Dolls, and unmarked. Courtesy Renie Culp.

Left: Apache Indian and right: Eskimo Indian. Dolls are not marked. Box tags: Heritage Dolls/A Sunbell Co. Courtesy Renie Culp.

12" Plastic and vinyl and has beads for eyes. Carries small all plastic doll. Purple suede material. Tag: Carlson Dolls/Made in U.S.A. Courtesy Renie Culp.

Standing: All hard plastic with sleep eyes Carlson Doll Indian. Sitting: purchased from Reno, Nevada and the boy is all plastic and was a mailing from an Indian Reservation asking for donations. Courtesy Renie Culp.

10" Plastic and vinyl with sleep eyes. Rooted hair. Girl has baby on back. Dolls aren't marked but tag: Carlson Dolls/Made in U.S.A. Courtesy Renie Culp.

INDIAN & ESKIMO DOLLS

4" Plastic and vinyl with painted eyes to the side. Rabbit fur and is even stuffed inside. Courtesy Renie Culp.

4" Tiny all vinyl baby dressed in real fur and in woven basket that is lined in fur. Doll not marked. Courtesy Renie Culp.

5" All hard plastic with large painted eyes to the side. Rabbit fur covered and carries leather gloves. Courtesy Renie Culp.

226

18" Plastic and vinyl with sleep eyes. Has double rabbit head and Eskimo Indian marking on hides. Courtesy Renie Culp.

12" Impish Eskimo. All vinyl doll that is unmarked. Bead set eyes to side and closed smile mouth. Real fur covered. Courtesy Renie Culp.

18" Cotton with rabbit fur trim and has a double hood. Marks: SM..something, on head. Courtesy Renie Culp.

INDIAN & ESKIMO DOLLS

5" Vinyl doll covered with rabbit fur and has plastic baby in middle. Courtesy Renie Culp.

18" Eskimo that is all vinyl with sleep brown eyes and rooted hair. Real fur covered. Doll has no marks. Courtesy Renie Culp.

8" All hard plastic with light brown sleep eyes and rooted hair. Has an Eskimo yoyo in one hand and a glove in the other. Courtesy Renie Culp.

12" Plastic and vinyl with rooted hair and painted eyes. Rabbit and seal fur outfits. Courtesy Renie Culp.

8" Eskimo doll that is all good quality hard plastic. Sleep brown eyes. Real fur. Marks: Carlson Doll, on tag. Courtesy Renie Culp.

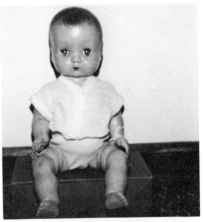

IRWIN PLASTIC CO.
5"-6" All plastic child - $4.00. 10"-11" All plastic child - $9.00. 16"-17" All plastic child - $25.00. Large all plastic bent leg baby, marked: Irwin. Sleep eyes. Not original. Courtesy Jeannie Mauldin: 6" All plastic baby - $4.00; 12" - $9.00; 16" - $25.00; 20" - $35.00.

Shows the full face view of the fine modeling on the Dick Clark doll. Courtesy Robin Schmidt.

26" Dick Clark. Marked: Juro, on head. All original. Cloth body and limbs with vinyl head and hands. "Dick Clark", in script on jacket. Courtesy Robin Schmidt.

JURO

Very little is known about this company, but the dolls that have been added to collections have extremely fine modeling, and are made with a lot of attention to detail of clothing. Dick Clark, 26", cloth & vinyl – $145.00. Pinky Lee, 24", composition hands, cloth body & limbs with a vinyl head and molded-on hat. Two pull strings in back operate the arms and legs – $145.00.

15" Baby Yawnie. Cloth body and limbs with vinyl head. Sleep eyes and rooted hair in front. Courtesy Jeannie Mauldin.

13" Bionic Big Foot by Kenner Products. The Sasquatah Beast. All rigid vinyl. Painted features with open/closed mouth and molded teeth. Courtesy Renie Culp.

KENNER

Baby Alive. Foam & vinyl, mouth chews. Price is for MINT doll only, 16" – $20.00.

Baby Bundles. 16" – $16.00. Black – $20.00.

Baby Yawnie. Cloth & vinyl. 1974, 15" – $18.00.

Big Foot: All rigid vinyl, 13" – $15.00.

Butch Cassidy & Sundance Kid. 4" – $6.00 each.

Blythe. 1972. Pull string and eyes change color and position. 11½" – $20.00.

Charlie Chaplin: All cloth with walking mechanism. 1973, 14" – $50.00.

Crumpet. 1970. Plastic & vinyl, 18" – $20.00.

Dusty: 11½" – $15.00.

Gabbigale. 1972. Plastic & vinyl, 18" – $20.00. Black – $35.00.

Garden Gals. 1972. Right arm and hand bent to hold watering can. 6½" – $9.00 each.

Jenny Jones and Baby. All vinyl. 1973. 9", Jenny, and 2½", Baby – $15.00 set.

Skye, 11½" – $18.00.

Sleep over Dolly & miniature Skye doll, 17" – $30.00. White with miniature Dusty doll – $25.00.

Steve Scout. 1974, 9" – $15.00. Black – $18.00.

Sweet Cookie. 18" – $20.00.

KENNER

16" Baby Bundles. All vinyl and strung, bent baby legs and bent arms with open hands. Painted eyes and rooted hair. Open mouth/nurser with molded tongue. Marks: General Mills Fun Group Inc. 1975, Cinn. Ohio. Made in Hong Kong. No. 2600, on backs. Courtesy Jeannie Mauldin.

13" Baby Heart Beat. All one piece vinyl body and limbs. Vinyl head with rooted hair, and painted eyes. Open mouth/nursers. Battery operated and doll comes with stethoscope so the heart beat can be heard. She also has a thermometer. Marks: GMFGI 1977, on head. Courtesy Jeannie Mauldin.

17" Baby Won't Let Go". Plastic body and legs with vinyl head and arms. Rooted hair and painted eyes. Open/closed mouth with molded tongue. Hold doll up by the fingers and her fingers close over yours. Also comes with a toy rattle. Both are original. Marks: GMFGI 1977, on head. GMFGI Kenner Prod. Div. Cinn. Ohio 45202. 26100-26150, on backs. Courtesy Jeannie Mauldin.

18" Sweet Cookie. Plastic and vinyl with jointed wrists and elbows. Rooted hair, painted eyes and open/closed mouth. Plastic and vinyl. Comes with battery box and many different items. All original. Courtesy Jeannie Mauldin.

18" Crumpet. Plastic and vinyl with rooted hair and eyes that open and close as she pours. Battery operated. Jointed at wrists. All original. Courtesy Jeannie Mauldin.

18" Gabbigale by Kenner. Plastic and vinyl with rooted hair and painted eyes. Both are original. Pull string operated talkers with the pull string coming out of the front of the doll. Courtesy Jeannie Mauldin.

KENNER

Dusty plays tennis. The wrists are jointed and the waist is jointed and the knees bend. (Author).

4'' "Butch Cassidy and Sundance Kid" action figures. Levers in back makes arm move. All rigid vinyl with molded on clothes and hats. Marks: CPG 1979/Hong Kong, on backs. Horses are marked: G.M.F.G. 1978, on legs. Made by Kenner. (Author).

Skye by Kenner shown in her all original fishing outfit and with accessories. Marked: G.M.P.G.I., on head. 1977 G.M.F.G.I. Kenner Prod/Made in Hong Kong, on back. (Author).

17" Clown. Cloth body with vinyl head, molded hair and painted features. The red plastic ball on the nose turns, and it winds a music box inside the cloth body. Tag: Joy of a Toy Knickerbocher Inc. Courtesy Jeannie Mauldin.

5" "The Lord of Rings" which is "Ringwraith" and made of all rigid vinyl with molded on clothes. Action figure that has excellent detail for such a small figure. Made by Knickerbocher. 1979-1980. (Author).

KNICKERBACHER TOY CO.

Bozo Clown. Vinyl head with molded red hair, plush body and limbs, 14" – $20.00; 24" – $38.50.

Clown, cloth, 17" – $10.00.

Composition child, right arm bent at elbow, 15" – $75.00.

Flintstones, 17" – $45.00. each.

Levi Rag Doll. All cloth, 15" – $16.00.

Lord of Rings, 5" – $9.00.

Pinocchio. All plush and cloth, 13" – $42.00.

Scarecrow. Cloth doll, 23½" – $45.00.

Seven Dwarfs. One piece composition body and head with jointed shoulders, 10" – $60.00 each.

Sleeping Beauty. All composition with bent right arm, 15" – $85.00.

Snow White. All composition with bent right arm, 15" – $85.00.

Soupy Sales. Vinyl & cloth, non-removable clothes, 13" – $75.00.

Two headed dolls with vinyl mask faces, one head crying, other smiling, 12" – $18.00. Cinderella with both bodies, all vinyl, one side sad, other with tiara, 16" – $ . . Awake and Asleep-face masks of vinyl, 12" – $20.00.

KNICKERBACHER
LEE, H.D.

17" Barney. Cloth and vinyl with molded hair and painted features. Marked the same as the Fred Flintstone. Courtesy Virginia Jones.

17" Fred Flintstone. Cloth with vinyl head, molded hair and painted features. Marks: The Flintstones/Hanna-Barbera Prod. 1961 by Knickerbocher, on tag. Hanna Barbera 1961, on head. Courtesy Virginia Jones.

13" Buddy Lee in original Phillips Gas uniform. All hard plastic with molded hair, painted features and black boots. One piece body, legs and head. Jointed shoulders only. Marks: Buddy Lee, on back. Courtesy Pat Timmons. Buddy Lee: 13" composition - $135.00; 13" All hard plastic - $100.00.

13"-14" Buddy Lee. All original and all composition. Wears Lee overalls with Lee marked buttons that fasten the strap over the shoulders, blue denim shirt, red tie around neck. Cap has the Seaboard Railroad emblem. This railway emerged with Coastline Railroad. The cross piece of the emblem says: Air line and the heart shape in center says: Through the Heart of the South. Courtesy Eloise Godfrey.

MAKER UNKNOWN

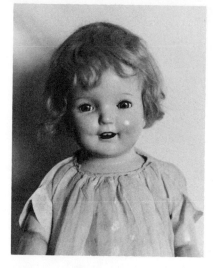

22" Unmarked beautiful composition shoulder plate head, composition arms and legs of a child and cloth body with cryer in back. Blonde mohair wig over molded hair, blue celluloid over tin sleep eyes. Original. Open mouth with two upper teeth, and tongue. Dimples. Courtesy Nancy Lucas. 22" - $125.00.

17" Composition head with loops in hair for ribbons. Excelsior filled cloth body, upper arms and legs are also cloth. Composition lower arms and boots. Jointed at shoulders and hips. Original romper suit, painted blue eyes to the side. Courtesy Nancy Lucas. 17" - $85.00.

20" Unmarked composition with green sleep eyes, open mouth and teeth. Original clothes. Definitely a Shirley Temple look-a-like, but of very fine quality. Courtesy Evelyn Samec. 20" - $125.00.

18" "Inemak the Greenlander" from books by Alice Allison Lide. Illustrated by W. W. Clarke. Cloth stuffed with wool dust body and legs. Composition arms and head. Painted blue eyes, eyeshadow, inset lashes. Mohair wig stapled on over molded hair and clothes are pinned on. Yellow snow suit with straps under feet. Oil cloth boots and real fur trim. (Author). 18" - $95.00.

17" Unmarked two faced composition doll with painted blue eyes, orange painted hair, cloth body and composition arms and legs. Cothing appears to be original. Courtesy Dottie Mulholland. 17" - $150.00.

17" Unmarked two faced dolls. This side of face "asleep". Courtesy Dottie Mulholland.

MAKER UNKNOWN

12" All rubber, fully jointed, Laughing Baby. Open mouth/nurser. Sleep eyes. Lightly modeled hair. No marks. Courtesy Shirley Merrill. 12" - $30.00.

8" Unmarked excellent quality hard plastic doll with vinyl head and rooted hair. Sleep eyes. Walker legs. (Author). 8" - $30.00.

8" Plastic key wind walker with over sized feet. Molded red hair, painted eyes to the side and molded on clothes. Head and arms move with the legs. Courtesy Jeannie Mauldin. 8" - $22.50.

14" Rigid vinyl body and limbs, soft vinyl head. Fully jointed and marked on back: CTNCI. Courtesy Phyllis Houston. 14" - $20.00.

15½" Sad Sack from cartoons by Sgt. George Baker who wrote for "Stars and Stripes," the G.I. newspaper. Vinyl head jointed at neck, one piece body and limbs. Molded shoes. Original, but missing cap. From World War II. Courtesy Nancy Lucas. 15½" - $75.00.

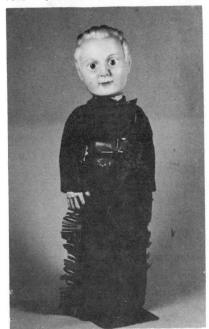

20" Davy Crockett. Early vinyl head, molded hair and inset glassene eyes. All one piece latex body and limbs. Original clothes with cap pinned in front. (Author). 20" - $42.50.

MAKER UNKNOWN

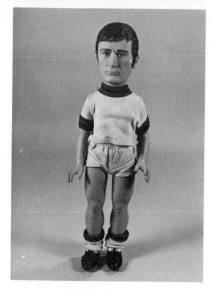

14" Socker player. Orange plastic body with paler plastic legs, vinyl head and arms. Very good face modeling. Brown molded hair and painted features with green eyes. Original, except missing playing shorts. Vinyl shoes have spikes. Marks: EFFE/Modello/Riva. (Author). 14" - $40.00.

15" without ears. "Funny Bunny" with vinyl face mask and very finely detailed vinyl hands and tennis shoes. Mohair plush hair and tail. Painted features. Not marked. (Author). 15" - $20.00.

18" Boy and girl pigs. Mohair over cardboard with squeaker in stomachs. Wire, felt covered tails. Felt at ends of noses. Pink Flannel inside ears, and brown felt feet. Non removable clothes. Unmarked. Courtesy Virginia Jones. 18" - $45.00 each.

12″, Allen – $25.00.

Baby First Step, 18″ – $25.00; Talking – $35.00.

Baby's Hungry, 17″ – $20.00.

Baby Pataburp, 13″ – $15.00.

Baby Say N See, 17″ – $12.00.

Baby Secret, 18″ – $20.00.

Baby Small Talk, 11″ – $8.00; Black – $16.00.

Baby Walk N Play, 11″ – $15.00.

Baby Walk N See, 18″ – $16.00.

Barbie. #1 - 11½″ MINT IN BOX – $750.00 up; Doll only – $450.00. #2 - Same as #1, but no holes in feet, 11½″ – $1,000.00 up. #3 - 1960 (still marked 1958 on body), 11½″ – $55.00. #4 - Soft, heavy material of new body does not turn light colored. Marked with Pat. Pend. mark. 1961, 11½″ – $55.00. #5 - Same as #4, but has one row of hair pulled through for bangs, and the bangs have a firm texture, 11½″ – $35.00. #6 - First Bubblecut, 11½″ – $35.00. #7 - Hard hollow Pat. Pend. body, rest same as #6, 11½″ – $25.00. #8-9 - 1962 and basically the same as #7, 11½″ – $25.00. #10 - Bubble cut with paler nails and lips. Midge marked body, 11½″ – $20.00. #11 - Fashion Queen with molded hair/band, plus wigs, 11½″ – $150.00. #12 - Swirl bangs (across forehead and to the side). Midge marked body, 11½″ – $75.00 #13 - Miss Barbie with sleep eyes: Midge marked body, 11½″ – $400.00. #14 - Side part with head band, 11½″ – $300.00.

Barbie Items: Car roadster – $250.00. Sports car – $100.00. Clock – $25.00. Family house, 1968 – $45.00. Plane – $200.00. Wardrobe – $35.00. #1 Barbie stand. Round with two prongs to fit into holes in doll's feet – $50.00.

Bozo, 18″ – $18.00.

Buffie, 10″ – $20.00; 6″ – $12.00.

Capt. Lazer, 12½″ – $20.00.

Casper the Ghost, 16″ – $28.00.

Chatty Brother, Tiny, 15″ – $18.00; Baby – $18.00.

Charming Chatty, 25″ – $45.00.

Chatty Cathy, 20″ – $22.00. Brunette/brown eyes – $35.00. Black – $75.00.

Cheerleader, 13″ – $12.00.

Cheerful Tearful, 13″ – $15.00. Tiny, 6½″ – $10.00.

Cynthia, 20″ – $20.00.

Dancerina, 24″ – $20.00. Black – $35.00. Baby, not battery operated – $18.00. Black – $27.00.

Dick Van Dyke, 25″ – $45.00.

Francie, 11½″ – $20.00. Black – $75.00.

Grandma Beans, 11″ – $14.00.

Hi Dottie, 17″ – $15.00.

Herman Munster, 16″ – $22.00.

Lil Big Guy, 13″ – $8.00.

Kiddles, Mint in packages – $9.00. Storybook with accessories – $20.00. Jewelry – $8.00.

Ken, flocked hair – $30.00. Molded hair – $25.00.

Midge, 11½″ – $20.00. Molded hair, 11½″ – $25.00.

Moon Mystic, 11½″ – $60.00.

Mother Goose, 20″ – $35.00.

MATTEL

Mrs. Beasley, talking, 16" – $20.00.
Randy Reader, 19" – $22.00.
Rockflowers, 6½" – $12.00 each.
Saucy, 16" – $45.00. Black – $75.00.
Scooba Doo, 21" – $45.00.
Skediddles, 4" – $9.00.
Shrinking Violet, 15" – $55.00.
Singing Chatty, 17" – $20.00.
Sister Belle, 17" – $28.00.
Skipper – $20.00. Black – $75.00. Grow-Up – $12.00.
Skooter, 9½" – $20.00.
Sun Spell, 11½" – $60.00.
Swingy, 20" – $18.00.
Tatters, 10" – $20.00.
Teachy Keen, 17" – $16.00.
Teener, 4" – $20.00 each.
Tinkerbell, 19" – $10.00.
Truly Scrumptious, 11½" – $45.00.
Tutti, 6" – $18.00. Packaged sets – $35.00.
Todd, 6" – $18.00.
Twiggy, 11" – $40.00.

This is the **only** Barbie that is worth up to $500.00. Then she must be MINT, in her BOX.
The eyebrows are inverted "V's" and the iris of the eyes are painted white. There are holes
in bottom of feet to fit metal stand with two prongs that must be with the doll and box, as
well as the first booklet, to command this amount of money.

#3 Barbie with regular ponytail and soft curl-
ed bangs. Marks: Barbie/Pat. Pend/-
MCMLVIII/by Mattel Inc. Made in 1960.
Courtesy Joan Amundsen.

#4 Barbie with large braided ponytail, soft
bangs and marked: Barbie/Pat. Pend./-
MCMLVIII/by Mattel Inc. Courtesy Joan
Amundsen.

#6 Barbie Bubblecut. 1961. Courtesy Joan
Amundsen.

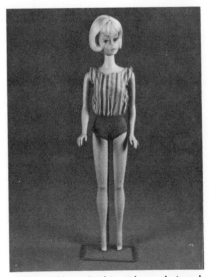

1965 Bend knee Barbie with new hair style
that is referred to as "American Girl".
Courtesy Joan Amundsen.

MATTEL

Miss Barbie with sleep eyes shown with wig stand and three wigs. Bend knees. Courtesy Joan Amundsen.

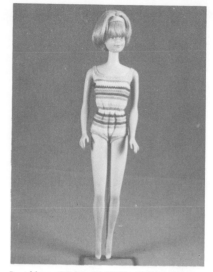

Bend knee Midge of 1965. Multi stripe suit, ribbon head band, long bangs and straight flip hairdo. Freckles. Marks: 1958/Mattel Inc/US Patented/US Pat Pend./Made in Japan. Courtesy Joan Amundsen.

#13 Sleep eyed "Miss Barbie" with molded hair and removable head band. She came with three wigs and was first doll to have the bendable knees.

Shows the eyes closed on the "Miss Barbie" of 1964.

Barbie "Hot Rod", finely detailed and just in scale for 11½" dolls. (Author).

Barbie "Mix 'N Match" Gift Set with blonde bubble-cut Barbie. 1962 booklet in box. Courtesy Pat Timmons.

Boxed Ken with blonde molded hair crew cut. #798 "Ski Champion" outfit. Courtesy Pat Timmons.

MATTEL

18" Baby Walk 'n See with roller skates. 1966. Dressed in white eyelet trimmed in hot pink. Walks on skates, eyes move all around. Vinyl and fully jointed. Battery operated. Courtesy Ann Wencel.

11" Grandma and twin Beans. Vinyl head, painted features and she has rooted white hair. The babies have painted curls. She has bean bag body and soft stuffed legs. The babies have soft stuffed unformed bodies. Velcro strips on arms hold the dolls. Non removable clothes. All three tagged: Mattel Inc. 1975. Grandma's head is marked: 1974 Mattel Inc. (Author).

18" "Bozo" talking clown. Red yarn hair, cloth body, felt hands and shoes and original clothes. Vinyl head with painted features. Marks: 1963 Mattel, Inc. Hawthorne, California, Made in Mexico/Pat. in U.S.A./Pat. in Canada 1962, other Pat. Pend., on tag. Courtesy Wendi Miller.

10½" Buffie and Mrs. Beasley. Buffie has a plastic body with vinyl head, and limbs. Rooted hair, painted eyes, open/closed mouth with two upper painted teeth and has freckles. Mrs. Beasley has a vinyl head, rooted hair and painted eyes. All cloth body and limbs. Buffie is a pull string talker. Marks: 1967 Mattel Inc/U.S.A. for Pat. Pend./Mexico, on back. Courtesy Jeannie Mauldin.

6″ Buffie and 3″ Mrs. Beasley. Both all original. Buffy marked: 1965/Mattel/Japan, on head. Courtesy Shirley Merrill.

15″ "Tiny Chatty Brother". Original aqua cotton romper suit, hat and slippers. Vinyl and plastic, rooted hair, although the Black version has a caracul wig, that is very nice, but must be a replacement. Pull ring talkers. Marks: Tiny Chatty Baby/Tiny Chatty Brother 1962 Mattel, Inc./Hawthorne, Calif USA-US Pat. Courtesy Ann Wencel.

18″ Chatty Baby redressed as a nun. Dressed by Bernice Pruett. Courtesy Margaret Mandel.

MATTEL

20" Chatty Cathy. All original in original box. Pull string talker. Blonde with blue eyes. Courtesy Pat Timmons.

20" Chatty Cathy. Plastic and rigid vinyl. Sleep eyes, open/closed mouth with two upper teeth and freckles. Pull string talkers. Left: Chatty has different hands and both White dolls are original. Marks: Chatty Cathy 1960-Chatty Baby 1961/ By Mattel Inc./U.S. Pat 3,017-187. /Other US and Foreign Pats. Pend., on back. Some Chatty Cathys are marked: Chatty Cathy Pat. Pend. MCMLX/By Mattel Inc. Hawthorne, Calif. Also circle with Mattel Inc, Toy Makers, in circle. Courtesy Jeannie Mauldin.

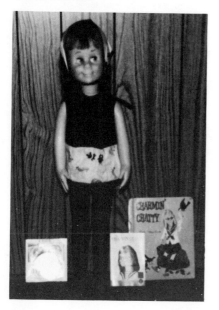

25" Charming Chatty. All original with records, book and clothes booklet. Battery operated. Courtesy Jeannie Mauldin.

13" Small Talk Cheerleader. Tag: 1970 Mattel Inc. Cloth with vinyl head and rooted hair. Painted features. Pull string talker. Sewn on leatherette shoes. Felt "O" for Oklahoma. Says things such as: "We want a touchdown", "Come on Big Red", etc. This doll was made for several different universities. (Author).

15" Singing Chatty. Pull string operated. Both dressed in red and both are original. Missing shoes and socks. One is brunette and other is blonde. Courtesy Sally Bethscheider.

24" Dancerina. 1968. Both are original, and battery operated. The smaller ones are not battery operated. Courtesy Jeannie Mauldin.

MATTEL

17" Hi Dottie. 1971. Plastic and vinyl with rooted hair and painted features. Both are original. Courtesy Jeannie Mauldin.

13" Lil Big Guy. Vinyl with painted blue eyes, freckles and has molded red hair. Dressed as Policeman with stop sign. Marks: Mattel Inc. 1975 Hong Kong, on back. Also came dressed as Fireman. Jointed shoulders and hips. Courtesy Mary Wheatley.

Herman Munster. Cloth and vinyl. Pull string talker. Tag: Herman Munster/1964 Kayre-Vue Productions/1964 Mattel Inc. Hawthorne, California. Courtesy Renie Culp.

11½" Sun Spell, Guardian Goddess. Very long gold and orange hair, painted features and vinyl and plastic. When arms are down, she has a snap on full length gown, as the legs are pulled apart, the arms fly up, the gown pops off to reveal her "Super" women's costume. Marks: 1978 Mattel Inc. Taiwan, on head. Mattel Inc. 1966/Taiwan, on lower back. Courtesy Renie Culp.

11½" Moon Mystic, Guardian Goddess. Has very black and deep blue hair, otherwise the description is the same as the other one. Courtesy Renie Culp.

16" Black and White "Saucy" by Mattel. 1972. Rotating arm makes eyes and face move to different positions. Original. Courtesy Jeannie Mauldin.

20'' Talking Mother Goose. 1970. All cloth and vinyl head, molded hair and hat, painted features and glasses. Pull string talker and says nursery rhymes. Courtesy Shirley Pascuzzi.

17½" Miss Seventeen. Hair inset into cutout scalp, painted features, and molded on earrings. Original. Marks: US Patent 2925664/ British Patent 8045664/ Made in Hong Kong, on lower back. All rigid plastic, with strung arms, high heel feet with holes in bottom for stand. Gold plastic cup marked: Miss Seventeen. Twelve high fashion outfits were available for this doll. Made by Louis Marx & Co. Courtesy Joan Amundsen.

10" Sundown Kid of the Ready Gang. Full action figure. Gun is above average for detail, as are the spurs. No marks on doll at all. Box: Marx & Co. All good quality hard plastic with vinyl head, painted beard, rooted blonde hair and painted blue eyes. Sundown's horse is named Dagger and is grey with black mane & tail. Other of Ready Gang are Trooper Gibson (black) with black horse named Midnight. Ringo & his appaloosa horse, Thunder.

10" Sundown Kid of Ready Gang. This doll is being called Clint Eastwood with no foundation, as no information on box indicates it was meant to be him. Most likely the blonde hair and pancho (Eastwood's "trademark") has started this among collectors.

MARX

16″ "First Love". All vinyl with swivel waist, rooted hair, sleep eyes with lashes. Original clothes. Marks: Made in USA & Italy/1979 Louis Marx & Co. Glen Dale, W. Va. Courtesy Carole Friend.

Archie. All vinyl, bend knees, 1975, 9½″ – $9.00.

Betty. All vinyl, bend knees, 1975, 9″ – $10.00.

First Love Baby, 1979, 16″ – $12.00.

Ginny Bones. All plastic interconnected tubing with modeled head, hands and feet, 40″ – $18.00.

Jughead. All vinyl, bend knees, 1975, 9½″ – $9.00.

Miss Toddler. All plastic, battery operated walker, rollers on bottom of feet, 21″ – $25.00.

Miss Seventeen, 18″ – $35.00.

Sundown Kid. Action figure, 10″ – $5.00.

Veronica, All vinyl, bend knees, 1975, 9″ – $10.00.

27" Deluxe Czechaslavokia. All cloth with oil painted face mask. International Doll Co.-Mollye Goldman.

27" Deluxe Dutch. All cloth with mask, oil painted face, braided wig and elaborate clothing. Made by Mollye Goldman of International Doll Co.

MOLLYE DOLLS

Airlines. Hard plastic, 14" – $125.00; 18" – $150.00; 23" – $175.00; 28" – $225.00.

Cloth. Children, 24" – $50.00; 29" – $85.00. Internationals, 13" – $65.00; 15" – $95.00; 27" – $110.00. Composition. Toddlers, 14" – $55.00; 21" – $75.00. Children, 15" – $85.00; 18" – $110.0. Young Ladies, 16" – $160.00; 21" – $250.00. Jeanette McDonald, 27" – $450.00. Bagdad dolls, 14" – $160.00; 19" – $300.00. Sultan, 19" – $365.00; Sabu, 15" – $385.00.

Vinyl children, 8" – $18.00; 11" – $22.00.

8'' Little Women using the ''Perky'' doll that is all vinyl and some are marked: Mollye, on heads. Uses two different heads, one with freckles. Second row, right is the other face used by Mollye Goldman of the International Doll Co. 1953.

MEGO

Batman action figures, 8″ – $8.00 each.
Cher, 12″ – $12.00.
Dianna Ross, 12½″ – $20.00.
Dinah-Mite, 7½″ – $8.00; Black – $12.00.
Happy Days set: Fonzie – $12.00; others – $8.00.
Joe Namath, 12″ – $45.00.
Our Gang set: Mickey – $20.00; others – $12.00.
Planet of Apes, 8″ – $9.00 each.
Pirates, 8″ – $12.00 each.
Robin Hood set – $12.00 each.
Sir Lancelot & others, 8″ – $12.00.
Star Trek set, 8″ – $15.00 each.
Soldiers, 8″ – $9.00 each.
Sonny, 12″ – $10.00.
Starsky & Hutch: Captain or Huggee-Bear – $15.00 each; others – $8.00 each.
Super women action figures, 8″ – $8.00 each.
Waltons, 8″ – $9.00 each.
Wizard of Oz: 8″Dorothy – $12.00; 15″ – $35.00. Munchkin – $9.00. Wizard – $12.00. Others – $10.00; 15″ – $35.00 each.

Rare Nancy Ann set. "Hush a Bye Baby" 4½″ tall twins dressed in pink and white sweater. Oval box is 9″ x 12″ x 6″. Babies are on pink, white flowered pillow. Courtesy Pat Timmons.

12½″ Dianna Ross. Same body as the Cher dolls, with bendable knees and jointed at waist and wrist. Plastic and vinyl. Inset long lashes. Marks: Motown Record Corporation, on head. Mego Corp/ 1975/Made in Hong Kong, lower torso.

NANCY ANN

NANCY ANN STORYBOOK

Bisque, 5" – $35.00 up; 8" – $38.00 up; Black – $60.00.
Plastic, 5" – $22.50 up; 8" – $25.00 up; Black – $50.00.
Bisque Baby, 3½" – $47.50. Plastic Baby – $32.00.
Nancy Ann, 10½" all vinyl – $35.00 up.
Muffie. All hard plastic, 8", Ballgown – $95.00; Dress – $75.00.

5½" #127 "Merry Little Maid." Eyes of baby blue Forget Me Nots in bloom, make me think of you. Bisque with one piece body, head and legs. Jointed shoulders. Original. Courtesy Pat Timmons.

Bridal Set. Plastic and shown with 4¼" Ring Bearer and Flower Girl. Courtesy Pat Timmons.

#87 of the Family Series. 5½" Bridesmaid. Bisque with jointed shoulders only. Courtesy Pat Timmons.

8" Muffie. All hard plastic and in original white gown. Courtesy Pat Timmons.

8" Muffie. All hard plastic and original in brown and yellow dress. Purse with name on it. Courtesy Pat Timmons.

8" Muffie. All hard plastic. Re-dressed and re-wigged by owner to the period of the dolls. Courtesy Glorya Woods.

NANCY ANN
THUMBS UP DOLL

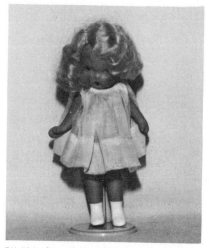

5" #111 "Here am I, Little Joan, when no one is with me I am alone". Bisque with jointed shoulders and hips. Has label made of paper glued to back of her hat that is oval shaped with silver lettering on a black background: Nancy Ann/100% wool/Dressed Dolls. Courtesy Pat Timmons.

5" #80 of Family Series, "Margie Ann". Bisque, jointed shoulders and hips and blonde hair. Blue dress and white painted shoes. Courtesy Pat Timmons.

5½" #60 of Big Sister Series. "Big sister goes to school". Plastic, red hair and blue eyes. Jointed at shoulders, neck and hips. Blue and white dress. Courtesy Pat Timmons.

8" "Thumbs-Up Doll". Flexible "lasticold" with one piece body and head. All original. Painted eyes and glued on wig. Tag: Your $1.50 purchase/ of this doll/helps in sending/ambulance to Britain and Her Allies and Vitamins to/ the undernourished children of England/ An original/creation of/Margit Nilsen Studios, Inc. Courtesy Pat Timmons. $65.00.

27" Rita Walking Doll. All hard plastic, saran wig, sleep eyes and open mouth with upper teeth. All original. By the Paris Doll Co. Doll is unmarked. Courtesy Marjorie Uhl. 27" in dress - $95.00; Ballgown - $125.00; Majorette - $125.00; Cowgirl - $125.00.

REMCO

5" Sweet April. Plastic body with rigid vinyl arms and legs. Vinyl head with inset blue eyes. Open mouth/nurser. Button in back makes arms move. Marks: Hong Kong/Miner Ind./New York NY 10010. Originally made by Remco and the molds, as well as the Remco trademarks & name was sold to the Miner Industries. Original majorette outfit was packaged for Sweet April while Remco was still in business. (Author).

6" I Dream of Jeannie. Plastic and vinyl with posable vinyl legs, rigid vinyl arms, softer vinyl head. Painted eyes to side, rooted hair and holes in feet for stand. Remco Toys, Inc/Made in Hong Kong, on back. Has 36 extra outfits and a plastic bottle case. (Author).

REMCO

Baby Crawlalong, 20" – $18.00.
Baby Grow a Tooth, 14" – $22.00; Black – $35.00.
Baby Laugh A Lot, 16" – $15.00; Black – $30.00.
Baby Sad & Glad, 14" – $16.00.
Dave Clark 5, 4½" – $45.00 set.
Heidi, 5½" – $7.00.
Jeannie, I Dream of, 6" – $7.00.
Jumpsy, 14" – $15.00; Black – $22.00.
Laurie Partridge, 19" – $30.00.
Little Chap Family: Set of four – $. Dr. John, 14½" – $40.00; Lisa, 13½" – $35.00; Libby, 10½" – $25.00; Judy, 12" – $25.00.
Mimi, 19" – $35.00; Black – $60.00.
Orphan Annie. Plastic & vinyl, 15" – $35.00.
Sweet April, 5½" – $6.00.

SAYCO

Billy Joe. 25″ Sculptured detailed hair, two upper teeth on latex body — $45.00.

Boy. Molded red hair, latex body: 20″ — $35.00; 27″ — $50.00; as Peter Pan, 20″ — $45.00; 27″ — $65.00.

Melissa. 20″ finely detailed, sculptured hair — $75.00.

Brother or Sister. Unusual faces, 16″ — $45.00 each.

Tuffy. One piece body and limbs, or all plastic body. Protruding lower lip, 20″-21″ — $27.50.

20″ Early vinyl head with detailed molded red hair. All latex body in one piece. Original little boy's outfit. Also came dressed as Peter Pan in green clothing and hat. Courtesy Marjorie Uhl.

SIMPLICITY & McCALL FASHION DOLLS
TERRI LEE

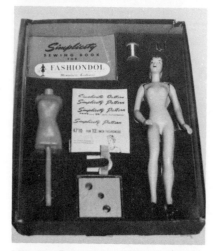

13" Simplicity Fashion-Doll. Composition with removable arms, composition dress form on wood dowel stick, patterns and wood stand. Painted features and shoes with composition pins to fit the stand. 1940's. Courtesy Pat Timmons. 13" - $28.00.

13" McCall Pattern Doll. Composition with removable arms. Painted features and molded hair. 1940's. Courtesy Pat Timmons. 13" - $28.00.

TERRI LEE

Terri Lee. 16" Composition – $125.00; Plastic – $95.00 up; Black – $325.00 up; Oriental – $350.00 up; Vinyl – $125.00; Talking – $125.00.

Tiny Terri Lee. 10" – $87.50.

Jerri Lee, 16" Plastic – $115.00; Black – $375.00; Oriental – $400.00.

Tiny Jerri Lee, 10" – $97.50.

Connie Lynn, 19" – $275.00.

Gene Autry, 16" – $500.00 up.

Linda Baby (Linda Lee), 10"-12" – $175.00.

So Sleepy, 9½" – $115.00.

Mary Jane. Plastic walker Terri Lee look-a-like with long molded eyelids – $75.00.

Clothes. Ballgowns – $40.00; Horseback Riding – $.   ; School dresses – $28,50; Skaters – $37.50; Brownie Uniform – $20.00; Coats – $20.00; Davie Crockett – $32.00; Suits – $20.00; Jerri Lee short suits – $40.00.

16" Terri Lee in black and white beach outfit, black slippers and vinyl yellow (other side blue) floating ring. Courtesy June Schultz.

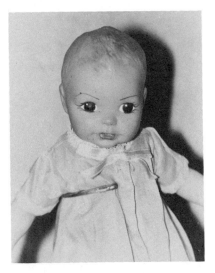

10" Linda Baby. All vinyl, with painted eyes and hair. Jointed at shoulder and hips. Long, thin limbs. Tagged gown: Linda Baby. Made by the Terri Lee Co. Courtesy Kimport Dolls.

18" Troll Bunny. All vinyl with long inset lashes. Dressed in yellow and black felt, white tail. Marked Dam Things/Establishment/1964, on foot. Courtesy Virginia Jones.

TROLLS

Dam Things. 3" – $9.00; 6" – $20.00; 12" – $20.00; 16" – $30.00; 18" – $52.50.

Uneeda. 3" – $7.00; 6" – $11.00.

Unmarked. 3" – $5.00; 6" – $8.00; 12" – $12.00.

Animals. Cow – $15.00; Large cow – $25.00; Horse – $30.00; Giraffe – $30.00; Turtle – $20.00; Monkey – $25.00.

Two headed troll. 6" – $16.00; 12" – $26.00.

Santa Claus Troll, 3" – $14.00; 6" – $19.00.

Grandpa & Grandma, 1977, 13" – $20.00 each.

TROLLS

6½" and 2" tall cow trolls. Large one: Bell around neck. Paper sticker on foot: Original Dam Things. Original 1964-1965. Dam Things Est. Mfg. by Royalty Designs of Fla. Inc. Jointed at neck. Small one: All one piece. Marked: Dam Things Est. 1964, on one foot. Design of Fla. Inc., on other. (Author).

13" Giraffe with jointed neck. Body is molded in two pieces, but is unmovable. Unmarked. (Author).

6" Turtle. All one piece and unmarked. Courtesy Virginia Jones.

Group of trolls that include a 3″ two headed one marked: Uneeda 1965, on back. One head has black hair, the other blue. Also in front is a 3″ Grandpa troll with white hair and beard. Unmarked. Courtesy Mary Wheatley.

13″ Grandpa and Grandma marked on backs: Dam Troll-1977. Courtesy June Schultz.

UNEEDA

Anniversary Doll, 25″ – $48.00.
Baby Dollikins, 21″ – $28.50.
Baby Trix, 16″ – $15.00.
Betsy McCall, 22″ – $42.00. Pre-teen, 11½″ – $35.00.
Blabby, 18″ – $20.00.
Bare Bottom Baby, 12″ – $14.00.
Dollikins, 8″ – $6.00; 11″ – $12.00; 19″ – $20.00.
Fairy Princess, 32″ – $65.00.
Freckles, 32″ – $65.00.
Lucky Linda. Composition, 14″ – $200.00.
Pollyanna, 10½″ – $28.00; 17″ – $40.00; 31″ – $70.00.
Pri-thilla, 12″ – $18.00.
Rita Hayworth, 14″ Composition – $165.00.
Serenade: Battery operated talker, 21″ – $28.50.
Suzette, 10½″ – $20.00; 11½″ – $25.00; 11½″, Sleep eyes –
$30.00.
Tiny Teens, 5″ – $7.00 each.

UNEEDA

13½" "Lucky Lindy". Represents the flyer Lindbergh who flew the "Spirit of St. Louis" to Paris. Cloth stuffed with large oil cloth attached shoes. Composition lower arms and composition head. Molded hair and painted eyes. Oil cloth helmet and olive green body suit and belt. Marks: Uneeda, on shoulder. (Author).

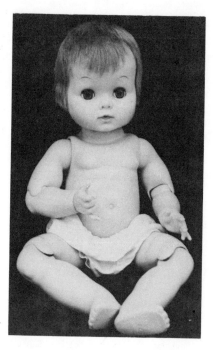

20" Baby Dollikins. Pin jointed elbows and knees, turning wrists. Red rooted hair, blue sleep eyes. Open mouth/nurser. Marks: Uneeda, on head. Uneeda Doll Co. Inc., on back. Courtesy Edith Evans.

8"-11"-19" Dollikins with extra joints at elbows, wrists, waist, knees and ankles. Large one has sleep eyes. All are marked Uneeda, on heads. Courtesy Jeannie Mauldin.

Marked Uneeda Ballerina with large painted eyes and rooted hair in upswept hairdo. Original blue leotards and tutu, blue ballerina slippers. Courtesy Jeannie Mauldin.

8" Virga's "Lucy". Comes in black patent case with compartment on top. (Pink lined). Has felt appliques on sides. Has additional wardrobe. Doll is hard plastic with vinyl head, molded on shoes, sleep blue eyes/molded lashes and rooted pale pink hair. Good qulaity pink satin gown with pleated net ruffles and lavender ribbon topless gown. Pink real fur stole lined in satin. Stole and gown tagged Schiaparelli. (red on white). Pearls in hair. (Author). $55.00.

12" Virga doll called "Chi-Chi". High heeled hard plastic body and limbs with jointed knees, vinyl head with rooted hair, small blue sleep eyes/molded lashes. Gown is rose satin with wide silver net ruffles and is topless. Real fur stole with rose lining. Wrist tag: Doll created by Elsa Schiaparelli. Comes in rose and black box. (Author). $68.50.

VOGUE

Baby Dear, 12" – $35.00; 17" 50.00; 1964, 12" – $25.00.
Baby Dear One, 25" – $125.00.
Baby Dear Two, 27" – $145.00.
Brickette, 22" – $65.00.
Ginny. Composition (Toodles), 7"-8" – $115.00; Hard plastic: Wool wig – $145.00 up; Bent leg baby – $145.00 up; Painted eyes – $130.00; Non-Walker – $115.00; Walker – $105.00; Wee Imp – $95.00 up. (Allow more for unusual outfits). Vinyl: Internationals – $22.00.
Ginny clothes: Ballerina – $18.00; Ballgown – $22.00; Bride – $18.00; Riding Habit – $22.00; Skater – $18.00; Prince – $26.00; Queen – $100.00; Hansel/Gretel – $26.00 each; Clown – $28.00; Easter Bunny (baby) – $25.00; Groom – $26.00; Majorette – $25.00; Skier – $22.00.
Hug-A-Bye Baby, 16" – $22.00.
Jan, 12" – $35.00.
Jeff, 10" – $35.00.
Jill, 10" – $35.00.
Lil Imp, 11" – $35.00.
Love Me Linda, 15" – $28.50.
Star Bright, 18" – $40.00; Baby, 18" – $40.00.
Welcome Home Baby, 20" – $50.00; Turns Two, 24" – $65.00.

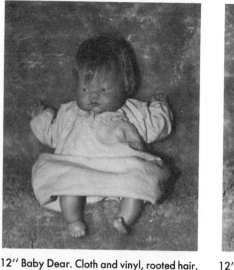

12" Baby Dear. Cloth and vinyl, rooted hair, painted blue eyes. Marked: E. Wilkin 1961, on back of leg. Vogue tag on top of body near neck. Original nightie. Courtesy Shirley Merrill.

12" Baby Dear. Cloth and vinyl, sleep blue eyes, rooted blonde hair. Not original. Marks: Vogue doll/1964, on head. E. Wilkin, on back of leg. Courtesy Shirley Merrill.

22'' Brickette. Vinyl head and arms, rigid vinyl body and legs, original rooted hair, green sleep eyes (flirty), freckles and has red fingernails. Jointed waist. Marks: Upper back: Vogue Dolls, Inc. 1959. Dress tagged: Vogue Dolls Inc. Courtesy Shirley Pascuzzi.

VOGUE

27" Dear Two. All vinyl chubby toddler with long rooted hair and sleep eyes. All original. Courtesy Virginia Jones.

27" Dear Two Boy. Chubby vinyl toddler. All original. Rooted hair and sleep eyes. Courtesy Virginia Jones.

16" Hug-A-Bye Baby. Cloth and vinyl with pixie-type face. Rooted hair, large sleep blue eyes/long lashes. Closed smile mouth. All fingers and thumb on right hand curled in, thumb extended and all fingers on left hand curled. Large toes separate. Clothes tagged. Lightly molded hair on forehead and back of head under rooted hair. Marks: Vogue/1975, on head. Courtesy Shirley Merrill.

18" Baby Star Bright. All original and marked: Vogue Doll/1966, on head. Rooted hair and large painted brown eyes to side with painted star highlights. Extended 1st finger on left hand with rest of fingers curled. All fingers curled on right hand with thumb on 1st finger. Cloth body, vinyl head and limbs. Courtesy Virginia Jones.

18" Star Bright. Plastic body and legs, vinyl head and arms. Large painted eyes to side with star highlights. Rooted hair and has small fingers wide spread. Marks: Vogue Doll/ 1966. Courtesy Virginia Jones.

15" Love Me Linda. All vinyl with large painted brown eyes, and has molded tear drop below left eye. She also was sold without the tear drop. Black rooted hair. Original tagged dress. Head marked: Vogue doll 1965. Courtesy Shirley Merrill.

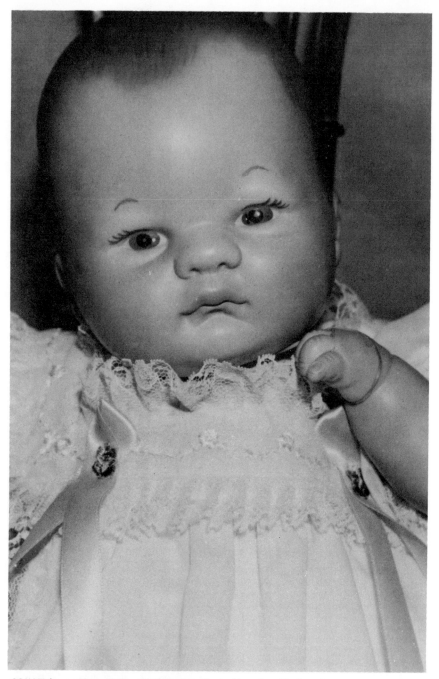

20″ Welcome Home Baby. Cloth body with vinyl head and limbs. Blue painted eyes, lightly molded, painted hair. Original. Courtesy Phyllis Teague.

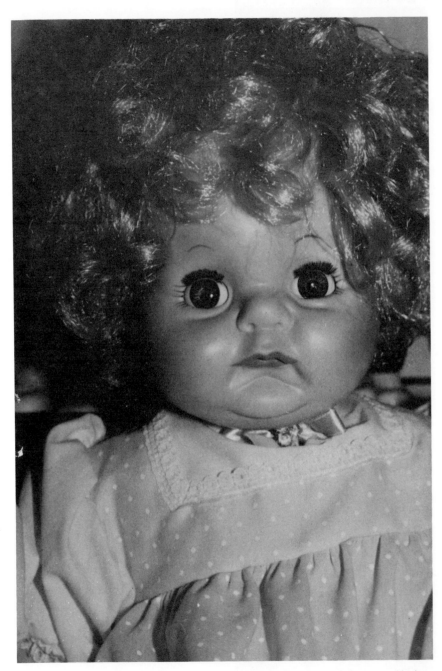

24" Welcome Home Baby Turns Two. All vinyl with rooted hair and sleep eyes/ lashes. Original. Courtesy Phyllis Teague.

VOGUE

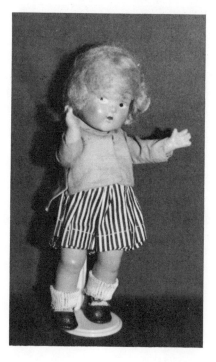

11" Lil Imp. All vinyl with blue sleep eyes, rooted hair, original dress, but replaced shoes and socks. Marks: 1964 Vogue Doll, on head. Courtesy Shirley Merrill.

7" Toodles-Ginny. All composition with painted eyes to side. All original. Courtesy Pat Timmons.

Crib Crowd Baby Series. 1950. Painted side glancing eyes. Printed organdy over cotton with tie string closing in back. Wool-caracul wig. Courtesy Pat Timmons.

Toodles-Ginny. All composition with painted eyes to side, bent right arm. Marks: Vogue, on head. Tagged Vogue dress. Courtesy Shirley Pascuzzi.

Ginny with red caracul wig poodle cut. 1952. From Kindergarten Series #26. All original. Courtesy Pat Timmons.

Crib Crowd, bent leg baby. All hard plastic with caracul wig, sleep eyes-no lashes. Check/lace romper suit. (Author).

VOGUE

Ginny as "Fairy Godmother". All hard plastic, sleep eyes-no lashes. Gown is orange with gold trim and dots. Courtesy Pat Timmons.

No. 54 Ginny dressed as Mistress Mary. Hard plastic, sleep eyes with no lashes. All original. Courtesy Pat Timmons.

Ginny as "Beryl #43" All hard plastic with sleep eyes and painted lashes. All original. Courtesy Pat Timmons.

Ginny #72 "School" Blue figured dress with yellow trim and yellow purse, straw hat with yellow ribbon. Courtesy Pat Timmons.

Ginny #26 "Carol". 1953. Red dotted dress with white figured border and bodice. Large white ribbon in hair. Courtesy Pat Timmons.

Ginny #74 "Party". Hard plastic and all original. White nylon dress with nylon lace ruffles. Flowers, ribbon and bow trim. Ribbon sash. Zipper closing. Straw hat with flower trim. Courtesy Pat Timmons.

VOGUE

Ginny in white satin top with red hearts, and attached black velvet pants. Courtesy Pat Timmons.

Painted eye hard plastic Ginny in cowgirl suit, old, but replaced shoes and socks. Should have boots. (Author).

Six Ginnys in various costumes, along with Ginny furniture, table, chairs, wardrobes. Courtesy Glorya Woods.